MISSION-BASED MARKETING

MISSION-BASED MARKETING

Second Edition

Positioning Your Not-for-Profit in an Increasingly Competitive World

Peter C. Brinckerhoff

JOHN WILEY & SONS, INC.

For general information on our other products and services, or technical support, please contact our Customer Care Department within the U.S. at (800) 762-2974, outside the United States at (317) 572-3993 or fax (317) 572-4002.

Wiley also publishes its books in a variety of electronic formats. Some content that appears in print may not be available in electronic books.

For more information about Wiley products, visit our web site at *www.wiley.com.*

ISBN 0-471-23718-3

Printed in the United States of America
10 9 8 7 6 5 4 3 2 1

For my wife and best friend, Christine Hargroves Brinckerhoff.
In a life filled with blessings, you are the one for which I am most thankful.

Acknowledgments

When you sit down to write the second edition of your third book, you begin to get the idea that you know what you are doing, and can handle the task at hand. Of course, you are wrong, or at least I was. I have many people to thank for bringing this project to completion, and the main recipients of my gratitude are the staff and volunteers of the not-for-profits whose examples bring so much life and credibility to the ideas found in the following pages. Any good consultant learns while he or she teaches, and I like to think that all of my training and publications are a way of sharing what I have learned. It is certainly true here.

About the Author

Peter Brinckerhoff is an internationally known expert at helping not-for-profits get more mission for their money. Since embarking on his consulting career by forming his firm Corporate Alternatives, Inc. in 1982, Peter has worked with thousands of not-for-profit staff and board members throughout the United States. He is a widely published author, with over 50 articles on not-for-profit management in such prominent journals as *Nonprofit World, Advancing Philanthropy, Contributions, Strategic Governance,* and the *Journal of Nonprofit and Voluntary Sector Marketing.* Peter is also the author of the award-winning books *Mission-Based Management* and *Financial Empowerment, Social Entrepreneurship, Faith-Based Management,* and the *Mission-Based Management Workbook.* Peter's books are used in the graduate and undergraduate nonprofit programs at over 70 colleges and universities worldwide.

Peter brings a wide array of practical hands-on experience to his writing, consulting, and training. He has served as a board member, staff member, and executive director of a number of local, state, and national not-for-profits. He understands all three of these perspectives and their importance in the not-for-profit mix.

Peter received his Bachelor's degree from the University of Pennsylvania, and his Master's of Public Health from the Tulane University School of Public Health. He lives in Springfield, Illinois, with his wife and three children.

Peter can be reached online through his web site, *www.mission based.com.*

Contents

1. Introduction 1
    A. A Competitive, Always Wired, World 3
    B. Who This Book Is Written For 5
    C. The Benefits of Reading This Book 6
    D. Preview of the Book 7

2. Marketing: The Competitive Edge 12
    A. The Characteristics of a Market-Driven Organization 13
    B. Meeting Customer Wants 15
    C. Treating Everyone Like A Customer 18
    D. Being Better Than Your Competition 19
    E. A Team Effort 22

3. Being Mission-Based *and* Market-Driven 29
    A. Which Is Right, the Markets or the Mission? 30
    B. Moving with the Markets, Maintaining Your Mission 33
    C. The Never-Ending Marketing Cycle 37
    D. The Results of Becoming Market-Driven 38
    E. Motivating Board and Staff 40
    F. Holding On to Your Core Values 46

4. Being Flexible and Changing with
   the Market 52
    A. The Need for Flexibility 53
    B. Retaining the Capacity for Flexibility 59
    C. Being a Change Agent 64
    D. The Pace of Change in a Competitive Environment 67

5. The Marketing Cycle for a Not-for-Profit 74
   A. The Marketing Cycle That Works 75
   B. The Marketing Disability of Most Not-for-Profits 88
   C. The Marketing Cycle and Your Competitors 89

6. Who Are Your Markets? 96
   A. Market Identification and Quantification 97
   B. Market Segmenting 105
   C. Focusing on Target Markets 107
   D. Treating All Your Markets Like Customers 109

7. Who Are Your Competitors? 114
   A. Identifying Your Competition 115
   B. Studying the Competition 124
   C. Focusing on Your Core Competencies 131

8. Asking Your Markets What They Want 135
   A. Surveys 136
   B. Focus Groups 144
   C. Informal Asking 147
   D. Asking Online 149
   E. Asking Mistakes 150
   F. After Asking 152

9. Better Marketing Materials 156
   A. The Problems with Most Not-for-Profits'
      Marketing Materials 157
   B. Solving Customers' Problems 162
   C. Things to Include in Your Marketing Materials 164
   D. Things to Avoid in Your Marketing Materials 166
   E. Developing Different Materials for Different Markets ... 168

10. Technology and Marketing 172
   A. Using Technology to Market in a Better, Faster, and
      More Focused Manner 173
   B. High-Tech Asking—High-Tech Listening 179
   C. Your Web Site(s) 183
   D. Better Marketing Materials 186
   E. Development 189
   F. Newsletters Online 192

11. Incredible Customer Service 195
A. Three Customer Service Rules 197
B. The Customer Is Not Always Right, but the Customer Is
Always the Customer, So Fix the Problem 198
C. Customers Never Have Problems; They Always Have
Crises, So Fix the Problem *Now* 198
D. Never Settle for Good Customer Service—Seek Total
Customer *Satisfaction* 202
E. The Unhappy Customer 207
F. Regular Customer Contact 209
G. Turning Customers into Referral Sources 211

12. A Marketing Planning Process 215
A. Developing Your Marketing Team 216
B. An Asking Schedule 219
C. Targeting Your Marketing Effort 222
D. A Marketing Plan Outline 224
E. Marketing Planning Software 230

13. Resources for Marketing 232
A. Books, Workbooks, Periodicals 233
B. Organizations 234
C. Software 235
D. Web Resources 235

Final Words 237

Appendix A: Survey Sample 239

Appendix B: Focus Group Questions 244

Index 247

1
Introduction

OVERVIEW

More competition. Social entrepreneurism. A competitive environment. The free market. An open market. Market-based pricing. Managed care. These terms are now nearly ubiquitous in the literature of the not-for-profit world. But what do they mean to you, your staff, your board, and the people that your not-for-profit serves? And, more importantly, how does your organization fit, survive, and, yes, prosper in an increasingly competitive and rapid-response environment?

And then there is technology. The wired world, always online, always expecting instant answers, quick responses, cures downloaded on demand. The pace of change, the pace of expectancy (how quickly we expect things to be done) has accelerated and will continue to. How will your organization react?

Since the first edition of *Mission-Based Marketing* was published in 1996, so much has changed, and yet the core issues and skills of marketing for a not-for-profit have remained the same. There is more acceptance of not-for-profit advertising, and of not-for-profits using business skills to pursue their mission. There is the advance of technology. For certain things, such as printing your own marketing materials, it has reduced costs drastically; in other areas, such as maintaining a worthwhile and appealing web site, it has increased costs in time, money, and the skill set you need on staff. And, of course, there is increased competition for good staff, good volunteers, donated dollars and goods and, most importantly, for grants, contracts, and people to serve.

How do you manage an organization in a "right-now" culture, when what most not-for-profits provide is not a "right-now" solution? You don't fix the environment, or stop child abuse, or improve pre-kindergarten education, or stop homelessness, or hunger, or discrimination right now. But

1

that doesn't mean you can't start right now, and perform your mission in a way that pays close attention to the right-now culture.

This book will show you how to react, respond, and reshape your organization into one that prospers using the best tools of twenty-first century not-for-profit management. How? By becoming market-oriented while remaining mission-based. By using the well-established and time-tested methods of marketing to do more mission. By treating everyone who interacts with your organization like valued customers. By developing a team approach to marketing, where customer satisfaction is everyone's job. By asking customers what they want and trying your best to give it to them.

In my lectures and keynotes I repeatedly contend that the skill of marketing is really a business skill translated over to mission. Many people are uncomfortable with the concept of marketing in a not-for-profit because they see marketing as no more than crass sales. Sales (crass or not, your choice) is *one part* of marketing, but not the whole thing by any means. And, to help you understand right away why this book, and the concept of mission-based marketing, is so important to you, let me assure you that marketing is a way of doing better mission, sooner, and in a more focused manner. Good marketing in a not-for-profit is good mission, and I'll show you how to do it.

In this initial chapter, we will look at why your world is "going competitive" and what the linkage is between competition and marketing. We'll look at who I have written this book for (the target market) and what the benefits are of reading the book, and of investing your time with me. Finally, I'll give you a brief preview of each of the remaining chapters of the book so that you will know what the sequence of our time together will be like.

There is little if any rocket science in the following pages. But there are scores of solid, practical ideas on how to bring your organization into a competitive frame of mind that will keep it in business in the twenty-first century. In the chapters that follow, you will learn why marketing is so fundamental to your mission and how successful mission-based organizations are simultaneously market-driven. You will view a marketing cycle and see how it can be adapted to your organization and your mission. You will learn how to identify and keep close to your customers, and how to identify and keep tabs on your competitors. You will see how technology has made marketing easier, cheaper, and much more challenging all at the same time. We'll walk through the key elements of incredible customer service and show you applications for your customers.

Marketing is not a discrete event with a beginning and an end. It is a continuing process, a cycle that becomes a discipline, part of your culture. To develop that culture may take months or even years in your organization, or it may be a very short journey. It will depend on your staff, your board, your funders, and your community, but most importantly on you, the reader. You will be the one who will have the tools to help the others cross the bridge from your current position to being mission-based *and* market-driven. It's a lot of work, but well worth it for your organization, your community, and the people you serve.

A. A COMPETITIVE, ALWAYS WIRED, WORLD

Throughout the not-for-profit community, the tide is has been changing for the past decade. And, like tides, the changes at first are barely noticeable, and more evident on some parts of the shoreline than others. But once the tide changes, the momentum is reversed and the outcome is irreversible. The forces at play are too big, too powerful, too global to resist.

In the not-for profit world, the tide has changed and the trend is inexorably, irreversibly moving toward competition, toward freer markets, and away from monopolies and restricted markets. Governments, particularly at the state and local levels, have discovered that competition works in the not-for-profit world, and that freeing up this part of the economy produces lower cost and better services just like in other sectors. And, like other transitions from a restricted market to a free market, it always produces a market shake-out: some organizations don't survive because they cannot adjust and compete. Will your organization be a competitor or a footnote in history?

I need to digress here for a moment. At the same time (1960–1990) that we were spending trillions of dollars fighting and ultimately winning the Cold War to keep the world safe for democracy and capitalism (or was it capitalism and democracy?), we prevented our not-for-profit sector from benefiting from the open market. We had one of each kind of human services or arts entity in each community and kept others out by not funding them.

❑ **FOR EXAMPLE:** Look at how we name our not-for-profits: The Adams County Mental Health Center, Springfield Chamber Orchestra, Denver Association of Retarded Citizens, Sacramento Animal Shelter. In our very names, we declare a geographic monopoly for these groups and local donors, and then the United Ways and other funding entities keep out competition under the excuse of "duplication of service."

When you think about it, this is not only incredible, it's also very patronizing and demeaning to the not-for-profits' staff and boards. It says, "We know you are nice folks, but you aren't very good managers and so you can't play by the same rules we do (the free market). But we need your services, so we'll protect you."

In fact, in all of the major not-for-profit arenas—the arts, research, the environment, human services, education, religion, and associations—only three areas are completely unfettered by this shackle of restricted markets: religion, private (usually higher) education, and associations. We see the best example of diverse organizations meeting the diverse needs of the population connected with places of worship. With no restrictions on size, location, theology, or services, religion has become a truly diversified "industry," with an order and denomination (or "flavor" as my minister puts it) for everyone. Churches, temples, synogogues, and mosques are free to compete, and many choices have evolved, but not in the arts or in most human services, where most of the government money is spent. These groups are protected, and at a high price. And the good news (for some) and the bad news (for others) is the same: this protection is eroding as governments, stuck in a perpetual budget crunch, try to find new methods of paying for the increasing demand for social and educational services.

Part of this evolution has shown up in the outsourcing or privatizing of traditional government services, such as prisons or even public schools. As that action has become more and more accepted, funders have taken another look at how they currently fund the original "outsourcers," not-for-profit groups. The funders have realized that they can get more for less by allowing competition to enter previously sacrosanct areas and, as long as their standards for quality are high, that it should be a win-win-win situation.

❑ **FOR EXAMPLE:** In Texas, the entire Welfare-to-Work initiative was taken away from government and their not-for-profit subcontractors and awarded (on a competitive bid) to Lockheed Martin, over a huge hue and cry that a for-profit would not be sympathetic. After the first three years of the project, the customers (the people going from welfare to work) were hugely satisfied with the program and the services they received. In Massachusetts, providers of services to adults with disabilities used to get calls from the state saying, "We are going to send you George (or Nancy or Bob)" as a client. Just because the organization was there, as long as they did satisfactory work, they got more people to care for. Not any more. Since 1995 the organizations must bid against other not-for-profit providers to demonstrate both their service and financial competitiveness to "receive" the client. In Indiana, for-profit providers of residential services are required to bid against not-for-profits.

❑ **FOR EXAMPLE:** The federal government, long a bastion of continuing contracts, is now bidding more and more work, particularly in the human service area. They are looking more at outcomes than at process, and are allowing for-profits and not-for-profits to bid on work that used to be set aside solely for not-for-profits.

❏ **FOR EXAMPLE:** Ask any development officer of any organization whether the fund-raising arena is more or less competitive, more or less outcome-based, more or less driven by the needs and wants of the funder. Their answer will be a resounding "YES!" I recently saw an article that noted that the ratio of corporate dollars applied for to those granted went from 1,500:1 in 1985 to 13,000:1 in 1995, and over 25,000:1 in 1999. Certainly the foundation staff that I know are deluged with applications from types of organizations that they had not even heard of five years ago.

This trend, from a taxpayer's view, and a donor's view, is good. We get more services, often of better quality, usually for less money. But from the viewpoint of your not-for-profit, how does it look? Scary? Exciting? Dangerous? Like an opportunity?

Probably some of each. If your organization is not market-driven, not ready for competition, probably the danger and fear are predominant. Hopefully, by reading this book and applying the ideas and techniques you will find here, you can turn the adversity into opportunity, and improve your organization's mission capability. And here's a note of optimism. You are already competing, and doing it successfully in some arenas. You probably just haven't noticed, or been willing to admit it! More on that in the coming chapters as well.

B. WHO THIS BOOK IS WRITTEN FOR

This book is written for the management and board members of not-for-profit organizations of all types. Whether your organization is in human services, environmental protection, the arts, education, religion, or an association, this book has something for you.

Your organization needs to be more market-oriented and, for many entities, that requires a culture change. Such changes are initiated only at the board and senior management level. And, changes of such importance need to be coached consistently over time to take hold. They need to be coached by those same board members and senior staff.

But, such cultural change will not be successful unless everyone in the culture adopts the new ideas, the new philosophy. As you will read over and over, marketing and competition are *team* sports, and when one person doesn't play well the entire team loses. Thus it is essential that the key ideas in this book be transmitted to the entire team. As a former staff member, executive director, and board member of local, state, and national not-for-profits, I try to provide ideas for all levels of your organization, not just for the executive director, or solely for the board. I believe that a strong marketing effort is put forth by a team—one of line staff, senior management, boards, and volunteers—since the more people that can see the ideas here, the easier and faster it will be to implement them.

The book is designed to give you practical advice on how to move your organization as an entire team toward a market-based philosophy. To help you, I have included dozens of real-world examples (which can be found by looking for the "❏ FOR EXAMPLE" tag), and specific applications for you to apply, in some cases, the same day you read them (which can be found by looking for the "☞ HANDS-ON" tag). At the end of each chapter, there is also a list of **"Discussion Questions"** that focus on the key points of the chapter. These questions are intended to help you generate discussion about the important issues raised in the book, and to provide a team forum to help you decide which ideas you can use right away, which will take some time, and which may not be appropriate for your organization.

NOTE: There is also another tool available for you to help implement the ideas in this book: The Mission-Based Marketing Workbook and CD-ROM, *which is available from John Wiley & Sons. The workbook is full of self-assessments, checklists, and action ideas for you to use as you work to realize your organizational marketing ambitions.*

C. THE BENEFITS OF READING THIS BOOK

By buying and reading this book, I know that you are making an investment of time and money. So what are the benefits of that investment? What will accrue to your organization? *I guarantee that you will get at least the following benefits from this book:*

- An understanding of why marketing is so crucial to being a mission-based organization.
- An understanding of why marketing is so important to your continued competitiveness.
- A new insight on what the marketing cycle is and how your existing and future services and customers fit into it.
- A series of methods to help you and your staff treat everyone like a customer.
- A clear understanding of the difference between needs and wants, which is crucial to a competitive organization.
- Ways to incorporate marketing concepts into your web site.
- Ways to utilize technology in producing better, more targeted marketing materials.
- Ways to incorporate e-mail into your marketing, communications, and inquiry efforts.

- Knowledge about the best ways to develop and conduct surveys and focus groups.
- An understanding of how and why to write a marketing plan.
- An understanding of why marketing principles are so important to better fund-raising.
- New insights on ways to improve your marketing materials and focus them on your many markets.
- An understanding, perhaps for the very first time, of who your markets really are.
- A list of ways to provide excellent customer service.
- Ideas on how to get your board and staff involved on your marketing team.

By the time you finish reading this book you should have an excellent hands-on understanding of marketing, competition, and your role on the marketing team.

To get the most from this book, or from any management text, I strongly recommend that you read it as a team of board and staff. By team reading and team application, there is a much higher likelihood that the ideas included here will get implemented. That is why I have included the **Discussion Questions** at the end of each chapter. Have your staff read the book, and then use the questions to generate a healthy discussion. Also at the end of each chapter is a list of online resources that were current as of the date of publication. Finally, remember the potential for implementation from the *Mission-Based Marketing Workbook and CD-ROM* discussed earlier.

D. PREVIEW OF THE BOOK

So now you know why you need to read this book, and what benefits will accrue to you because of your investment of time and money. But what is in the book? Let's look at how the book is constructed and then at a brief summary of the chapters.

I have split the book into two major areas. The first four chapters are really about philosophy and getting you to change your ideas about the intersection of marketing, competition, and your not-for-profit mission. These chapters contain the big concepts, as well as some hands-on ideas for initiating needed changes in your organization.

Beginning with Chapter 5, we get into the more technical aspects of marketing and competition, including your markets, your competition, using technology, ways to ask, methods of improving your marketing materials, customer service, and developing a marketing plan. These seven chapters are the "how-to" part of the book, where I offer specific ideas to help you embrace the concepts provided in the first five chapters.

Let's look at the chapters in more detail.

Chapter 1: Introduction

This chapter provides an overview, a method of getting the most from the book, and some focus for you on marketing and competition.

Chapter 2: Marketing: The Competitive Edge

In this chapter, we will review why good, consistent marketing is a competitive edge. We will first review the six characteristics of not-for-profits that are truly competitive. You will see that competitive organizations consistently meet customers' *wants,* not just their *needs.* You will get your first ideas on how to treat everyone (including your funders) like valued customers. We'll also take an initial look at how your organization can be better than your competition. Finally, we'll explore why marketing is truly a team effort and show you some ways to bring everyone in your organization onto that team.

Chapter 3: Being Mission-Based *and* Market-Driven

At some point your organization will be faced with a dilemma: Follow the mission or follow the market. What do you do? This chapter will deal with ways to decide what the best path is for your organization as well as for your own personal ethics and values. The chapter will cover how to move with the markets, but maintain your mission. I'll also show you how to delineate and then use core values to make staying on track easier. Another challenge is, how do you bring the rest of the staff and board along for the ride? This chapter will cover that by giving you some tools to motivate the staff and board, and will reiterate the six mission benefits of becoming and remaining market-based and customer-oriented. Also included are some suggestions for how to settle into the marketing culture for the long term.

Chapter 4: Being Flexible and Changing with the Market

Flexibility is the key to marketing and competitive success. The wants of your markets will change—in unpredictable ways and not always on your schedule. This chapter will show you why you need to stay flexible, provide some examples of the pace of changes in the market, show you seven workable methods of becoming a change agent in your organization, and identify the ways that you can retain your organizational flexibility in the right-now environment.

Chapter 5: The Marketing Cycle for a Not-for-Profit

The cycle for marketing is endless, and it starts at a place that may surprise you. This chapter will show you in detail the proper sequence for marketing, and will also go through the marketing cycle of competitors. Additionally, we will review what may be the biggest barrier standing in your way to becoming a competitive marketer: the marketing disability of most not-for-profit staff.

Chapter 6: Who Are Your Markets?

In order to serve the many markets of your organization, you need to first know who they are. This chapter will walk you through the surprising process of market identification, and then will show you how to segment those markets to decide which ones you want to pursue most avidly. Once that is accomplished it will then be time for you to select and focus on target markets. The discussion here will show you how. You will see that you can use this technique in both the provision of mission, and in your fund-raising activities. Finally, we'll make sure that you, your staff, and your board all understand why all of your markets (even your funders) should be treated like valued customers.

Chapter 7: Who Are Your Competitors?

The flip side of identifying your markets is to identify who is going after those markets—other than you. This is already occurring in fund-raising, volunteer recruitment, and hiring of good staff. How do you compete? You start by looking at your competition. This chapter will show you how to identify and continually monitor your competition. Then, we will review ways for you to focus on your core competencies so that you can successfully compete.

Chapter 8: Asking Your Markets What They Want

You need to give your markets what they want, within the constraints of your mission and marketing strategies. But you can't know what they want until you ask them. This chapter will cover asking in detail, including surveys, focus groups, informal asking (and common mistakes), and what to do after you ask. We'll talk about asking online, and how to ask your customers for key information about your competitors. Finally, you'll learn critical ideas on what to do *after* you ask.

Chapter 9: Better Marketing Materials

With as many markets as you have, it makes little sense to have one or two pieces of marketing material. It makes even less sense to have those marketing pieces focus on your services rather than on your customers' problems. This chapter will show you some specific ideas on how to improve your marketing material, seven things to include in your material, seven things to *avoid* in your material, ways to customize your materials for various markets, and how to use the latest (inexpensive) technology to develop very focused and very inexpensive marketing materials.

Chapter 10: Technology and Marketing

Technology has affected everything we do, and this includes marketing. I'll show you some ways that your peer organizations have utilized technology to find markets, meet the wants of their markets, and save money and time in doing so. We'll also cover some online issues such as improving your web site, asking customers online, and providing an online newsletter.

Chapter 11: Incredible Customer Service

When you have attracted people to your organization, whether as employees, volunteers, or to utilize your services, you need to keep them. To do that, you need to employ top-notch customer service methods. This chapter will reiterate the three core rules of customer service, show you how to empower all your staff to solve customers' problems *now,* help you instill the necessary attitude of what I term "compassionate urgency," provide you eight ways to do better customer contact, and show you tried and true methods of turning your customers into referral sources.

Chapter 12: A Marketing Planning Process

Like other key functions, marketing should be planned, with strategies, goals, and objectives. This chapter will show you how to develop your marketing team, plan your asking, target your marketing, and utilize the best current marketing planning software, and it will provide an outline that you can use as you develop your organization's marketing plan.

Chapter 13: Resources for Marketing

If you are serious about becoming a market-driven yet mission-based marketer, this book can get you started, but you will undoubtedly need to have more information, more tools, more specific help in particular areas. That's why I've included a chapter with lots of resources for you. Here, I've included information on books, software, publications, organizations, and web sites that can help you boost your marketing effort starting today.

RECAP

In this initial chapter, you have had your first exposure to the more competitive, more wired, always online world that your not-for-profit is entering. We have discussed the ways to get the most from the remainder of the book, and previewed the chapters for you.

There is no question that marketing and competition go hand-in-hand. If you don't know who your customers are, how can you find out what they want? If you don't know what they want, how can you attract and keep them as customers? And you fail the competitive test without customers!

The challenge for you is to bring your organizational culture, which for a variety of valid historical reasons may have less than a fully focused marketing worldview, into a world where such an outlook is critical—essential to success and to survival.

2

Marketing: The Competitive Edge

OVERVIEW

You have already read in Chapter 1 about the changing, increasingly competitive and "right-now" world that your not-for-profit organization will be working in for the remainder of your career. If you work for an organization that you consider competitive now, how can you stay ahead of the competition? However, as you look objectively at your organization, if you do not see a competitive player, what do you do?

The answer to both questions is: You market. At its most fundamental level, marketing is the competitive edge for both for-profits and not-for-profits, and this chapter will start you on your journey to becoming a mission-based *and* market-driven not-for-profit manager.

CHAPTER THUMBNAIL

➤ **The Characteristics of a Market-Driven Organization**
➤ **Meeting Customer Wants**
➤ **Treating Everyone Like a Customer**
➤ **Being Better Than Your Competition**
➤ **A Team Effort**

We'll begin with the characteristics of market-driven, mission-based organizations. These six characteristics will allow you to look at your organization and see some potential weak points that you can focus on as you read the remainder of the book. They are drawn from my experience with successful not-for-profits in all parts of the not-for-profit sector.

After we lay that groundwork, we will look at the difference between meeting needs and wants and show you a number of examples of how not-for-profits are working hard to gear their services to wants, not needs. Then, we'll go over tried and true methods of treating everyone, including your funders, like valued customers. Your attitude, and more importantly, your staff attitude toward service recipients as customers, is absolutely essential to your organizational transition.

Next we'll turn to ways to be better than your competition, and give you your first glimpse of how your competition views you and ways to measure yourself against competitors. Finally, I will show you how to start bringing everyone onto the marketing team. Marketing is everyone's job, not just for the executive director or the public relations manager.

By the time you finish this chapter, you will have a good initial handle on the principles that will guide the remainder of the book: that good marketers meet wants, not needs; that competitive organizations must market aggressively; that every one of the people in every one of your markets deserves and needs to be treated like a customer; and that everything everyone does in your organization is marketing: everyone is on the team.

A. THE CHARACTERISTICS OF A MARKET-DRIVEN ORGANIZATION

So where do I want you to end up? How do I want your organization to eventually look? What comprises a market-driven, and still mission-based, organization? Let's look at the characteristics of not-for-profits that are successful at this difficult and challenging mix of high priorities. The six characteristics below work together, as a comprehensive whole. Don't delude yourself into thinking that, if you pick 1, 3, and 5 that you will be okay. You won't. You need to move toward complete implementation of *all* of the six.

Not-for-profits who are successful at marketing:

1. Understand Their Markets

They realize that their markets extend beyond just the people that they serve. They identify, quantify, and target the markets that they want to serve and can serve well. They study the market as it is, and as it will be. They get to know the people that are in the market, and evaluate constantly the changes in the market's wants. We'll investigate market identification and understanding in Chapter 6.

2. Treat Everyone Like a Customer

Funders, board, staff, and people that receive services are all thought of and treated like customers. Even difficult customers are treated as well as possible. Customer satisfaction, solving customer problems, and a sense of compassionate urgency are high priorities organization-wide. Customer satisfaction will be the subject of Chapter 11.

3. Have Everyone on the Marketing Team

They work at the attitude that everyone, every staff person and every volunteer, is crucial to the success of the organization's marketing, its customer service, and its competitive edge. They know that the smallest mistake or indifference or lack of understanding can result in a lower perception of value from a particular market or customer. There will be more on the marketing team later in this chapter.

4. Ask, Ask, Ask, and then Listen

No one knows what a customer wants until they ask, and ask regularly. Successful organizations shape their services to meet customer wants, and they are constantly asking so they can stay in tune with how those wants change and develop. We'll look at asking in depth in Chapter 8.

5. Innovate Constantly

They are flexible. To respond to changing market conditions and customer wants, these organizations are extremely flexible, with staff and board encouraged to take reasonable risks on behalf of the people that they serve. We'll look at innovation more closely when we consider flexibility in Chapter 4.

6. Embrace Competition

They don't fear competition (though they may not revel in it): they focus on their customers' wants and doing the best possible service. They know that competition ultimately makes their services better and more market-focused. Chapter 7 will discuss competition in depth.

How do you feel your organization meets these benchmarks? If you feel pretty good about where you are, great! You will learn some excellent techniques about how to turbocharge your organization in the coming pages. If you feel that you don't measure up as well as you'd like, don't despair! All of the characteristics will be addressed in the remainder of the book with hands-on suggestions for you to implement.

B. MEETING CUSTOMER WANTS

As I hope you have noticed, I repeatedly have used the term "wants" instead of "needs" when describing the target of your marketing interest. Why have I done that? Because there is a *huge* difference between needs and wants. You may need to rethink your traditional view of working to meet customers' needs. What you must target is their wants.

Let me start by describing the difference between the two. We all have needs: to sleep, eat, breathe, work, socialize. We also have wants: chocolate, new clothes, time with our family, a new job. What is the difference? People *have* needs. People *seek* wants. There is no more fundamental, no more important foundation for successful marketing than those six words: *People have needs, people seek wants.* Let's look at some examples of what I mean, both for wants and needs.

❑ FOR EXAMPLE: If you have ever had a friend, family member, or employee who abused alcohol or drugs to the point of becoming dysfunctional, you know that that person *needed* treatment, often intense and immediate treatment, long before they *wanted* it. In fact, every one around the abuser—their friends, their family, their employers, and their neighbors—all knew what was *needed.* But as long as the abuser didn't *want* help, he or she wouldn't seek help. A sad example, but one that is played out every day in nearly every community. Wants rule.

❑ FOR EXAMPLE: We all need water, or at least some liquid to survive. In the United States most of us get our drinking water from municipal water treatment systems or, in rural areas, from wells. Some systems have "hard" water, some "soft." But nearly all our water is safe to drink, and while the taste varies widely from system to system (as a frequent traveler I can attest to this fact), neither medical nor safety reasons mandate or even suggest that we avoid our tap water.

So why the incredible popularity of bottled water? This product is expensive, un-*needed,* but yet obviously *wanted* by millions of American consumers, so much that the product now comes not only in about forty brands, but five or six primary sizes and innumerable flavors. It's a case study in wants surmounting needs. Again, wants rule.

❑ FOR EXAMPLE: Think for a moment of a chocolate milk shake. Who needs one? Nobody. Who wants one? Millions of us, enough so that every major fast food chain carries them, and in many flavors and varieties. Those yummy wants get the better of us—and wind up as unwanted baggage around our waists!

❑ **FOR EXAMPLE:** I may have a need for transportation to school or work. But I decide from many choices which method of transportation I will purchase. Car, truck, van, bus, motorcycle, or even Rollerblades. And within those choices are many makes and models. I have a need, but I buy what I want, within my budget. In fact many people *want* a particular car that they don't *need* so badly, they buy well above what they can afford. Wants rule.

I'm sure that you can come up with your own examples by the dozens of how people have wants that are not really needs, but that they are willing to pay serious money for. Now, what can you do to meet your customers' wants? How can you be competitive with other providers of services like yours or for each increasingly competed-for donated or earned dollar?

First you have to ask. The biggest mistake people make in marketing is saying "I've been in this business 20 years and I know what customers want." Wrong. No one knows what any customer wants until he or she asks. You need to develop a culture of asking, and this cultural shift is so important that we will spend an entire chapter on ways to ask, when to ask, and how to ask.

Second, you listen, and try to meet as many wants as you can. This may mean providing services at new times, in different places, in new settings, in different languages. Let's look at some examples:

❑ **FOR EXAMPLE:** Churches throughout the United States are developing more and more "family night" activities as well as expanded youth activities, and building the buildings to house them. Particularly popular are open gym times, volleyball and basketball leagues, family aerobics, and family activities. What wants do these activities meet? They address the want of parents for a safe environment for their kids as well as a common ground for planned family interaction and time. Usually these activities have little if any religious overtone or content other than the location. Church and non-church members are welcome. The benefit for the church is straightforward: by meeting a want in the community they get people in their facilities where inevitably some will take an interest and join the congregation.

❑ **FOR EXAMPLE:** Museums and zoos are providing classroom "experiences" for elementary, junior high, and high schools. These traveling "road shows" expose the students to art, history, archeology, and zoology in their schools. The wants met? Enhancements to the traditional curriculum without the cost (in both time and transportation) of a field trip. The benefits? Often the organizations are paid for this type of work, and it gets some of the kids interested enough in the museum or zoo to talk their parents into a visit.

How did these organizations find out what their customers wanted? They asked, they observed, they read aggressively, they watched their competition as well as organizations that were not competing with them, and then they asked again. What they didn't do was assume that they *knew what people wanted or, worse, what people **needed***.

And, we are so good at giving people what they need that we forget to worry about what people want. I call this the Not-for-Profit Marketing Disability, and we'll cover it in detail in Chapter 5, but suffice it to say here that we have to break out of the mold of assuming that because someone needs it, or worse, because we "know" they need it or tell them they need it, that they will want it. Doing a needs assessment is not enough. The job of a mission-based marketer is to make the person want what they need.

This brings up an interesting and important point. Once we diagnose, or test, or interview, or observe and decide what a person needs, many not-for-profit staff have a moral and professional responsibility to see that the customer gets what they need. Doesn't this negate the adage that you have to give people what they want? Not at all: both the want of the customer and the responsibility of the professional can be met.

❑ **FOR EXAMPLE:** A psychologist has a patient who has been evidencing more and more erratic and sometimes self-abusive behavior. The standard medications and outpatient therapies are obviously not working, and the psychologist's professional opinion is that the patient *needs* inpatient treatment for weeks if not months. Without the treatment, the patient may become suicidal, or violent toward others. But the patient is an adult, and has the choice of being admitted or not admitted. And, at this point, he doesn't *want* to go into a treatment facility.

What should the psychologist do? All the professional knowledge of *need* is powerless in the face of the ability of the patient to follow his *wants*. But the psychologist does not turn away. She works to convince the patient that he *wants* to go into the facility. She does her best to turn the *need* into a *want*. By doing this, she is using an age-old marketing technique, the one that convinces people that they really want a product or, in this case, a service. The technique is called *sales*.

I would not be surprised if you were uncomfortable with the idea of "selling," and you have a lot of company in the not-for-profit sector. Let me put this another way, one that may ease the discomfort a bit: For-profit organizations can and do spend marketing dollars to make us want what we don't need. We don't really *need* a new car (or SUV) every three years. My teenage daughter doesn't *need* to wear only clothes from The Gap or Limited. No one, not even my wife, *needs* chocolate. Such mixing of needs and wants is understood and accepted in the free market. Buyer beware.

The difference between for-profit marketers and not-for-profit marketers is crucial: while for-profits make people want what they **don't** need, *not-for-profit marketers should always strive to make people want what they do need.* So you see the difference? And, just as importantly, do you see that the skills required are essentially the same? Good marketing *is* good mission. Organizations that have good marketing skills can do better mission. And it all starts with understanding—and accepting—the difference between needs and wants.

Work with your staff to help them to understand that no matter how correct they are about needs, customers have the right to want something. Show them that marketing, turning needs into wants, can lead to *more* mission, not less.

This realization that people seek wants, even people that we serve, is the first step in really treating everyone like a customer, which is the subject of our next section.

C. TREATING EVERYONE LIKE A CUSTOMER

This is such an important concept that I will dwell on it more than once in this book. Successful and competitive organizations realize that everyone in and out of the organization needs to be thought of as a valued customer (even when they are wrong). This is often tougher for not-for-profits, for a variety of reasons that we should review.

The not-for-profit community is the only market that I am aware of that often thinks of its biggest customer as the *enemy.* Those of you with major funding sources from local, state, or federal governmental sources know what I am talking about: You look at these payers as organizations to do battle with, to lobby with, to argue with. This perspective is, to put it mildly, shortsighted. *The people who pay you are customers,* and deserve to be treated that way. They may be the customers from hell, but they are still customers.

☞ **HANDS-ON:** Look at your organizational attitude now. Get out your income and expense statement. Look at the four largest sources of income. Now think of the people at those organizations who you deal with the most. Is your image of them as a customer or as a pain in the neck? Are they, in your opinion, an opportunity to serve—or a barrier to service? Now ask your senior staff the same question. If you, like so many organizations, tend toward thinking of your funders as a problem, rather than as a person who your organization can help, you're in trouble in a competitive world.

Now let's look at the other side of the ledger—the people that you serve. If you are like most not-for-profits you don't call these people customers, which is fine. You call them students, patrons, consumers, clients, patients, parishioners, recipients, tenants, the congregation. The labels, as I say, are fine. However, if the labels are joined to an attitude that doesn't acknowledge that these people are also customers, you've got trouble.

A competitive, market-oriented organization, whether for-profit or not-for-profit, thinks of *everyone* outside the organization, and as well as those *inside* the organization, as customers. We'll discuss this at greater length in Chapter 6, after we identify all your markets and their differing wants. Then, I'll show you how to treat every customer with "Incredible Customer Service" in Chapter 11. For now, just remember (and begin to preach to your staff and board) that in today's environment *everyone* is a customer, and that those organizations that fail to appreciate this truth will not do as much mission as those that do. The techniques of marketing will help you tremendously in this effort, but the attitude that funders, staff, board, and the people you serve are really, truly customers has to come first, and it has to be believed, reinforced, and, like so many values, led by example, by you.

D. BEING BETTER THAN YOUR COMPETITION

But what about the other guys? In a noncompetitive environment, you don't need to worry about competition. Either there isn't any or there isn't much and you really are protected by your funders from worrying about the market's whims and changes. No more. Not only do you have to pay attention to your markets, ask what they want, and give it to them (as we will detail in Chapter 8), you have to compete for the good graces of your customers with other organizations who are trying to lure them away from you.

Competitors come in all shapes and sizes, provide great and innovative services and awful ones, have lots of money and are broke. Obviously, knowing the competition is a critical component of both marketing and becoming competitive, and we'll spend an entire chapter (Chapter 7) just on this subject. Right now, I want to make two important points about marketing and your competition.

First, the competitive marketing skills you will learn by reading this book will go a great distance toward helping your organization maximize its effectiveness in a competitive market. You can outresearch, outsell, outproduce, outsmart, and be more responsive than your competition (even really well-run organizations) if you apply what you learn in these pages. On the other hand, if you ignore the marketing part of your job, if you don't ask your markets what they want, if you just decide that what you are doing is fine and that you know what's best for all the people you serve, then even the sloppiest competitor who applies a little marketing smarts is going to eat your lunch. You can be better than your competition if you pay attention to what they are doing, if you innovate, and if you are willing to be flexible as the market changes. Most importantly, you need to be better than your competition not just in your eyes, but *in the eyes of your customers.*

❑ **FOR EXAMPLE:** Let's assume you are trying to retain your physical therapist staff (which for readers not familiar with the human service arena is a *very* tough job; there are many more jobs than there are therapists). You check around and find that your salary is very competitive, and your fringe benefits are great. You thus assume that you are competitive, that you are giving the customer (in this case, the therapist) what they want. And then they leave for a job at a *lower-paying* competitor. Why? Because the competitor has traditionally invested in regular staff training and has the best therapy equipment, which is what your therapists value. Why didn't you know this? Because you didn't ask; you assumed that money was the issue. You were better than your competition on the financial scale, but not on the scale that was important to the therapist: training and equipment. You lose.

My second point is that you have to begin to preach (or if you are already there, regularly reinforce) the underlying philosophy with your staff that you have to *compete.* Many, many not-for-profit line staff, midmanagement, and even senior staff feel that they are professionals and thus it is unseemly, undignified, somehow *dirty,* to compete. That's the director of marketing's job. I just do what I am trained for. If I go after other organizations' clients (patients, customers, students, members), I will not only sully my reputation, I will anger all my friends at that organization. Sound familiar?

This was fine and honorable thinking in the past, but it's deadly in the current environment. Attitudes like that will keep staff from believing that they are on the marketing team; it will keep them from accepting the need for flexibility, accommodation, and rapid change to meet customers' wants, it will impede their thinking of everyone as a customer. And, since marketing is a team sport, it will cause the team to do poorly as a whole.

☞ **HANDS-ON:** For many readers, this will be a tough cultural change. Here is how to start. Talk to staff in groups of eight to ten about the changes in the business environment, and demonstrate how what you have done in the past is competitive, and discuss how your environment is becoming even more competitive. Show them who your competition is and how the competition can now take away customers, clients, volunteers, and donated dollars. If you have had customers leave (or not return) recently, use them as case studies. Then ask, "How can our organization respond?" Let the staff (hopefully) come to the realization that marketing and competition, while difficult and perhaps distasteful, is the only way that your organization is going to survive to *continue to do more mission.* Like so many other discussions of change, if you can emphasize the mission connection, that marketing is good mission, that competing is good mission—you will have a much better chance of convincing the skeptics. Repeat the exercise for the whole staff, and as you go through your sessions, note which staff are on board and which are holding back. Encourage the people who are buying in to coach and cajole their hesitant peers. Remember that cultural changes like this take time, and that slow and steady repetition, reminders, and training are the essential tools. In Chapter 3 I'll provide you with seven specific ideas on how to motivate and bring along your board and staff.

Repeat after me: Competing is not bad. Competing is not immoral. Competing means continuing to be there to do good works. Competing makes us better. Competing means doing more mission, in a more focused and effective way. But in the new more competitive environment, you have to believe in your mission, your skills, and in the quality of your outcomes enough to be *willing* to compete. Remember when you were called back inside from recess in grade school? Did you run faster to the door when you were alone or when you were racing one of your friends? Me too. Competition does that; it pushes us to achieve things we couldn't on our own.

One other note: Competition does not always result in military analogies: conquest, vanquishing, total victory. Often it means carving out enough market share, enough customers—more importantly, enough of the customers that you can serve the *best*—to keep you financially healthy, innovating, and prospering. You do not have to be predatory to be competitive. But you do have to be proud enough of what you and your organization do to *not be ashamed* to tell the customer of another organization how good you are.

❑ **FOR EXAMPLE:** An excellent demonstration of this is in America's churches. I have long contended that they provide an excellent example of what not-for-profits can do where the free market exists. No United Way or government funder says: "There are too many churches in this community, we have duplication of services." And thus we have lots and lots of spiritual choices, with more springing up every day.

I know a lot of ministers, rabbis, and priests. All of them devoutly believe in their church's or synagogue's theology. Few of them would think of themselves as competitive (except against evil), but in truth all of them are competing to attract and retain members for their congregation. Our church recently completed a major building project, moving into a new sanctuary. In the first weeks that we were in the new facility, we had many more visitors than normal, as people came to see the new building. Our minister used the opportunity to give a series of sermons on "What We Believe," detailing the key points of our denomination's value structure. While he never derided other churches, he was performing another age old marketing ritual—product definition. *"Look everyone, here is what makes us different. We believe in it and we hope you will. If you share our beliefs, come join us."*

Were our minister's words from the heart? Absolutely. Was it sales? Without a doubt. Was the minister moving the mission of the church forward? Yep. You see, marketing does not have to be flackery. Just because you believe something deeply does not prohibit you from selling it, and to deny that you are selling is simply self-delusion. Once you accept marketing as mission promotion, you can study marketing (as you are doing by reading this book) and use the techniques to promote more mission. Once you realize that striving to be the best does not necessarily mean boasting about being better than your competition, you will have made the first big psychological leap toward becoming a mission-based competitor.

But you can't do that alone. You need help, and that comes from your staff, board, and volunteers. Let's look at their impact, and how you can get them to move with you toward a market-oriented future.

E. A TEAM EFFORT

Marketing is a team sport. And, since competition is a most often win-lose proposition, your organization wins or loses together. One of the major mistakes that noncompetitive organizations make (both for-profit and not-for-profit) is allowing any employee to think that their job has nothing to do with marketing. These are the organizations where you call with a question and are left on hold for half an hour only to be connected to the wrong person, who says they know nothing about your problem. These are the restaurants who cannot accommodate someone with a special dietary need. These are the airlines where the baggage handlers are rude, or the grocery stores where the staff send you on wild goose chases looking for products that the store doesn't even stock.

The truth is: *marketing is everything that every one in your organization does every day.* It is the way that the phone is answered, the grass is cut, the building is maintained, the bills are paid, the bills are collected—not just how the services are provided. It is the way that customers' problems are solved, the way inquiries are followed up, the way that the staff interacts with each other. All staff need to develop a perspective that what they do, and how they do it, affects the whole team, not just the people within their immediate field of vision.

❏ **FOR EXAMPLE:** For those readers who cling to the idea that the senior management is solely responsible for organizational marketing, consider this: when you interact with a business organization, an airline, hotel, car rental agency, restaurant, quick lube shop, who do you come in contact with? What kind of people are responsible for ensuring that you are a well-served, happy customer? The *lowest-paid people in the organization,* that's who. At the airline, it's the reservation agent, counter staff, flight attendant. At the hotel it's the desk clerk, housekeeping, restaurant servers. At the car rental agency it's the bus driver, counter staff, check-in staff. At all of these organizations it is the people on the "bottom" of the organizational ladder who make or break your experience with the company. If any one of them screws up, the entire experience takes on a bad taste.

And, in each of these cases, there are people, also in the lowest paid tier, who *never see customers,* but who also affect their satisfaction. For example, at a car rental agency, the people who clean the cars and service them are critical. Get into a dirty car, or have a breakdown on the road, and you will not be a happy camper. At the airline, the baggage handlers, the operations staff, the aircraft service crews all go about their work anonymously, but have enormous impact on customer satisfaction. The gate agent may bump you up to first class, and the pilot and flight crew may get you to your destination on time (or even early!), but if the baggage crew doesn't get your luggage on your flight, or if they trash your bags, how happy will you be?

So it is not just the people who deliver the service, nor is it the top management who are in charge of marketing. Everyone is on the team, everyone has impact, even those who don't deliver the mission in person.

But even though all your staff are on the team, many may not want to be a member. What do you do about them?

☞ **HANDS-ON:** Some of your staff may not get this, or, as I say, they may not want to. They will fear yet another addition to their job description, a function that they aren't sure that they understand: marketing. Assure them that they are probably doing many of the things that they need to already. Are they polite and helpful to the people you serve? Do they try to solve their problems? Are they making suggestions to you about what they hear from customers? Are they watching what other organizations like yours are doing and bringing the ideas to the table? Are they continuing to read and learn about innovations in your field? All of these things are part of the marketing continuum. The greatest resistance to being on the marketing team that I see is people who assume that they will have to *sell*. My advice is that you specifically tell your staff that it isn't that their job will change, it is just that everyone needs to realize that everything they do *matters*, both in terms of mission and in terms of marketing.

The question is: do your staff know, understand, *believe* that their actions affect the entire organization? If they do, then the way that they do their job, their attitude and commitment, will carry them. If they don't, no amount of marketing technique and training will help.

❏ **FOR EXAMPLE:** My sister is a woman with severe mental retardation who lives in a small group home in northwest Connecticut. When I visit her at home, I look at many things: How is the physical condition of the building, the yard? How well-dressed, clean, and healthy do *all* of the residents look (not just my sister)? How helpful are the staff to me, and to the residents? And, how do the staff get along with each other? All of these things are going through my mind before, during, and after a visit. So, a staff person who thinks I will be happy if my sister is neat, well-dressed, and happy (all of which are important to me) will miss the boat if the rest of the indicators I listed are broken. While they (the staff) may not agree with me that the lawn being mowed or not matters, it does to me (as I believe that maintenance of a property is an indication of organizational commitment to total quality), and what *I* want as the customer is the bottom line.

Remember, the customer perception of quality is what ultimately counts. In Chapter 5 we'll discuss the marketing disability that most not-for-profit staff suffer from, a disability that makes it hard to focus on what the customer wants. Your staff may be ignorant of how customers perceive your organization, or they may feel that, since no one has complained, customers are happy. Another big mistake.

☞ **HANDS-ON:** To get an idea of how customers perceive your organization, try this. Find a good friend who can act as a potential consumer. Arm them with a few key questions, such as: "What services do you offer? What kind of payment do you accept? What are your fees? Are you handicapped accessible? Do you have references that I can call? Why should I join (come, purchase, etc.)?" Have the friend first call your organization, and carefully record what happens from the most critical viewpoint possible. How many rings did it take before the phone was answered? How long before the caller was connected with someone who knew this basic information? If the caller was promised a call back, or was told information would be sent in the mail, were they ever called, did the material ever arrive, and did it answer the questions? Was there follow-up? Ask your friend, "Based solely on this interaction, would you pursue using our services further?"

Now, phase two. Have the friend present themselves at your organization's door, asking the same questions, perhaps overlaying it with being a bit difficult, or asking unusual questions. Again, debrief the friend to find out the result of the visit. Was the information given in person and over the phone the same? What did you think of the part(s) of the facility you saw? How were you greeted? With a smile and a welcoming word, or as if you were interrupting something *really* important (like the receptionist's coffee break)?

If you want, add questions for staff that would target a new market that you are after. For instance, if most of your clientele is paid for by Medicaid and you want to move toward people who are covered by private insurance, have your friend present themselves as a "covered life." Try to have them pose a little different question, and see how your people respond. One corollary for this is asking a fast food clerk for a special order (hamburger, rare, no ketchup, double mustard, two pickles).

Finally, if your wonderful friend is up to it, have them present their experience (good or bad) to your management team or marketing committee in person. Try to have them explain their perspective on the interaction. This is a scary but valuable exercise. You and your staff will learn a lot, and you will gain important insight into how things look on the other side of the admission desk or entryway. It will also reinforce the fact that everyone is on the marketing team, all the time.

What about your board members, and your other volunteers? Are they on the team? Of course. Boards are representatives of the community to your organization, and they are also ambassadors back to the community. How they act and interact is important, both at board meetings and elsewhere. Volunteers are also involved in many key tasks, ones that, if done well, enhance the mission and the reputation of the organization. But if they are done badly, or with a poor attitude, or with the feeling of "I'm just a volunteer . . ."

❑ **FOR EXAMPLE:** Good friends of ours recently began looking for a new church. Their current church had grown too big for them, and they focused their search on smaller, more intimate congregations. Denomination was not as important to them as how much opportunity there was to get to know the people, to work on church activities, to sing in a good choir, and to have group discussions rather than lectures in Sunday school classes. Over lunch, I asked the couple which churches they were considering, and they rattled off four or five that they had visited, and two or three more that were on their list. I suggested one more church that was in the geographic area of their search, and got an immediate and vehement response: "No way, their board of elders is the most divisive, political group I have seen. We know three couples there and they constantly talk about the divisions at the governance level and how much friction and tension there is." That church, despite its small size, active volunteer program, and excellent music ministry, was a nonstarter. Why? Because the board couldn't get its act together.

There is another point that I have to make from this story. Twenty years ago when someone changed churches, they went to another church of the same denomination. A Methodist (Episcopalian, Lutheran, Catholic) was that for life. The large denominations counted on this and many took their "flocks" for granted. And, in the past two decades, their numbers have shrunk dramatically, with people flocking (no pun intended) to small, new, often fundamentalist denominations. Why? Because those churches gave people what they *wanted,* and what they wanted wasn't necessarily what the traditionalists at the mainline denominations felt they *needed.*

Team, team, team. Everyone is on the marketing team. The executive director, the receptionist, the janitor, the volunteer. And everyone in between. Make this your mantra. Repeat it until you, your staff, and your board instinctively act that way.

RECAP

In this second chapter, we have covered some key preparatory ground. We first looked at the six characteristics of a market-driven, mission-based organization. To quickly review, these are:

1. Know your markets
2. Treat everyone like a customer
3. Have everyone on the marketing team
4. Ask, ask, ask, and then listen
5. Innovate constantly
6. Embrace competition

After this initial benchmarking, we then went over why marketing and all of its components are such a critical edge in the increasingly competitive world you will inhabit. We then discovered the core truth about marketing: *People have needs, but people seek wants.* Meeting needs is not enough in a competitive world. Finding out what the wants are and meeting them should be your organization's focus from this day forward. We also discussed the ways that you can turn a need into a want, a particularly important skill for some readers.

Next, we looked at ways to change your mindset about some of your markets so that you can develop a culture where everyone is treated like a customer. This includes your funders, which I acknowledge may be a stretch for many readers. We went through your internal and external markets and discussed why all of them are customers.

We then turned to the issue of being better than your competition, and why "better" needs to be defined by your customers, not just by you. I showed you some examples of how organizations that compete do not have to be predatory, but how all of them have to meet wants by listening to their markets and responding.

Finally, we discussed how marketing is first, last, and always a team sport. Everyone in your organization must play, and be aware that they are always playing, if you are to compete successfully. In a competitive world, there is no sideline, no injured reserve. Everyone is always on.

Mission-based organizations can use marketing as the competitive edge. The tools you will find in the rest of this book can help you compete, help you do more mission, more efficiently, more effectively. Do not fear competition. Do not shy away from it. Competition will make your organization a better one, but only if you survive to get better. Good marketing will give you the edge, the time—to not just survive, but to thrive. Good effective marketing is not just haphazard selling. And, you need to move your organization from what may well be its current monopoly status (or attitude) to being market-based. That's not easy, but it needs to begin now. It's the subject of the next chapter.

Discussion Questions for Chapter 2

1. How does our staff view marketing? How can we make ourselves more market driven?
2. Do we have some, all, or any of the characteristics of a market-driven organization? Which ones? How can we improve against this benchmark?
3. Do we meet needs and wants, or just one or the other? Do our staff and board know the difference between needs and wants?
4. Can we really compete? Are we of a mindset to be competitive? Do we say "Oh, no!" or "Bring it on!" when confronted with a competitor?
5. What percentage of our staff and board understand that everyone needs to be on the marketing team? How can we improve/maintain that percentage?

3

Being Mission-Based *and* Market-Driven

OVERVIEW

As you read this, you are probably in one of two positions. You are ready to move toward becoming market-driven, convinced that a competitive marketplace is upon you and that the only way for your organization to survive is to listen and respond to the marketplace. Or, you are still hesitating, unsure of whether becoming market-based is the right thing for your organization at this time, unconvinced that you can bring your board and staff along.

In both cases, you should be asking the penultimate question: Can we *really* be both mission-based *and* market-based? Can my organization be responsive to the whims, trends, and even the folly of the marketplace and still be considered true to our mission? Can we even hold onto our identity, much less our core values, over time?

CHAPTER THUMBNAIL

➤ **Which Is Right, the Markets or the Mission?**
➤ **Moving with the Markets, Maintaining Your Mission**
➤ **The Never-Ending Marketing Cycle**
➤ **The Results of Becoming Market-Driven**
➤ **Motivating Board and Staff**
➤ **Holding on to Your Core Values**

All of these are important questions, and ones that I want you to carefully consider, even if you are convinced that market-based operations are the path to the future for your organization. In this chapter, we will discuss them, and give you some tools for wrestling with these dilemmas as they come up. Because they will. Today, tomorrow, next week, or next year, you will have a market opportunity that pulls you away from your mission. What will you do? Now is the time to set the guidelines.

First, we'll look at which of the two powerful forces is correct: the market or the mission. One is right, but one should be your focus and your guide, and I'll show you which is which. Then we'll look at a number of examples of not-for-profits who have moved with the market while maintaining their mission, and use their experiences to guide you as you proceed. You will see how some organizations adapted their mission to the market, and how others bent the market wants to meet their core mission.

Also in this section, we'll review the important ways that you can use your mission to strengthen your market-based efforts, and to keep you on course. Next, I'll show you why the marketing cycle never really ends; why you never truly satisfy all the market wants; how you can constantly challenge yourself, your staff, and your organization to attain new heights of quality and customer satisfaction.

We'll continue by figuring out how to make sure that your board, staff, and volunteers are enthusiastically contributing to the transition. You need to motivate them, and I'll show you how. Then, we'll examine the positive results of becoming market-based. This list will be one that you will want to discuss thoroughly with your board and staff, as will our next topic, the results of staying where you may be now, a service-based organization. Finally, we'll go beyond the mission, to your core values. Each organization has them, and you should be able to list yours and refer to them often as you try to ensure that you don't stray too far from what you believe. Here too, we'll look at some examples of organizations that had to decide whether to accept the market want, or to say no.

By the time you are through with this chapter, you will be able to start the transition to being mission-based and market-driven, which I completely believe is crucial to your organization's continued survival and ability to continue providing your important mission.

A. WHICH IS RIGHT, THE MARKETS OR THE MISSION?

If your organization moves toward the market, if it listens to what the market wants, some day, some week, some month, you will be confronted by a market want that conflicts with your mission, your organizational history, or even your personal values. What are you to do? What should be your guide? Which, in such a conflict, is "right"—the market or your mission?

Let me put it as succinctly as I can in three sentences:

1. The market is *always* right.
2. The market is *not always right for you.*
3. The *mission* should be your organization's ultimate guide.

The market wants what it wants, and there is no denying it, no ignoring it, no trying to make it not so. The people that you serve want what they want, but you can, and in some cases *should,* give them only so much. The people who fund you want what *they* want, but you can, and in some cases *should,* give them only so much—even to the point of turning down their money.

And here is the point: *The choice is always yours as an organization.* You can choose not to meet a market want whenever you feel that it is in conflict with your organization's mission or values. And, further, you have to evaluate whether or not such a market move is in conflict with your personal values and ethics.

❑ **FOR EXAMPLE:** A good friend of mine was the director of patient education for a set of rural health centers in the Southwest. As she did her market surveys, talked to patients and community members, and reviewed data from focus groups, she saw repeatedly that the community was concerned about a rapid rise in teenage pregnancies and in what seemed to be an epidemic of girls dropping out of high school to care for their babies. She brought this information, along with the other identified concerns, to her marketing committee and eventually to the board of directors.

The board decided to expand the organization's already broad educational role in the community by working with the community's public and private schools to offer more effective classes and counseling on pregnancy prevention, to both boys and girls. This supported the organization's mission of primary care prevention, treatment, and community education, and its core value that prevention was a priority. And, this was fine with my friend. The idea was good, it was something that she could do well, and the board had given her the resources she needed.

But the board had added one point she could not abide. In working with the teens, the board directed (after a long and acrimonious debate) that *all* options should be discussed—that all choices, including terminating an unwanted pregnancy, should be presented objectively and without endorsement. My friend has very strong personal feelings about abortion, and she stated that she could not endorse, encourage, present, or even develop such a presentation. After a great deal of personal soul-searching, she resigned her position.

Whether or not you agree with her on the very controversial subject of abortion, you have to admire her willingness to sacrifice her job to preserve her own sense of morals, ethics, and values. Two key markets, the board and the community, had indicated their wants, so the market had spoken. The board's method of meeting the community's wants was not the only choice, but it was the option that they selected. And my friend thought it through and said, "I cannot, in good conscience, do that."

My point here is that, if you find yourself being drawn into territory where you feel uncomfortable, stop. Talk it through with friends, coworkers, family members, or a spiritual counselor such as a minister, priest, or rabbi. Don't let the market drag you into a place where you no longer feel good about yourself. As a not-for-profit manager, you have to feel good about what you do; you must exude enthusiasm and commitment to the mission to do your job well. It is that selfless, idealistic energy that makes not-for-profit staff special. It's that same enthusiasm and commitment that gets the organization over the hurdles and barriers it confronts, and that keeps everyone on the team we discussed in the last chapter. If you feel you are being forced into a position of doing something wrong, even if your competition is doing it, even if the markets are screaming for it, you will lose that edge—that extra effort, extra sacrifice—you are now willing to make to pursue your mission. Don't lose that by following the markets into a dark place. You *can* say no. Others, in other organizations, will be there to meet the want, and that's fine. You need to do, first and foremost, what you feel is *right*.

That having been said, how do you decide? Look at the sequence shown below. It shows some checkpoints that you can use to assure yourself that you are not being drawn into a place that is wrong for you or your organization.

Checkpoint 1: How does this change fit with our organizational mission and values?
Checkpoint 2: How does this change fit with my personal ethics and values?
Checkpoint 3: How does this change coincide with and support our organizational strategic plan?

Notice that the first checkpoint is your mission, the second checkpoint is your personal values, and the third is an organizational capability check. While I think that this is an appropriate ordering, you really can answer the questions in any order, because, if you find that the answer to *any* is negative, you should not proceed. So if you are more comfortable putting the personal issues first, fine. If you feel that they should be the final checkpoint, that works as well. Just check them *all.*

☞ **HANDS-ON:** For a new service or even a major service expansion, here is a checklist that you can run through:

- Does this action support our mission?
- Does it support or conflict with our organizational values?
- Does it support our strategic plan goals and objectives?
- Does the action wind up with net income or net cost? If it is a loss center, can we afford it?
- Is this something we can do well?
- Is this action something I can personally support?

If there are other issues that are important to you, add them to the list. Go through the list considering the mission, values, and ethical issues carefully.

The bottom line in this discussion is that, to be effective, you need to move with the markets whenever you can, but you need to use your mission, your values, and your personal ethical compass to guide you and set appropriate limits.

That having been said, don't let your the mission be the excuse to *never* change. Something new or different is not by definition *anti-mission.* If you hear yourself saying, "We've never done it that way," that doesn't mean you shouldn't. *Use* your mission, don't *hide behind it.*

B. MOVING WITH THE MARKETS, MAINTAINING YOUR MISSION

So what are some practical ways to move with the market and still maintain your mission? The most important skill in this area is learning how to say "no" to a good idea, and even to a real need. Even though a market may want you to provide a service, you need to back away if you can't do it well, or if doing the service would jeopardize everything else you are doing. More and more not-for-profits are learning that they cannot be all things to all people, that they cannot solve all the problems in their community, and thus that they need to pick and choose what they do well, what they can afford, and not just chase every dollar out there.

❑ **For Example:** How often has your organization faced a dilemma like this: You are awarded a $1 million contract for services. Not often enough, you say? Well, read on. Let's assume that the contract is for one year, and is designed to reimburse all your costs, and thus is a breakeven for you. The funder wants you to start the first of next month. You have no start-up expenses and can just open your doors on the first and start doing business. (Having no start-up costs would be *extremely* unusual, but it makes the example more understandable.) You will bill the funder monthly on the first of the month and they will take 45 days to pay. Is this great or what? Only if you have $125,000 to invest. That's the cost of the contract for the 45 days that you have to operate before the funding kicks in. You are lending the funder $125,000 *interest-free* for the year of the contract—real money that really disappears for that time.

What do you do? The market (the funder and the service recipients) really want this contract to take place. It supports your mission. But it does not support your organizational value of at least breaking even on every piece of work, and your strategic planning goal of not letting your cash on hand drop below 40 days' operating expenses. Since this contract does not recognize the expense of the "loan" to the funder, you lose money (the opportunity cost or interest that you can earn on the $125,000 for the year). And the use of that money to finance the contract draws down all your cash reserve.

The market said move. The mission said move. But your values and goals said stop. Frankly, this problem confronts not-for-profits every day. Should you take the money or not? The market says yes. What do you say?

A second challenge in following the market is that you may not realize the problem until you are already deeply involved with the market change. None of us can predict the full outcome of implementation of new methods of service, different payment methods, or new strategies for identifying and meeting community needs.

❑ **For Example:** In heath care, managed care puts health care providers into the incentive/risk loop, pushing them to keep people healthy, to treat them faster, with more outpatient care. It is a payment strategy that has literally swept away old concepts in medicine and dramatically changed the relationship between providers, insurers, employers, and patients. Managed care has moved the markets—seismically.

Most hospitals and physicians grudgingly accepted managed care, convincing themselves that the quality of care would not suffer too greatly. And they jumped into programs wholesale. The managed care intermediaries looked first at where the greatest savings were to be found, and it was easy to identify hospital inpatient costs as a huge percentage of overall health care expenses, and a place where significant savings could be quickly realized. So admissions were questioned, stays were shortened, and the hospitals and physicians went along.

Until the insurers crossed an invisible "morality" line, one that no one could have foreseen: they started limiting new mothers to 24, even 18, hours in the hospital after the birth of a child. This policy generated a huge number of complaints which were picked up by the media and outraged the public. Money had overcome basic mission, and people were angry. But what could the hospitals and physicians do? They were contractually obligated to follow the managed care intermediary's rules. Yet they felt morally and mission-obligated to do *something.* Some hospitals let mothers stay and didn't charge for the extra day or two. But there is only so much uncompensated care that any hospital can absorb. So the hospital and medical industries lobbied Congress and state legislatures to change the law and set low-end limits that everyone could live with. They met their mission benchmark, the market want of their patients, *and* the market want of the funding intermediary.

Your next challenge is to make sure that when you move with the market, you don't lose your organizational identity. If you move so far afield from the service, group, or community that people identify you with, you can put your organization into a bind, particularly in fund raising and board recruitment. No one will know who you really are; no one will be able to join you to a core cause.

❑ **FOR EXAMPLE:** In the 1980s the Xerox Corporation was expanding its product line, trying to diversify its income and lower its reliance on its central product: photocopiers. Its strategy was to move away from thinking of itself as a copier company, and move toward the identity of a manufacturer of office machines. Suddenly you could buy Xerox desktop computers, printers, even answering machines. The slogan "Office Xerox" was plastered all over the business press, and ads appeared in general circulation as well as business magazines.

The problem was that the attempted identity change left the consumer behind. People had a strong image of Xerox as a copier manufacturer, not a computer maker. And not only did they think of Xerox as *a* copier maker, they thought of them as *the* copier maker. "To xerox" was and still is a commonly understood verb. By moving away from a core identity, Xerox not only lost a lot of money on products that didn't sell, they confused their customers, some of whom thought that they were abandoning photocopiers completely. At just this time, rival copier firms such as Mita were able to tell people that *they* would be focused on photocopiers for the long haul, but that Xerox was no longer centrally committed to that product line. Xerox lost market share.

Don't follow a market want either into anonymity or far enough afield to fundamentally confuse people; but, again, don't automatically discard any idea that changes your traditional services or service population.

❑ **FOR EXAMPLE:** A good example of success in such an identity transition is the YMCA (remember, the "M" stands for "Men's"), which moved across gender lines in the 1950s to expand its potential customer base. (I should point out that the age and religious labels have also been surmounted. You don't need to be under 30 or a practicing Christian to use a Y, be on its staff, or volunteer for a board position.)

Thus, identity-drift is okay, but you need to carefully think through how people think of you now and how they will think of you as you change. And, in some cases, it won't matter.

❑ **FOR EXAMPLE:** Chaddock is a residential school in Quincy, Illinois, that serves children who come from broken or abusive homes, and who have not been able to succeed in a family foster care environment. Its original name was Chaddock College, and it has gone through a series of name and service changes since its incorporation in 1853, including the Chaddock Methodist Boys School. It ceased using this name in 1983 when it admitted girls for the first time. Yet, in 1995, Chaddock received over 100 donations where the check was made out to "Methodist Boys School." It didn't matter that the organization now serves boys and girls, or that it is no longer closely affiliated with the Methodist Church as it was in its early years. Its image, its identity remain the same.

Finally, I want to show you a tool with which to maintain your mission while you move with your markets. You don't even have to go to a hardware store to purchase it. It's in your office right now. It's called your mission statement.

Successful managers use all the available resources to get the job done. Our mission statements are truly our central tool, our most valuable resource. So why don't we use them more? Here are some ways that you can get more use out of your mission, and have it help you keep your organization mission-based, even while you are in the heat of discussions on how to meet the changing wants of your target markets.

1. Have the Mission Visible—Everywhere

If you don't already, get your mission statement printed up attractively and hand it out to everyone in the organization. Put it on the wall by your reception area as well as in your staff lunchroom. Have a copy on the table in your conference room, and print it first in your strategic plan, annual report, and even in your newsletter. Have it relentlessly around, a constant reminder of what the point is at your organization.

2. Use the Mission Statement Constantly at Management, Board, and Committee Meetings

Now that it's around, you need to put it to use. If you don't, the mission will just become another essentially invisible wall decoration. So, make copies of your mission statement and have them literally *on the table* at all board meetings, committee meetings, and staff meetings. Then talk the mission up. In staff meetings when there is a program or policy choice to be decided, ask, "Which one of these choices is more mission-based, or makes us more mission-capable?" Lead by example and show staff that you rely on the mission to help make your decisions, and that you expect them to do the same. Duplicate this action at board and committee meetings. Will having copies of the mission end all disputes? Hardly. But it will help to make sure that everyone in the organization is mission-focused.

3. Use the Mission in Your Decisions About New Markets and New Services

Using the checklist detailed earlier in this chapter, use the mission as one of your most important benchmarks in deciding when (or when not) to move toward a new market, provide a new service, or serve a new clientele.

You already have the entire organization invested in the mission. That's why you are all there doing the good works that you do. So use the mission as a tool to help you keep your organization on track. Not only will it help guide you in marketing, but it will get you into the habit of using the mission in all of your major decision making, your staff and board meetings. It's a good mission-based habit to get into.

C. THE NEVER-ENDING MARKETING CYCLE

So where does all this lead? When do you get to the promised land of becoming a mission-based and market-driven organization? How do you know when you have arrived? And, when you arrive, can you stop and rest a bit?

Not really. Once you embark on this journey, it becomes a philosophy as crucial to the performance of your charitable purpose as any other part of your mission statement. For example, you may, as an organization, believe in prevention, early intervention, a particular method of education, or in a particular environmental cause. Those beliefs are closely related to your organizational identity; they describe in large part who you are. Now you need to become a market-based organization that also has those same values, one that puts credence not only in your own beliefs, but also in the beliefs and wants of your many markets.

How will you know when you have become market-driven? You will know when you can quickly tell me how your five most important funders feel about you, based on survey or focus group data. Or when you can rattle off the four or five most recent adjustments you have made to your service array, or to the delivery of services, based on information gathered from your customers. When I can walk into your organization and you are sure that I will be greeted with courtesy on my arrival and asked about my experience on my departure. When your marketing material is targeted, and when you can quickly list your target markets, your key competitors, and your core areas of competence.

But even when you can do all this, you won't have *arrived.* Because there is always a little further to go. Always a market in flux, a new want in development, a new competitor to face. Marketing is a tease really, a horizon that you can see the shape of, but that is always just out of reach. It is moving ground, constantly reshaping itself in ways that you can't really predict until you are there.

So you never really arrive, but you still cannot afford *not* to embark on the journey.

D. THE RESULTS OF BECOMING MARKET-DRIVEN

What good things happen if you go through all the work, effort, and discipline to become and remain market-driven? How can you tell if it is worth the investment? There are some real and tangible results from making this change, and the six listed below are the ones I see most often.

1. You Will Have Happier Markets—Particularly Consumers and Government Funders

If you ask and listen, ask and listen, ask and listen, and then make a reasonable effort to accommodate the wants people have, they will have a better feeling about you. First, simply because you asked. That action shows that you care, are more businesslike, and, in the case of perhaps a poor historic relationship with your funders, want to improve the relationship. Second, because you take action and try to accommodate them. Happier customers mean more return customers, more referrals, less hassles from funders, more sweep-up funds and pilot project grants, and being given a little slack in a crisis. You want happier service customers and happier funders. Marketing can help you get both.

2. Your Organization Will Have a Better Image in the Community

People will talk about you as a "businesslike charity," one that is using what they perceive as their money (from donations or taxes) in a more efficient, effective manner. You will have a higher visibility in the community, because you will be out there asking all the time. You will gain a reputation as a responsive organization, not one of those not-for-profits that hasn't changed since the Roosevelt Administration (Teddy's, not FDR's!). This image will mean more customers, more donations, better morale for the staff and board, easier board recruitment, more designated donations through United Way, and even, if you are lucky, a better press.

3. You Will Retain Your Current Markets

If it is not already happening, it will soon: Someone will show up to compete with you for your core business. They may, as we discussed earlier, just "cream" you, taking the most lucrative funders, donors, families, or service recipients. But come they will. By doing good marketing starting *now,* not after the competition shows up, you will cement the long-term relationship with many of your core markets. And, by competing and being responsive to changing wants when the competition does arrive, you have a much better chance of keeping those customers on board and loyal. If you think that this doesn't apply to you, ask your fund-raising staff if they need those donors who reliably contribute every year: those people who are retained customers. You don't want to lose them.

4. Your Organization Will Be More Efficient and Effective in the Provision of Services

By definition, if you are a market-based organization, you are doing things that your markets want, and not doing things that they don't want. This will allow you to focus more and be more efficient and effective in what you do. You'll get more mission for the money, because you will be putting your money where it has the most impact.

5. You Will Develop New Revenue Sources

Success breeds success. You will find that happy customers will tell others, and this will result in more business, more customers, and new funders. Organizations that are good marketers attract new revenue like a fully pollinating flower attracts bees. Your business skills will be tested deciding which work to take and which not to, and it will be important to stay focused on your core competencies. But I have seen organization after organization reap the financial rewards of marketing by having new and previously untapped sources of funding within 18 to 24 months of kicking off their marketing effort.

6. Your Organization Can Become and Remain More Financially Stable

As a result of being more focused and effective, and as more funding sources are developed, you can become much more financially stable. Notice that in the five previous points I say you "will," but here I say you "can." Why? Because just having more income doesn't mean you will be more financially stable. More income gives you the means to stability, but you still need to manage those funds well, ensuring your growth doesn't outstrip your cash, that your new expenses don't exceed your new income, that you put some money aside for capital improvements and repairs. But good marketing gives you the opportunity to become financially stable. (For a whole book on this subject, see my book *Financial Empowerment, More Money for More Mission.*)

If you do your marketing well, consistently, and with the entire staff and board on the marketing team, these results will accrue to your organization. They are the tangible benefits of all the work and money that you will put into your organizational change. Some are measurable, some are not, but if you are sensitive to them, you will be looking for the rewards in the right places.

E. MOTIVATING BOARD AND STAFF

You cannot make this change alone. For some people in your organization (perhaps including you), this will be the first time you have ever encountered, or had to deal with, competition. For others it will be "old hat." For some, there will be an easy transition. For others, there will never be complete acceptance that the "charity" days are long gone and never returning.

But you can do it. Your organization, if well led, can make the transition to a mission-based and market-based entity. Look around. You have lots of company.

❏ **FOR EXAMPLE:** Thirty years ago, American hospitals had a pretty good deal. In most communities there were a stable number of hospitals, with a slowly growing number of beds. They often shared physicians, and even certain resources. Rarely did hospitals openly compete; certainly they never advertised. There was often an esprit de corps and an elitism at a larger institution that perhaps was associated with a medical school but, in general, a hospital was a predictable entity: a not-for-profit, community-based organization that provided a wide range of different inpatient care and was a user of community resources including donations and volunteer time. Walk into a primary, secondary, or tertiary care hospital in New York, Des Moines, or Phoenix, and you would see basically the same array of services, the same equipment, and the same approximate size.

Today, you get anything but the "same." Over 20 percent of American health care is delivered in for-profit hospitals, when it is delivered *in* the hospital at all. Hospitals have shrunk; many are not even in business. Hospitals have specialized, "creamed," and focused on particular things that they can do well. They have merged, acquired, and been acquired to meet the wants of the markets, who in their cases are not only their patients, but also their physicians (the classic model of a referrer), the managed care insurers (who duplicate many of your funders), and even some tough-to-recruit staff, such as physical and occupational therapists.

The hospital that you and your family visit now is by definition market-based. I can say that with assurance because the ones that are not market-based are gone.

Was this an easy transition? No way. But the change was coupled with a huge increase in the business expertise and education of hospital administrators. Dozens, even hundreds, of master's programs in hospital management and administration sprang up all over the country as people worked hard to learn how to manage these multi-million-dollar not-for-profit businesses in a competitive environment.

❏ **FOR EXAMPLE:** If you are as old as I am, you can remember "the phone company." You received your local and long-distance service from one carrier—in fact, everyone did. You didn't own your phones, the company did. It was the perfect monopoly, until an upstart company named MCI sued AT&T and won. In the mid-1980s long-distance phone service was deregulated, and AT&T was, in fact, broken up by a federal judge. Local phone services have followed down the deregulation path. Some of the "Baby Bells" have flourished in the new competitive environment, and our telephone service, except at the local level, is now less expensive, more efficient, and carries much more information. Each company has its own strategies, its own array of products and services (some of which are *very* confusing to the customer) and is reacting to its own market's wants, sometimes well, sometimes not.

To appreciate the magnitude of the changes this monopoly caused inside AT&T, you need to understand that *everyone* in the senior and midmanagement levels at AT&T and the Bell System had spent *all or nearly all* of their careers working for a monopoly. This was a Fortune 100 company with 300,000 employees and not a clue about marketing. All they had to do was connect people's phones and make sure that service was dependable and reasonably fast. But there had never been an MCI or Sprint or any other of the dozens of small long-distance competitors that there are today.

At AT&T, prior to the breakup, there was no culture of asking, no system to monitor customer satisfaction, no method of recruiting customers. Why? Because there was no need to have them. Now, think of all the people that the long-distance providers alone have hired just to pester you during dinnertime hawking their wares! Think of the boost to the advertisement market to carry all the television and print ads! They have adjusted and adjusted quickly. But it wasn't easy, even though they were a for-profit.

❏ **FOR EXAMPLE:** Speaking of utilities, a similar overhaul is under way in the selling of electric power. Particularly in the Northeastern states, different companies are now competing to provide the electricity you use. While the network of wires, cables, transformers, and switches will remain the property of the local utility, the actual power that you use may come from any of a number of sources. One CEO even envisions selling power like cable television, with a fixed rate per month!

Talk about a major change! Utilities have *never, ever* had to worry about a customer choosing someone else. If they lived in the utility's service area the choice was to have power or not to have power, but never did the consumer have *choice!* Again, *nearly all* of the staff on board when the market changed had spent *nearly all* their lives in the comfort and relative safety of a monopoly. Now they would have to adapt or perish. And again, just as in hospitals and telephone communications, there are mergers and acquisitions by the dozen. The market is going through a shakeout. Some organizations—those that learn to adapt to a market-based philosophy—will flourish, but those that don't will fade away.

All of these examples have themes similar to the dilemma you face: they had a staff and board that had been raised in a monopoly, not in the more frantic, more variable competitive arena. Just like you, they had a choice: Adapt or die. Just like you, they were faced with the possibilities of merger, or acquiring, or even being acquired.

And there was one other thing that all of these industries did: They got outside help. Hospital administrators hired marketing staff from the for-profit arena. When that didn't always work, they set up master's programs in administration to learn from within. The utilities and phone companies relied heavily on consultants and outside hires who understood the whims of the marketplace. They spent a great deal of money retraining employees, focusing on customer service, learning how to solve problems quickly, efficiently, and even *politely.*

The point is this: You can too. As you enter the competitive arena, many of your staff will seize up and resist the change. They will bemoan the fact that they took their job to serve, not to sell. Many, in fact, sought the shelter of the not-for-profit environment precisely because they did not want to enter the hurly-burly of the business world.

However, some of their resistance will not be solely for philosophical reasons. Many staff will correctly assume that they don't know *how* to act competitively. And, like most people, they would rather do nothing than mess up. So they will resist.

☞ **HANDS-ON:** Get your staff and board the help that they need. Specifically:

- Send people to courses on marketing, customer service, quality control, surveying, focus group development, and making better marketing materials.
- Have an outside marketing consultant come in and provide you with a competitive assessment. Have him or her tell you what you need to improve, and where your strengths and weaknesses are in terms of expertise and readiness.
- Hire from outside your discipline. Particularly in the marketing area, a fresh set of eyes, a fresh perspective, can be invaluable. Having this new expertise in-house will be vital in the coming economy.

Most of your staff and board, if they feel that they are properly "equipped" to compete, will do just fine. But you have to get them the "equipment."

What else can you do to motivate the staff and board and to get them over the inertia of resistance?

☞ **HANDS-ON:** Try one or more of these ideas:

1. Talk to them about the reality of competition.
Engage the staff and board early and often in discussions about competition. Show them information about the competitiveness that is oc-

curring in your sector. Target your information as closely as you can to your own discipline, and your income and service array. For example, if you get 25 percent of your income from small donations, you can show your staff and board members information on how many groups in your community have increased their development efforts. If you only get 1 percent of your income from fund raising, don't bother with making a case for more competition in that arena.

Have senior staff and your board read this book, and then use the questions at the end of each chapter to walk them through topics relevant to the issues developed in the book. This will allow you and your management and policy team to more easily coalesce around the reality of increased competition as well as the need for increased marketing efforts.

2. Talk about your mission.
Discuss the people that your organization has helped. If you can, use real names of real individuals to highlight the value of what your organization does. Note that if you don't compete there is a good chance that you will not be around much longer to help those people who depend on you. If you have a much-disparaged competitor, talk about what happens if the people you serve must start going to them because you are no longer around. Use your mission as a tool for reflection on your value, and for motivation to try competing.

3. List organizations like yours that are in trouble or out of business.
If you can, prepare a list of organizations in your area of work who are in financial trouble. National examples are good, but local or state ones are much better for underscoring the potential outcome of not paying attention to the market forces that are shaping the future of your organization.

4. Get them comfortable with the idea of marketing.
Review with them who your markets are, using the chart you will see in Chapter 6. Help them understand that everyone, even your funders, are really your markets. Remind them that, while mission is always first, if there is no money, there is no mission!

Most importantly, help them see that they are already marketing, and have been for many years. This will help remove some of the "change" and "new" labels from the idea. For example, if you have "nontraditional" hours for services designed to meet the needs of two-income families, you are marketing—designing a service distribution to meet the wants of the market. If you already ask about customer satisfaction in any way, you are marketing—testing the wants of your customers. If you have started up a new service, or opened a new location in response to a customer-stated desire, you are marketing—responding to the markets. I'm sure you have some examples with which to allay the fears and concerns of your staff. Use them.

5. Get them comfortable with the idea of competition.
Show them areas where you have competed in the past, including fund raising, grant applications, or United Way funding. Note that as service recipients become more and more the focus of funding streams and choice is increased, you will need to compete for those recipients in just the way that you have competed for funding in the past.

Go through the exercise of developing a list of competition using the sample tables in Chapter 7. Make sure you emphasize your organization's strengths at some point, or your board and staff will think that you are facing unbeatable competition.

6. Recognize and acknowledge their fears and concerns. Admit your own.
Acknowledge that this is new turf for all of you, and that many staff and board did not come to the organization to take part in the competitive marketplace. Talk about your fears, concerns, and the need for more training and help. Note that change is inevitable and that, while you don't have the power to change the marketplace, you do have the power to shape your own destiny within that market. Discuss your options and your choices, and then look at the result of becoming market-oriented and the fallout that occurs if you stay service-oriented.

7. State clearly and forcefully that you need to move ahead and do it now.
After this discussion is complete, end on a firm, forceful, and assured message: We need to move the organization ahead, and get ourselves ready to compete. Look for agreement, and if you sense that it is not there, note that you are regrettably sure that this direction will alienate some members of the staff and board. And, for those whose discomfort is too severe, you would recommend that they go elsewhere with their time, energy, and skills.

This is a hard part of the discussion for nearly all of us. But it is true. You are embarking on a long and difficult journey through a countryside that many of your staff and board never thought that they would set foot inside. Dragging them along against their will will slow everyone down, distracting you from the job at hand: leading your organization through the change. It is better to make the hard choices now; for people that you feel cannot come along and support the new direction, it is better to recommend that they get out now. The train is leaving the station. Better to have these folks leave voluntarily now than to have them derail the train later on. Or for you to have to throw them off.

These seven steps, if discussed with empathy and understanding, but with a clear sense of where you are going, will bring on most of your staff and board. Is there any other information that you can give these good people that might motivate them? Certainly, and I've made a list below of the results of becoming market-based. Show it to your staff and board and ask if these are outcomes that your organization would like.

F. HOLDING ON TO YOUR CORE VALUES

We've talked endlessly about mission, mission, mission, and markets, markets, markets. Ask, ask, ask. Listen, listen, listen. Obviously, you can see I believe in the value of repetition. I have learned other things to value in writing: the use of examples, trying to give readers ideas that they can put into use immediately (Hands-On), and telling the reader the whole truth, not just the part that they might want to hear. I value clarity and brevity but, even though they are values and things that I value and aspire to, I do not always attain them to the level that I would like. I get distracted, get lazy, or just like a certain story too much to cut it short. My writing values are not always as tightly held to as I would like.

The same is true for your organization. Beyond your mission there is a set of core values that guide the way that you do the things you do. If you are a school, you might put a high value on teaching the students to work in teams, or on high discipline, or on faculty esprit de corps. As a church, you might strongly value community service, political application of your spiritual beliefs, a literal interpretation of the Bible, or the funding of overseas ministries. As an art museum, you might focus on the avant-garde, or on traditional masters, or on teaching children, or on reaching out through the schools. Your organization may put a high value on teaching people to help themselves or on a certain theory of therapy.

These values take you part of the way from your mission to the implementation of that mission. They give you guidance on the more practical month-to-month and year-to-year implications of how to stay true to your mission.

❑ **FOR EXAMPLE:** Here are the mission and values of a state child welfare agency that I worked on with the staff to develop a number of years ago:

MISSION: The Department of Child Welfare, in partnership with others, will provide services to children and families to protect and advocate on be-

half of children and youth who are, or who are at risk of, being abused, neglected, or removed from their families.

VALUES:

➤ *That children have a right to a safe, secure, permanent living arrangement, preferably with their own family.*

➤ *That we should act quickly, competently, and professionally to protect children, prevent harm, and advocate for their well-being.*

➤ *That children and families are served best in homelike settings in their own community.*

➤ *That we should recognize the humanity and importance of each individual, and treat them honestly, with fairness, dignity, compassion, and cultural competence.*

➤ *That we should foster a stable, supportive workplace which will allow for each employee to grow, develop, and participate in the fulfillment of the mission.*

➤ *That we are accountable for the work we do, and thus, must effectively and efficiently utilize all available resources to carry out the mission of the department.*

You can see that the values spoke not only to the mission, but also to the staff, the way the mission would be accomplished (not in institutions), and that everyone should be held accountable. This is a good set of values for a public organization.

National Public Radio's Mission and Values Statement reads as follows:

The Mission of National Public Radio is to work in partnership with member stations to create a more informed public—one challenged and invigorated by a deeper understanding and appreciation of events, ideas, and cultures.

The fundamental values that guide our mission are:

➤ *Reporting with accuracy, thoroughness, and fairness;*

➤ *Using sound creatively to engage the intelligence, curiosity, and imagination of listeners;*

➤ *Encouraging innovation;*

➤ *Honoring cultural diversity;*

➤ *Upholding the tradition and prerogatives of public radio as a local medium;*

> ➤ *Making the most of advances in audio technology; and*
> ➤ *Encouraging the talent, dedication, creativity, and productivity of our staff.*

The uses of these values in your marketing are many. They can help you select a core market to serve, avoid a funder, take a certain spin in your public relations, and focus on certain organizational outcomes.

They can also help you solve the painful puzzle of which tug to follow—the market or the mission.

❑ **FOR EXAMPLE:** Local not-for-profit community hospitals throughout the nation are in a terrible moral bind. There are more and more people with no insurance (and few funds) who are presenting themselves at the emergency room door with real (and sometimes life-threatening) injuries or illnesses. If the hospitals let everyone in (regardless of their ability to pay), they will be out of business and of no help to any one. On the other hand, the hospital mission is to help the sick and injured. How can they turn someone away?

This dilemma is exacerbated in small towns where it seems that everyone knows everyone. Thus, the board and staff are well aware as they set the policy for what is called "uncompensated care," that they may well be taking an action that will result in refusal of service to a friend, neighbor, or relative. How do values help? In most of the hospitals where I have helped board and staff through this moral mire, there was a value of "maintaining fiscal stability" which balanced the "ease the pain and suffering" value.

Often values do keep each other in balance. I have long held that the first rule of not-for-profits is "Mission, mission, and more mission." And that the second, balancing rule is "No money, no mission." The same is true for your organization: You can have "competing" values.

❑ **FOR EXAMPLE:** In our jurisprudence system we have many values (mostly listed in the Bill of Rights) such as the right to an impartial jury of our peers, the right to a fair and speedy trial, and the right to face our accusers. In certain situations, though, we violate these values to meet more compelling values, such as the right to life, liberty, and the pursuit of happiness. For example, in the case of an abused child, certain courts have allowed the child to act as a witness against a defendant without actually doing it in the same court as the accused. The value of the child's well-being and mental health takes precedence over the value of the right of the defendant.

In all of these examples, the values of the organization (or system) helped people to decide which path was right for them. And, in the examples, there was a lot of wiggle room to let certain circumstances result in certain interpretations.

☞ **HANDS-ON:** If you don't have a set of organizational values, now is the time to develop them. With your board and key staff (and an outside facilitator), look at your mission statement, and then make a list of the key things that set your organization apart, that make your organization special, that you believe in. Print this list up with your mission statement and use it along with your mission in management and policy discussions.

Your values are important guides in solving the moral, ethical, and mission quandaries that inevitably result from change, especially if that change is externally initiated. Formalize your values and use them as the moral and mission compasses that they are.

RECAP

In this chapter, you have learned the methods—and the dangers—of being simultaneously market-based and mission-based. You have seen the temptations that will tend to draw you into the world that chases money rather than mission, and I hope you now know the techniques to resist the temptation.

First, we went over the crucial question of which is right, the market or the mission? You learned that, at least in my opinion, the market is always right, but that responding to that market in the way that it wants will not always be the right thing for you. I showed you that your mission should be your guide, and that, while you need to listen and respond to the market whenever you can, the ultimate limit on your flexibility should be your mission. I also cautioned you not to let your mission be the rationale for rejecting any response to the market. The market wants will mostly be very appropriate for you, and you shouldn't hide behind the mission.

Next I told you how to move with the markets while maintaining your mission. I showed you some examples of organizations that are doing just that, and gave you some management ideas of how to get more use out of your mission statement to help you reinforce, remind, and refresh the mission every day.

Finally, we turned to the issue that moves past your mission and into your core values. I suggested that you list those values, discuss them, and use them as an additional framework within which to operate. We looked at examples of organizations that rejected new market opportunities that conflicted with their core values, and I provided you with a checklist that your staff and board can use to measure your comfort with a new or modified service based on your values.

Third, we looked at the never-ending cycle of marketing and competition, noting that your move from being service-based to being market-based is really not a move; it is the beginning of a philosophy of action—an endless process that constantly adapts, changes, improves, and adjusts to the changes of the marketplace. In short, you are starting a journey that never ends.

We next covered some important ground by reviewing the benefits of becoming a market-based organization. You can use these points in your discussion with board and staff to motivate and convince them that competition is real and marketing is a mission-based strategy. To quickly review, the six results were:

1. You will have happier markets—particularly consumers and government funders.
2. Your organization will have a better image in the community.
3. Your will retain your current markets.
4. Your organization will be more efficient and effective in providing services.
5. You will develop new revenue sources.
6. Your organization will become and remain more financially stable.

After that review, we talked about ways to motivate staff, board, and, yes, even you to make that journey. First, we talked about team development and I gave you seven discussion threads with which to convince any hesitant staff or board that you are going in the right direction. These discussion topics can also help make them more comfortable with policies that they may know are correct, but not yet feel are *right*.

To review, these seven ideas were:

1. Talk to them about the reality of competition.
2. Talk about your mission.
3. List organizations such as yours that are in trouble or out of business.
4. Get them comfortable with the idea of marketing.
5. Get them comfortable with the idea of competition.
6. Recognize and acknowledge their fears and concerns. Admit your own.
7. State clearly and forcefully that you need to move ahead and do it now.

By using these topics steadily, and with some empathy for the massive change you may be embarking on, you will bring most, but probably not all, of your staff and board along.

Now you know the yin and yang of making the change to a market-based not-for-profit. You have the skills and the techniques in front of you to convince your staff and board that it is the right choice. But, even after all of this work and motivation, you still have one more issue to think through before we move on to identify your markets, and look at ways to deal with their wants. The question is: Are we flexible enough to meet the wants of so many different customers? That's the subject of our next chapter.

Discussion Questions for Chapter 3

1. Are we mission-based? How can we be more so?
2. Are we market-driven? Can we improve our response to the markets? How?
3. What are the biggest barriers we face to achieving and maintaining market-driven status?
4. What are our core values? Should we add them to our mission? Who should be involved in setting them?
5. What are our core competencies? What is it that we do really well? Do these things enhance our mission or distract us from it?
6. Do our board members feel competition is a real concern? Why or why not?
7. Do all of our staff members feel that competition is a real concern? How can we regularly underscore this issue?
8. Do board and staff feel that marketing is related to mission? How can we do more to make the connection?
9. Can we take the actions suggested to make staff and board feel "equipped" to compete? How? When?
10. Looking at the benefits of being a market-driven organization, if these came true for us, what would it mean to our mission delivery?

4

Being Flexible and Changing with the Market

OVERVIEW

If you use the ideas presented in this book, you should wind up asking all your customers what they want, and asking regularly. If you do that asking well, you, your staff, and your board will be constantly confronted with small, medium, and even large changes in the wants of your many markets.

Here is the problem: Can you adapt to these changes? Can your staff? Can your board? Are you flexible enough that your organization can re-shape itself constantly to meet the changing environment outside your doors? In the old order, the protected economy, change came slowly and you had lots of second chances. The community, the funders, the people you serve, all gave you a break since you were a not-for-profit. No more. You need to adapt, adjust, change, improve, and innovate constantly to keep up with (if not ahead of) your competition. There is no point in going through all the marketing rigmarole that fills these pages if you are not going to change based on the information you have gathered.

So, can you change? If you are like most readers, you probably have your doubts. Some of you are concerned about whether or not you can drag your organization kicking and screaming into the *1980s,* much less into the twenty-first century! Others see not only a problem with staff being willing to change, but with the board acquiescing to fund the changes.

Additionally, there hangs over all of us the common wisdom that "we all resist change." This "wisdom" has been pounded into our heads for so long that we have all accepted it as profound truth, and that "truth" has become the number one excuse of managers who don't want to make the ef-

52

fort. Get over it. Yes, it is tough to overcome inertia, but once you do, and the momentum is in your favor, it gets easier and easier.

CHAPTER THUMBNAIL

➤ **The Need for Flexibility**
➤ **Retaining the Capacity for Flexibility**
➤ **Being a Change Agent**
➤ **The Pace of Change in a Competitive Environment**

In this chapter, I'll show you how to overcome that inertia, how to develop and use the momentum you need to be constantly changing and improving your organization. First, I'll try to make a strong case for the need for flexibility, providing you with examples that you in turn can use with any staff or board members who are indeed resistant to change. Next, we'll go over some important things your organization needs to do to retain its flexibility. As we get older, we get less flexible. I'll show you how to stretch organizationally. Then, in the third section, I'll provide you with seven ideas on how to be a change agent for your organization, showing you some hands-on ideas for keeping change moving throughout the organization. Finally, I'll really get your attention by showing you the increasing pace of change in a competitive environment. As I said above, in the old order we could slog along. No more.

By the end of the chapter you should have a real feel for ways to keep that momentum going. You'll need to. Outside your organization, the inertia has already been overcome and the changes you will need to adapt to are occurring right now. They will occur with or without you. As a good friend of mine likes to say, "The train is leaving the station. You are either on it, or under it."

A. THE NEED FOR FLEXIBILITY

So what is all this talk about change? Why do we need to be changing all the time? What's wrong with what we're doing now? Change is such a hassle, and there is no guarantee that when we change we're going to be any better. I like things the way they are. If we do good work, people will continue to use us. What choice do they have? We've done just fine doing the things we've been doing. If it's not broken, don't fix it.

Do any of these sound familiar? Have they come from your board? Your staff? From you? Probably. And, you have a choice. You can be flexible and survive to do more mission another day. Or you can be inflexible and not be around very long. In *Mission-Based Management,* I included "organizational flexibility" as one of my nine criteria for organizational success. This was underscored in *Financial Empowerment,* where I noted that retaining the ability to be flexible financially was a key element of empowerment. Today, in a competitive market, flexibility—the capacity to regularly, and on increasingly short notice, adjust your directions, methods, service mix, and size—is essential.

When we discuss change and flexibility, I am not always talking about huge changes, epic conversions such as new buildings, massive changes in program methodology or reimbursement methods. More often we are talking about small, steady, regular improvements in services, adaptations to the changing wants of your markets. These are what I call small improvements around the edges, and these incremental changes provide most of the increased value for your markets—and with the least change pain for you and your staff.

Most people see the word *change* as the word

☹CHANGE!!!!!!!☹

It rarely is that dramatic. Nor is seismic change always good. There is a Japanese philosophy of 100 percent improvement—1 percent at a time. This is the core of what is commonly called Continuous Quality Improvement or CQI. It doesn't focus on wholesale change, discarding all the "old" ways to embrace the "new." In fact, it builds on the best of the old, making steady improvements every day, every week, every month.

There are many, many examples in the not-for-profit sector of incremental flexibility based on changes in market wants. Let's look at a few.

❏ **FOR EXAMPLE:** Back to managed care, the huge change that we discussed in the last chapter. During the 90s managed care was the buzzword for many human services providers. It was seen as a momentous change in the way that business is done in the human services both by funders and by providers. It was not universally welcomed (to understate) and did require a rethinking of the way services are viewed. Managed care values outcomes rather than process. It puts incentives and disincentives in place that push efficiency and effectiveness.

But for many, many readers of this book, managed care is what the market, the funder, wanted then and still wants today. Looking only at the outcome measure component, this requires that service providers set outcome goals and document the outcomes rather than the process that got them there. In other words, did a patient get well, not did the patient spend 14 days in treatment.

In working with many organizations who are still adapting to this change, I hear gnashing of teeth, wailing about how awful this is. The conversation often goes like this. I ask, can you document the outcomes that you have had? *Certainly, but we don't keep a record of it now.* How difficult would it be? *Not hard at all.* So really, what is the big deal? *The big deal is that they want us to do what we have done in 21 days in 14.* Can you change what the funder wants? *No.* Then figure out how to do what they ask. Look at other organizations who are accomplishing it and emulate them. Or close.

This example points out two things. First, the documentation of outcomes, something the market wanted, was, in fact, easy (for some groups—for others measuring outcomes accurately and with some meaning is a first-class conundrum). Resisting documenting was just that: pure resistance—putting up roadblocks to what the organization *really* didn't want to do: more outcomes in less time. Here is the second lesson. Once the market has made up its mind, for whatever reason, you are simply wasting your time whining about the philosophy or the change. You can't worry about what might have been. You need to deal with what *is*. The train is leaving the station.

❏ FOR EXAMPLE: Many United Ways realized a number of years ago that allowing donors to target where their money went was a competitive advantage for those donations. This was a change, one that reduced the number of dollars that the United Way committees could allocate, which really upset some people. It also caused initial accounting headaches, and these were overcome. But the change allowed the United Ways to compete in the donation marketplace. I have also seen other local and state fund raisers, including churches, that allow donors to select the programs that they are giving to. Obviously, choice sells. But some groups never learn. In early 2000, the United Way of America wrote all of its affiliates strongly suggesting that the locals end the policy of donor choice, as such choice, to paraphrase, "put too much power in the hands of the donor." Well, shoot, and I thought that was a *good* thing! The good news from this is that most locals refused to change their policy, and the United Way of America got thousands of angry letters and e-mails deriding their suggestion.

❏ FOR EXAMPLE: Local colleges and universities have needed to expand their student body numbers to include part-time students. This means having classes in the evenings on weekends, which is a major scheduling change. More instructors have to be recruited; janitorial duties must be reset for late at night. Maintenance activities that once could take all weekend now have to be compressed. But the market for part-time students is not nine-to-five, five days a week, and the successful organizations have accommodated. Universities have also found ways to use their biggest asset, their campuses, during their off-season. Over 200 now offer four- to six-week programs for high school juniors to both expose them to life away from home, and give them a course or two of college credit. Again, this requires adaptation, as you can't just cut 200 17-year-olds loose; they are, after all, still in high school. But university after university has found this a dual-purpose use of their facilities: It brings in revenue, and acts as a recruiter for potential students.

❑ **FOR EXAMPLE:** If there ever was an industry that had many market segments it is the hotel industry. From the Ritz-Carlton to the Motel 6, the range of what people want in lodging is amazing. Marriot Corporation alone has seven different "levels" of hotels. Within the industry there is intense competition, and hotel operators are always looking to build both brand loyalty and loyalty to a particular hotel. So, you see small, steady changes that appeal to the target customer: the businessperson during most of the year and families during vacation seasons. There are frequent-stayer programs, premium room upgrades, coffee makers in the rooms, express checkout, video checkout (that you can do on your room's television set), free newspapers, courtesy transportation to the airport— or to major local attractions, business-only floors, and, of course, pools and exercise rooms. Two recent additions to these customer-pleasing ideas are interesting. At many hotels, you now get a call in your room from the front desk within 10 minutes of checking in. You are asked if everything is in order in your room. This accomplishes two things. First, you know the hotel is concerned about your stay and it gives them a quick opportunity to hear any problems from you while they can still fix them, rather than at checkout. Second, it is a quality assurance (QA) checkup that the housekeeping and maintenance people know will be made with every check-in.

The other interesting "perk" is the environmentally correct policy of only washing bed linens every three days or when there is a new guest in a room. This policy, which five years ago was remarkable, and is now so common it is ubiquitous, allows you to get clean linens every day if you wish, but allows you to help save the planet while, of course, saving the hotel money. A double winner for them. As a footnote, I recently heard a guest checking out of a hotel I had stayed in that did not have this linen policy, chewing out the manager because the hotel was so environmentally unfriendly, and promising never to stay there again. It was a great example of a good innovation at one chain becoming a must for all of the chain's competitors to stay competitive.

All of these small, usually inexpensive changes meet the markets' wants and add value to the stay, making it more likely that a customer will return.

❑ **FOR EXAMPLE:** Other examples of user-friendly changes instituted by companies that listen to their customers:

Airlines have *much* healthier food choices (when they serve you at all), particularly in first and business classes, than they did 10 years ago. People are more concerned about their nutrition and health, and more women (who are more nutrition-conscious as a group than men) are traveling for business. In the past three years, food has vanished from many flights, and so airports have responded by placing more delis and fruit stands near departure gates so that passengers can take food on board with them.

Nearly every automobile you see now has cup holders, a rare luxury as recently as 1993. Why? Because people love them, and they are relatively inexpensive to design into a vehicle. A large value added for little cost.

Computer software is now *much* easier to install and run than five or six years ago, and indeed, when you buy a new computer, most now have a lot of pre-installed software. Why? Because people *hated* getting their new hardware home and spending hours installing software, printers, and so on before they could use it. "Plug and play" is the standard now. Indeed, the software and hardware industries are leaders in constant adjustments and improvements.

"Free" refills for soft drinks at fast food restaurants have gone from a competitive edge when Hardee's introduced them in the early 1990s to a standard today. The expectations of the markets have changed. It is not a loss, by the way, for the industry. They simply have raised the prices for their sodas slightly. But they had to make a cosmetic change to accommodate a market want.

All of these examples point to the constant adjustment, accommodation, and willingness to be flexible in successful organizations in both the for-profit and not-for-profit sectors. And, it gets me to a crucial point (and secret) about change.

> *It's the steady change, the small improvements every day, not the huge makeovers, that make the difference. Not only are they more effective, they are easier for staff and board to accommodate.*

Put another way:

> *Incremental change is less painful. Less pain means less resistance.*

Why is this true? Because if you are market-driven, if you are asking, listening, asking, and listening in relentless persistence, then you will hear of a thousand small ways you can make your customers happier for every one major change. If you change 1 percent a day, in just 100 days, or one-third of a year, the entire organization is renewed, but at a pace that your staff can adjust and adapt to. Steady change is the secret.

But you do need to make that change within the context of a plan, to make sure your improvements and changes are moving you toward your overall organizational goal. Otherwise your 1 percent daily improvements can wind up with you going in circles.

Has your organization already changed while you weren't looking? Of course. You should not think for a moment that you are not changing. You are. And your staff is. And your board is. You have made accommodations to market changes, and you need to feel good about the changes you have made.

☞ HANDS-ON: To emphasize how many changes you have made in your organization in the recent past, do this exercise with your staff and/or board members: Look at your organization five years ago. If you have pictures, policies, staff lists, board lists, marketing material, audits, and annual reports, use them to make a comparison of then versus now. Specifically, look at:

- *Size:* How much income do you have per year now versus five years ago?
- *Programs:* Do you have more programs? Are the ones that you have provided in the past different now? How?
- *Location:* Have you moved? Have you purchased or sold a building?
- *Staff:* How many new people have been added to the staff? How many of those on staff five years ago have left?
- *Board:* What changes in the board have your seen?
- *Policies:* How have your personnel, financial, quality assurance, and other policies and bylaws changed?
- *Funders:* What is your funding mix? Do you get funding from dif-

ferent sources than five years ago? What changes have there been in reporting and accounting? In auditing and oversight?

- *Technology:* Do you use the same computers and software as five years ago? Cell phones? Faxes? Internet provider? How much has your web site changed? Did you have your own organizational URL two years ago? Five?

As you answer these questions as a group you will see that you have changed *a lot.* Talk about these changes. Some were easy, some were painful. But reinforce the fact that your organization has *successfully* changed in many, many ways and that you can continue to do so in the future.

Feel good about how far you have come, and don't feel that you have been static while the world has moved on. You may very well feel that you have not kept pace adequately. And, it is true that the pace of change is accelerating. But don't for a minute let yourself, your staff, or your board think that you are going to start changing from a standing start. You are already moving. But how do you stay flexible while you are moving?

B. RETAINING THE CAPACITY FOR FLEXIBILITY

All of us are born flexible. As we age, we all lose our flexibility. I'm sure you have watched toddlers bend in ways that would put you or me in the hospital. As we get older, we have to work hard on flexibility or it disappears, much to our disadvantage.

Mentally we can get inflexible as well. By not continuing to learn, not continuing to consider new ideas, or new ways of doing work, our mental processes get set in a rut just as surely as our muscles, tendons, and joints. When you hear yourself saying (or thinking), "Ah, that new stuff doesn't interest me. We're doing just fine," you should set off all the alarms. Sometimes the "new stuff" *is* questionable, but more often there is progress there to be embraced. Even if all of a new idea, process, or protocol is not completely applicable to your organization, some of it may be, and thus regular study and reading to both stretch your brain and learn something that may be of value to you later is important. Fight mental rigidity.

Organizationally we get inflexible as well. We get invested in our buildings, a syndrome that I call the "edifice complex." This complex results from having so much of our assets invested in our building that the building *becomes* the organization. We become product-oriented, and the product is what we do in the building. If we have classrooms, or inpatient beds, or display space, or even offices, we *have* to fill them—whether or not the market wants what goes into those spaces.

❏ **FOR EXAMPLE:** I'm sure you can think of any number of not-for-profits that have provided services out of a particular location for years. In many cases the building is deteriorating (another problem, but not the point for this example), and the neighborhood has changed, perhaps for the worse, perhaps for the better. But in either case, it is no longer the ideal place from which to reach people. What do most for-profits do in this situation? The successful ones move. They realize that if their customers are not going to come into the neighborhood where they are located, there will be no business at all soon. So, even if the sale of a piece of property means taking a loss, a loss with the realistic expectation of meeting customer wants is a good move.

What do the not-for-profits do? Come up with excuses about why they should stay where they are. Again, in the old economy this was fine, because there was no competition for their clientele. In the new economy such rigidity is a quick but painful method of organizational suicide.

You need to remain flexible as an organization, and not just in your buildings. You need flexibility in your programming, your service array, your methods of reaching people, and your methods of recruiting, managing, and retaining staff.

But how do you, your staff, and your board attain and maintain that flexibility? I've already shown you some suggestions on being a change agent, and I have some more suggestions in this area.

1. Retain Financial Flexibility

Earlier, I mentioned the edifice complex, that terrible financial disorder that requires organizations to feed their buildings rather than pay attention to the marketplace. Part of financial flexibility is having the cash that will enable you to make strategic and tactical moves promptly. Part of financial flexibility is not having all your assets in your buildings. Part of it is making money each year as an organization so that you can reinvest in your mission. Part of it is starting and maintaining an endowment.

But financial flexibility empowers other kinds of flexibility, including risk taking, which we will cover in a moment. Suffice it to say here that financial decisions need to be looked at not only through the lens of getting enough financial and mission return on investment, but also that of retaining enough flexibility to allow you some "wiggle room" later. (There is much, much more on this subject in *Financial Empowerment*.)

☞ **HANDS-ON:** Take out your most recent balance sheet and a calculator. Look at your fixed assets, and divide them by your total assets. Are fixed assets more than 75 percent of all your assets? Now, look at your cash and cash equivalents. Does it exceed 60 days' operation? If you have too many fixed assets, and too little cash, you are hamstrung when it comes to quickly accommodating changes in the market.

2. Use Risk Taking as a Flexibility Tool

Social entrepreneurship, taking risk on behalf of the people you serve, is another of the nine characteristics of successful not-for-profits that I examined in *Mission-Based Management,* and expanded on in *Social Entrepreneurship, the Art of Mission-Based Venture Development.* This important characteristic can be used here, to retain flexibility.

One of the things that people don't like about change is that it is a threat: There is danger in the unknown. The Chinese symbol for change has two parts: one meaning "danger," one meaning "opportunity." The Chinese got it right; there are both in any change. But where I see people putting up the most resistance is from the danger of the unknown, the entering of a dark room with only a puny flashlight.

In going through change, we are taking risk. That means we are almost certainly going to make mistakes. Everyone does. Mistakes by themselves are no big deal. We all learn better from our mistakes than from our successes. But if your culture is one where anyone who makes any mistake is punished (a blame-friendly environment) people will, or course, not want to try anything new. Why? Because there is a higher likelihood of error in doing new things than there is in doing things that are already known and practiced. If error, any error, means getting chewed out, why take the chance?

Are you risk-aversive as an organization? Do you have a mantra of 100-percent quality? While I have nothing against high-quality services, you need to remember: *Organizations that have a zero tolerance for error, have a zero tolerance for innovation.* Innovation, that essential competitive skill, is all about risk and reward. You try something new (a change) and you risk failure. But you also may succeed and then get rewarded.

You need to encourage prudent risk, regular innovation, and trying new things. Once your staff and board get the idea, you will see them stretching more and more. What do I mean by "stretch"? That's my next suggestion.

3. Stretch: Make Regular Small Changes

I'm a runner. Before I run, I stretch. Every time. If, for some reason, I forget, I can really tell. You and your organization need to stretch as well, and do it regularly. How? By making small regular changes *and noting them.* Remember the exercise I suggested of listing all the changes that have occurred in staff, board, service, location, and the like? From here on out, not only make the small changes but make note of them, so that people get used to hearing the words, and will realize that not only are things changing, but that they are not getting hurt by those changes. What you want to seek is a culture that is constantly refreshing itself, trying new things and taking on a new "look." Here are some small changes that you can make without too much trouble or expense. *Don't* do all of them at once! Dole them out over time, so that some change is *always* going on. I've divided the changes into two groups: *Low Impact* and *High Impact.* Changes in the first group are generally less expensive and less threatening to staff or board members; those in the latter are more so.

☞ **HANDS-ON:** Try these changes:

Low Impact

- *Change your letterhead.* Not now, but when your supply runs out. I'm not talking about changing the logo or the entire look (which may be timely as well) but rather moving the lines, changing the color, etc. I know that this may require changes in business cards and other materials, but those can be phased in over time.
- *Repaint, repaper, put down new carpet.* Don't ever think that a change of appearance is unimportant. If you have the money, give staff an allowance to buy wall decorations for their offices.
- *Upgrade your software.* Most software has regular upgrades, and many are available online to download. If yours are functional but not completely up-to-date, consider upgrading. It is often not expensive, sometimes even free, and you can be more productive after the change.
- *Rethink your meeting schedules.* Do you need staff meetings every week? Team meetings every month? Are the location, duration, and content of the meetings appropriate? Ask those who regularly attend and make the changes that they suggest.
- *Start with your own environment.* Move your own office furniture, add a plant, remove a picture. Buy a new coffee mug, eat lunch at a different time each day, drive a new route to work. As I wrote the second edition of this book, I moved my office furniture around for—I admit it—the first time in five years. The positive change in my attitude on arriving at my office every day (and I *like* coming to work) was amazing, and I resolved to move things around more of-

ten. Get used to difference, to adapting, to change, and lead your people as you do.

High Impact

- *Change offices.* Whoa! Here is a big one. Perhaps a change of location will help some people, or be an avenue for better communication, more effective supervision, or improved access to your clientele.
- *Change titles.* Starting with your own. Perhaps you have been thinking of moving to a corporate model where the executive director has the title of CEO and where people who were directors become vice presidents. Perhaps now is the time to implement that.
- *Reorganize your table of organization.* Not just to do it, but if you have been putting a needed change off, get on with it. Perhaps there will be a major reorganization, perhaps just a few people will be affected.
- *Change your committee makeup.* On the staff level this is pretty easy. I have always encouraged organizations to have representation on their committees from all levels of the organization both vertically and horizontally. This means from all levels of management, and all parts of the organization. If you haven't done that, start now. If you have, shuffle some staff from one committee to another (asking them first, of course, if they have any preference). At the board level, talk to your board president about implementing a needed new committee, or changing the job descriptions on existing ones, or moving board members around, or even changing the staff who are responsible for particular committees.

Please, don't misunderstand me here. I am not urging you just to stir things up. Don't make changes just to make changes. Any of these that you do implement should be done for a reason, and thoughtfully considered before starting. But a pace of regular change keeps the organization stretching, and thus more flexible.

4. Don't Always Call Change "Change"

Change is what it is. And it is inevitable. But if the word change really gets in the way, if when you say "change" the staff or board hear "trouble," switch the nomenclature. Use terms such as improvement, adjustment, innovation, refinement, shift, or variation. There is only so much cajoling, training, coaching, and being helpful that you can do. Some people get very hung up on words, hung up to the point that their engines seize. If that is true for you, go around the barrier instead of through it. Use different terminology, and perhaps it will help.

A final note about the retention of flexibility and change agency. Despite all of your efforts, all of your enthusiasm and spirited advocacy for moving your organization ahead, it is inevitable that some people just won't get it. They will continue to resist, or they will act out in other ways, some passive-aggressive, some morale-killing, some even outright rude.

When you have given your best effort to bringing these people on the team and they have decided, for whatever reason not to join, it is time for them to leave. Once the organization has made a decision to go in a certain direction, it is up to them, whether they be staff or volunteer, to get with the program and support it, or find other things to do in another organization. What happens when a basketball player refuses to run windsprints? Or a cellist refuses to play a certain piece with feeling? He or she is off the team or out of the orchestra. The same is true with your organization.

If you have read *Mission-Based Management,* you know that I am a great believer in participatory, inclusive management, a system where ideas flow from the point of service to the managers, and where decisions are made as close to the point of service as possible. That having been said, I do not in any way support staff insubordination or refusal to follow policy. Decisions still need to be made. And if we have entrusted those decision makers, whether they are the board, executive team or line workers, to make a decision, it is up to the rest of us to support it. Those who can't need to go elsewhere.

In *Leading Without Power,* (a book I highly recommend to you), Max DePree discusses not-for-profit decision making with this terrific insight: "We spend too much time looking for consensus, when we should be looking for agreement." I love that, and what it means is that yes, you should get input, but that committee work is not jury deliberation; you don't want to let one person who doesn't want to move forward control the organization's destiny. Rather, you ask for input from everyone, decide, and then ask if that support I discussed above will be there. The train is leaving the station—are you on it or off it?

C. BEING A CHANGE AGENT

As a key staff or board member, you need to lead in terms of the changes your organization pursues. You need to develop plans that outline the way your organization is going, and then delineate what needs to happen to get there. You need to set internal policies that support those plans. You must identify issues and discuss them fully, including staff, volunteers, and even the community in those discussions when appropriate.

But when all is said and done, when all the dust settles and the decisions are made, you need to *lead* on the changes you have just initiated, not just tell people to go do them. You want to be not just the initiator of change but the facilitator of it. A change agent is someone who helps people through the process, overcoming the barriers to change. To do this, I have found that the following seven steps are essential.

1. Show the Mission Outcome of the Change

We're back to the mission. People will resist new stuff. We all know it. But if you can show a relationship between the change and doing more and better mission, *some* of the resistance in *some* of your staff and board will be eliminated. Notice that I did not say *all* of the resistance in *all* of the people. But showing the mission connection will help. And, if you have been with your organization long, I'm sure you have dozens of human interest stories or success stories that you personally savor and that keep you motivated day to day. Share them.

2. Go Through the Change Together

Here's the lesson in a nutshell. People will change much more readily *with* you than *for* you.

❏ **FOR EXAMPLE:** Imagine yourself brought into a large room that you have never seen before. The room is an office for 10 people, and thus full of furniture. There is no one else there except you and your supervisor who brought you in. The supervisor points to a door on the far side of the room and says, "That is where we're going now. Get there." And then he or she turns the lights out and leaves. You have to negotiate the new terrain in the dark. You decide not to move at all. You don't want to get hurt, and you didn't really get a good look at the location of all the furniture before the lights were turned out. An hour later, your supervisor returns and says, "Why haven't you done what I asked? I showed you what to do!"

The new room is the change. When you tell people what to do and then leave them to their own devices, if they have never been there before, they will naturally be concerned about making mistakes. If, however, you are there for them, and you show them how to make the change, they are much more likely to comply, and with much less resistance. Imagine that same supervisor offering to come with you across the dark room and, better yet, bringing a flashlight.

Stay with people through change. Check in. Be available. Do your changing as a team.

3. Talk Regularly About Competition

I have spent many pages already talking about competition, your place in it and the need for continual asking and adjusting. Your staff need to hear the same message to lower their resistance and to see the need for change. At the end of this chapter there are specific discussion points on competition and the need for change. Don't, however, have just one session on this. Make it a regular part of staff meetings, board meetings, your newsletter, or other methods of communication with your staff and volunteers.

4. Point Out Changes Outside the Organization

Stay informed. Read widely. Pay attention to the outside environment, the world in general, and not just your industry. Learn to make connections between the changes in the outside world and your organization. Then share this information with staff. Be a role model for them of lifelong learning.

5. Don't Wait for Big Changes to Make Any Changes

If the only change your organization ever makes is monumental, you won't do it very well, because you won't have practiced much. Don't save up all your changes to "do it all at once." Incremental regular change is much less threatening. Remember the exercise I wanted you to do with your staff so that they would realize how much you had changed? If you did that, people probably said things to you like, "I had no idea we had come this far." Why didn't they notice? Because the changes were incremental. Now, use that low-profile, incremental approach to make your own organizational changes less threatening. If you do have a big change, can you break it down into more steady, small changes? If you can, it will lower anxiety and resistance.

6. Don't Criticize the Past—Look to the Future

When you announce a change, do it positively, not negatively. Too often I hear people say, "Now we're going to get it right," which of course implies that your people have been doing something *wrong.* Talk about fostering resistance! Instead of criticizing the past, talk about how this will be even better, do even more mission, help in your continual quest for higher quality. Look forward, not back.

7. Be Patient

Change takes time. Nearly any change you initiate, from a large one like a modification of your program policies, to a small one such as a change in a reimbursement form, requires a behavioral change on someone's part. And behavioral change takes time, a lot of time. You need to use your coaching skills to keep people on track. You need to be around so that you can catch small mistakes before they become big ones. You need to encourage and cajole and not expect perfection the first time out. Be patient.

These seven elements, when used together, will make for a much easier change process for your organization. And, the more your leadership team, managers, and supervisors practice them, the better.

D. THE PACE OF CHANGE IN A COMPETITIVE ENVIRONMENT

"The hurrieder I go, the behinder I get" is an old saying that speaks well to the feeling we all have at times about the world we live in. No one can possibly keep up with the changes in their profession, workplace, in fashion, sports, music, technology, entertainment, politics, and local, national, and international events. So we have a tendency to throw up our hands and say "OVERLOAD!" and find excuses not to pay attention.

The old refrain: In the "old" days, you could get away with that for a number of reasons. Change was slower paced, you got a break from people if you weren't "cutting edge" since you were a not-for-profit, and, most importantly, you probably had a relative or virtual monopoly. Thus it didn't matter how much you accommodated to changes in the "outside" world. You could accommodate at your own more leisurely (more "professional") pace. Remember when attorneys and physicians berated those in their professions who advertised? Unseemly. Unprofessional. Now you go down the road and see huge billboards advertising for law practices, medical groups, clinics, hospitals, and even individual practitioners. And some of those who refused to advertise are out of business, or have been bought out by their competition.

There are two key points I want to make here and they are both contained in the header above. First, there is the *pace of change*. It is accelerating with the explosion of information available, the speed of communication, and the general pace of our lives all being more and more intense. Second, is the *competitive environment*. This environment is one that your organization may already be in or may just be entering. But you and your organization cannot avoid it. Imagine you are at a huge airport. You are walking down an immense concourse to your plane. Suddenly you come upon a moving walkway, and are forced by the crowd to get on. Your pace has just picked up. Now the walkway speeds up ever so steadily until you are nearly racing. Things go by faster. You have less time to study them before they are behind you. And the end of the walkway comes up very, very fast. That is the transition from noncompetitive to competitive environments and from the slower pace of yesteryear to the rapid pace of today.

So both items affect you, as do some cultural shifts that we should touch on.

1. The Average Attention Span Is Down

I have no "hard'" data to back this up, just observations. Look at the length of the average television advertisement, the shortening of the average article in newspapers and magazines (or the entirety of *USA Today*), the shorter stories on the evening television news. We are a short-attention-span, and immediate-gratification, society. The point for you? People don't just leave this urge when they get up from their television. They bring it with them when they seek the services you provide. How many Americans would wait weeks or months for surgery? In England, people are used to it. How many people do you see frustrated at not being the first in line at the checkout counter in the grocery store? I see lots, including myself.

The issue here is that, to be competitive, you need to be as fast, as responsive, as fulfilling as your competition. And, the competition is always looking for ways to speed up their service.

❑ **FOR EXAMPLE:** The rental car industry has long sought to speed people from airplane to car. The bane of any renter is a long line to get a car, and even more, a long line to check the car back in at the airport. You want to get on your way. Hertz, Avis, Budget, and the rest have all experimented with ways to speed up the process. They tried express check-in, where you drop your rental agreement in a box and the company sends you a bill. But some people didn't like that—either they didn't trust the company to get it right, or they needed their receipt for accounting purposes immediately. So in the early 90s Hertz experimented with and then implemented a system (using what was then advanced technology) to accomplish both wants: a fast return and a receipt. When you pull up in a Hertz lot at an airport, a Hertz employee with a handheld computer approaches you, and while you are emptying the car of your belongings, takes your rental agreement, enters the mileage, and then prints out your receipt on a small thermal printer hanging off their belt. The handheld unit is connected by radio and phone lines to the central Hertz computer system, and you are on your way with little or no delay, and no line! What did Avis and Budget do? Imitated the system as fast as they could.

What can you do to accommodate this change? First, value your customer's time. Think through how you can do things more efficiently, more effectively.

2. Louder, Brighter Advertisements and Media

This is directly related to number 1. If you saw a retrospective on television ads from 10 to 15 years ago, you would be bored silly. The ads were, by comparison to today's machine-gun-style messages, bland and *long* (one whole minute!). You get inundated with electronic ads on nearly every web site, on the shelves at the grocery store, in nearly any environment you can imagine. Today, you have to nearly grab people by the throat to get their attention. And with the explosion of inexpensive PC-based design and printing software as well as dirt-cheap high-quality color printers, the spread of really bright, classy-looking material is everywhere. The issue for you in a competitive environment is that your marketing, advertising, and promotions have to look "current," which means constantly updated. If they don't, you won't get people's attention. If you don't get their attention, they won't use your services. "It was boring"—referring to your marketing material or your services—is the ultimate pejorative, and a deadly one in a competitive world.

3. The Product Cycle Is Now Down to Months Rather Than Years

Used to be that the time from "Eureka!" to the marketplace was many years. Now, the turnaround is much, much faster. Just look at the rapid pace of updated hardware and software. They are often literally outdated when they arrive on the shelves. We recently went to a new Windows operating system at my office and at home. After buying and installing the software, the installation program automatically went online to look for updates—and there were nearly 40 patches and add-ons. Innovation and improvement is a daily issue for software and hardware manufacturers.

Now, the fact that they are outdated does not mean that they are useless, but that is not the issue. The perception of not being new is the key. The auto industry did this for years, putting out new cars to replace perfectly good ones, and we all fell in line because we wanted the new look. But remember when all the new models came out in the fall? Now they arrive at different points in the year. The television "season" also used to start after Labor Day and go through the spring. Now the season is shorter, has more cancellations and midseason replacements, and is broken up by more "specials," all in an effort to keep our attention, and to turn out something new.

The point for you? Just like their attention spans, people bring their focus on the new to your organization. Is what you do *exactly* as it has been for many years? Strike one. Is your pace of change so slow that you could gear up now for a service adjustment to meet a market want—in two fiscal years? Strikes two and three. People won't wait that long, because your competition won't and then they will have choices of places to go other than yours. The admonition from you—"We'll be right there!"—doesn't work any longer.

4. The End of Annual Cycles

In the old economy, people in the not-for-profit world lived on an annual cycle, usually based on their state's or the federal fiscal year. We had annual budgets. We knew what our year "looked" like well in advance. No more.

❏ **FOR EXAMPLE:** In Chapter 1, I told you that in Massachusetts, when a person with a disability is placed in a community agency, the state gets bids based on the needs that the individual has. In telling you about it before, I used it as an example of previously noncompetitive services becoming more and more competitive. In this case you should know that not-for-profits that wish to provide services must respond in 15 days with a full service plan, and one of the competitive issues is how quickly they can begin providing actual services. This often means that, to be competitive, and to get the work, the staff must drop other things that they are doing to meet the 15-day response clock. This is called meeting a customer want. The example also shows that budgets are not always static and predictable. It also emphasizes that there is a vastly greater emphasis on a customer/vendor relationship, where the government is a customer and the not-for-profit is a vendor who must be responsive to keep its contract.

Thus, your organization must be responsive and reactive to meet customers' wants, even when those customers are the long-disliked major funder.

5. There Is Much Less Sympathy for the Not-for-Profit Who Can't Keep Up

I've touched on this a number of times already, but it has impact here as well. Ten years ago, when you had crummy service (or pitiful marketing, or obsolete buildings), people said, oh well, they are just a not-for-profit. What do you expect? Now they expect much, much, more. People see the funds you use as *theirs,* and often, they have a point. The money may be from tax revenues or it may be from donations, or both. And people want outcomes from their investment in you. So you don't get the break you did before. You need to compete, and more importantly, you need to be seen as competitive, up-to-date, and fully professional by your community.

You are in a rapidly changing, competitive environment. You know that.

Before we move on, however, I would be derelict if I did not discuss two important points. Up to here, I have been making the case for new, new, new. To some of you it may read as trendy, trendy, trendy. In some cases, there is a real and valid reason for not constantly reinventing yourselves, in *not* having the latest and greatest. Let's look at two such situations:

1. The case for stability

In some organizations it is important to have at least the appearance of sameness, of stability. For example, if your organization treats chronically mentally ill individuals, a predictable, comfortable, consistent environment is often important. If you go changing the office decor every six months (as if you could afford it), you could hurt your mission, rather than help it. In other cases, donors want to give to the "same" organization as they always have, and a major change in appearance of logo, stationery, or other materials could negatively affect that. In both of these cases, the stability of the appearance or of the program is important to key market segments. Respect that. Again, I don't advocate change for change's sake. But I do want you to be aware that your organization is being held to an increasingly rigid standard to keep up with the rest of the world. And a change of availability—for example, adding evening hours to accommodate new customers—would not offend people who are used to being served during the daytime. Again, ask your markets, and adapt. But don't let the adage "But we've always done it that way" allow stability to overcome market sensitivity.

2. The belief in poverty-chic

Poverty-chic is the still widely held belief that it is unseemly, if not immoral, for not-for-profits to have any appearance of wealth. Another way of putting this is "you can't do well doing good." There is a long, long story behind why this unfortunately still common belief is out there, but it does present real conflict with all of the exhortations that I have just give you about being up-to-date, professional, and responsive. For example, if you are like most of my clients, you have been criticized about your computers. They are too fancy, too expensive for an organization like yours, some say. And the *same* machines get criticized by your accountant or board members for being so out-of-date. You can't win. If you have professional marketing materials, some people assume you have lots of money and don't need donations. If you have new carpet in the lobby you are seen as frivolous; if you don't, you are hassled for having crummy space.

It seems you can't win. Well, you can, but it takes some time. First, you need to have your board and staff behind you when you "upgrade." By upgrade I mean the carpet, your vehicles, your computers, your office furniture. The staff and board have to agree that this is a good, mission-related investment. You have to have the people inside the organization on your side. Then, you can begin to make the case outside, but at least your staff and board shouldn't be taking shots at you.

It's a slow process to convince our friends and neighbors to let us be part of the rest of society. As long as they continue to treat us as poor brothers and sisters, we will, at least in part, act that way. And that way is not good mission.

But enough with the evangelism, let's get on to what a real marketing cycle is. That's the subject of Chapter 5.

RECAP

In this chapter we have covered an important facet of competitive marketing: flexibility. Maintaining flexibility and welcoming positive change are difficult organizational skills, and I showed you a number of things that may help attain and maintain them.

First, we looked at the need for flexibility, and I provided you with a number of examples of organizations that were and were not flexible in the face of changing market wants. Second, I showed you some methods of retaining organizational flexibility, including retaining financial flexibility, using risk taking as a flexibility tool, stretching by making regular small changes, and not always calling change "change." We reviewed the fact that incremental change is less painful and thus often less resisted.

Third, we examined seven specific ways for you to be a change agent. To recap quickly, these included:

1. Show the mission outcome of the change
2. Go through change as a coach
3. Talk regularly about competition

4. Point out changes outside the organization
5. Don't wait for big changes to make any changes
6. Don't criticize the past—look to the future
7. Be patient

Finally, we spent some time going over the pace of change in a competitive environment. The pace is picking up, and I pointed out that in the "old" days, people would give you a break because you were a not-for-profit, but those days are long gone. You need to keep pace because, as the environment becomes more competitive, people will have more choices and they may just choose to go somewhere else.

There is no substitute for flexibility. Remember the old story about the grasses on the shore during a storm. They are flexible, they bend, and they survive the storm. The strong, inflexible oak can survive many a wind, but will eventually meet a storm that will knock it down.

The competitive storm that you are entering is bigger than you are. Market wants change as fast as winds in a swirling gale, and you need to be flexible to remain standing. Finally, flexibility is not something that we naturally get better at with time; we get worse. Both as individuals and organizations we get set in our ways, we have our traditions ("the way we do things here") and our investments in certain paths. The older our organization gets, the bigger it becomes, the more difficult it is to change the path. But you must be able to change direction promptly and with a positive attitude if you are to succeed in the markets of tomorrow.

Now that you know how to retain your flexibility, we've really covered most of the preparatory steps of competitive marketing. Now let's get to the technical stuff, starting with the real markets you are serving.

Discussion Questions for Chapter 4

1. How averse are people here to change? Why? Do we as managers lead through change?
2. How much can we morally change with the market? Are there things that we do now that we couldn't have considered five years ago? Why are they okay now?
3. The list in Section B shows how to retain our flexibility. Can we do these? When?
4. Do we encourage or discourage prudent risk taking? How?
5. Is the pace of change in our markets accelerating or stable? What can we do to accommodate it? Can we encourage regular, persistent improvements?

5

The Marketing Cycle for a Not-for-Profit

OVERVIEW

Marketing is not an event, it is a process, and one that never ends. Unlike a linear process with a beginning, middle, and end, marketing is more cyclical, with familiar steps repeated over and over as the organization regularly responds to changes in the markets, customer wants, competition, and strategic issues.

And, even though it is important to know that the marketing cycle is just that, a cycle that goes around and around, it is even more important to understand the hub on which the cycle spins. That axis is the customer. *First, last, and in between, the marketing cycle for your organization should revolve around the people you serve.* Not around your existing services, not around your current building or staff or board, but around your customers.

CHAPTER THUMBNAIL

➤ **The Marketing Cycle That Works**
➤ **The Marketing Disability of Most Not-for-Profits**
➤ **The Marketing Cycle and Your Competitors**

This chapter will show you how the cycle works, and why it is important to attend to each part of the cycle in the prescribed order, as well as with regularity. I will cover a marketing process that I like and then move our discussion to the marketing disability that really impedes most not-for-profits as they market. This disability is a long-standing one, one that has been well ingrained in the minds of most not-for-profit staff and board members, and thus will be difficult to dislodge. If it cannot be overcome, however, the organization that you work for may be permanently behind the competitive curve.

In the last section of the chapter, we'll look at the marketing cycle and how it affects some of your for-profit as well as your not-for-profit competitors. You will learn how they view your organization, how they think about competing with you, and, most importantly, how you should view them. In Chapter 7, we'll cover the competition at much more length, but in this chapter we'll limit our discussion to your competition and their reactions to and interactions with your marketing cycle.

By the end of the chapter, you will have an excellent understanding of a marketing cycle that can work for your organization for existing products and services as well as for start-up ideas, new ideas, and even the business development cycle. You will know the disability you have to overcome, and that knowledge will be the first step in successfully responding to it. And finally, you will be able to see the markets through the eyes of your competitors, a key competitive advantage in an increasingly competitive world.

A. THE MARKETING CYCLE THAT WORKS

Most people seem to think that the marketing cycle starts with the product or service. If I know what I am selling, the theory seems to go, then I start from there. I then can decide how to sell, who to sell to, what way to convince them, and how to price. As noted in the introduction to this chapter, that sentiment is wrong, wrong, wrong, and wrong again. Marketing doesn't start with the product, or the service. Marketing starts with the *market:* the people to whom you are trying to sell, or to serve. If you start by deciding who you are serving, follow that by asking those people what they want, and then respond by giving it to them, that's marketing. If you start with a product or service and back into a market by asking "How can I sell this wonderful product or service to these people?" you are destined to succeed only for a very short time and then only if you are a superb salesperson.

Marketing (the verb) has to start with the market (the noun) to be effective over the long haul. And, by putting the appropriate marketing activities together in the correct sequence you can change the way your organization thinks of its markets and ultimately the way those markets think of you, hopefully for the better! The cycle that we're about to review works for new products and new services, and for honing and improving existing

Exhibit 5-1   Marketing Cycle

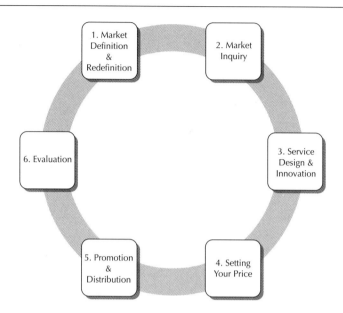

products or services. It works in human services, the arts, education, religion, environmental action, and legal aid. It works, because at its core it is sensitive to people's wants, not their needs, and it puts those wants first.

With no further delay, let's review this marketing cycle. Exhibit 5-1 depicts the cycle at its purest and simplest, in a generic form that can be used across disciplines. Later we'll apply it in a few "**FOR EXAMPLES.**"

As you can see, the cycle starts with the identification of the target markets, works its way through asking about the markets' wants, and then, and only then, designs or modifies the product or service you are going to provide. Nowhere in the display do you see the word "need." There's a reason for that, and you should know the answer if you read Chapter 2: Needs are different than wants, and wants are what people buy, not needs.

Let's dissect the cycle and go through it item by item, discussing each point in some detail. Then we'll reassemble the cycle and look at its application in some real world not-for-profits.

1. Market Definition and Redefinition

This sounds so basic that it creeps up on people. But the first question to ask is, who am I serving? Who are the people, the individuals that I am selling to? How many of them are there? Where are they? Are they as a group, as a market, growing in numbers or waning? As you approach this question, do not get sucked up into what I call "the census trap." You get caught in the census trap when you assume that your market is all the people in a geographic area. It never is. This assumption comes from historical not-for-profit monopolies. Many organizations had (and some still have) cachement areas, areas that were their "territory," their monopoly. In many cases funding for these organizations was based on population (capitated) so that the illusion that an organization worked for everyone in the cachement area was reinforced.

Nothing, of course, could be further from the truth. Your market is not everyone; it is a much, much more defined group of people. If you are a private school, it is the parents of children in the age groups you teach, who are interested in non-public education and who have the resources to send their children to your school. If you are a health department, for health screenings it might be just people who don't have private physicians, or if it was for lead screenings, just people with very small children who lived in older homes with lead-based paint. If you are a church, while your dogma may suggest that the world is your market, in reality, you are most likely going to appeal to people within five to eight miles of your church. Who are looking for a church. Who do not already have a church home. A much smaller number than "everyone" in the community, or even within your five- to eight-mile radius.

The action statement in Exhibit 5-2 says "Market Definition & Redefinition." Defining a market is pretty straightforward: You identify who you are going to serve. But what do I mean by redefining? It is an important term, because for most readers it will be the more common task. Redefining your market(s) means to periodically go back and look at your markets, assuring yourself that they are still there, that they are the ones you want to serve, and that they still have wants you can meet. For example, if you are a YMCA and one of your markets (for your athletic summer camps) is kids from 8 to 18, you might reexamine this market and redefine it to be *kids 8 to 18 from homes that have incomes over $30,000,* or *kids from public schools* as opposed to private schools, or *kids who played in your regular youth athletic leagues.* This regular redefinition is crucial since conditions change: Markets mature, and wants change along with them. Only by regularly reviewing and redefining who it is that you are serving can you accurately ask those whom you hope to serve what they want.

I hope that you get the idea that you need to identify your target markets carefully, developing as detailed a definition, as particular a description of them, as you can. The more accurate and finite your definition of your market, the more accurate your market projections will be, and thus

Exhibit 5-2   Action Statement

---

1. Market Definition & Redefinition

your estimates, assumptions, and plans. This technique should be used for all of your services, for all of your markets, so that you can recognize the many, many different markets that you serve. This activity is so important that we will spend the entirety of Chapter 6 solely on this subject.

2. Market Inquiry (or: What Do Your Markets Really Want?)

Having identified your market(s) as closely and finitely as you can, what is next? Is it to figure out how to sell your product or service to this newly identified group? Is it to blanket them with literature so that they will want what you have to sell? Is it to offer coupons to entice them into your doors the first time? No, not yet.

What is next in the marketing cycle is to figure out what the market wants (see Exhibit 5-3). How do you do that, you ask? By doing just that, *asking.* By asking, asking regularly and then, of course, *listening* and *responding,* you will find out what most people want. And remember our discussion in Chapter 2—people seek wants, so meet those wants and people will seek out your organization.

You can ask formally or informally. You can ask in surveys, in focus groups, in interviews, in one-on-one conversation. You can ask in person, or online. However you do it, you need to ask, and ask, and ask again. Because asking once is not enough, since people's wants change, and change

Exhibit 5-3   Market Inquiry

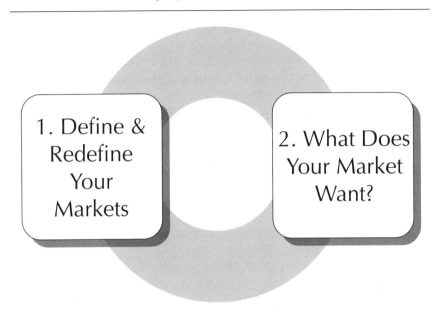

regularly. This is also a critical issue, and we'll spend the entirety of Chapter 8 on asking in all of its variety of ways.

Suffice it to say that you cannot meet markets' wants if you don't know what those wants are. And, you cannot know what the wants are unless you ask. The biggest mistake you can make in marketing is to say, "I've been in this business 20 years and I *know* what customers want." Wrong. No one knows until they ask.

❑ **FOR EXAMPLE:** In 1995, then Vice President Gore oversaw a widespread reevaluation of the way that the federal government did business. Called Reinventing Government (named after the excellent book of that title by David Osborne), this effort included customer service surveys in many federal agencies that had never before considered asking. The results were predictable: People wanted a whole lot different things than the "experts" anticipated. My favorite story from the effort was that of a senior administrator (with 25 years of service) at the Veterans Administration who was supremely confident that veterans didn't mind waiting to be seen at the VA hospitals because "they get to sit around and swap war stories." The survey showed, of course, that veterans, like the rest of us, *hate* to wait, and that the long waits were their biggest complaint!

Ask, ask, ask and listen!

3. Service Design and Innovation

Only now that you know who your target market is, and only now that you know what they want, only now can you shape (or reshape) your product or service to meet the wants of your target market (see Exhibit 5-4). This may mean starting from scratch to develop a new product or service, or, more likely, the constant amendment, innovation in, and improvement of, products and services already in place. Remember, not only will you be re-defining your markets regularly, but wants change with time. Even within static markets, wants change. As a result, you need to assess and reassess and reassess your services to ensure that they meet the current wants of the markets.

❏ **FOR EXAMPLE:** The staff of your organization is a market, and one that you should pay close attention to. Let's assume that you are going to survey staff about what kinds of benefits they would like as a precursor to making changes in your benefits package. What a great idea! You are asking the market what they want! The survey asks each respondent to rate each of 20 potential benefits on a scale of 1 to 10. You collect the in-formation and make the changes, trying your best to fit the benefits package to the wants of the staff. Now, go five years into the future. As-sume the unlikely, that every staff person that took the previous benefits

Exhibit 5-4   Market Service

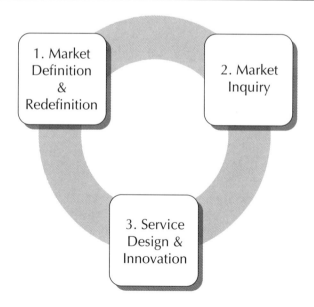

survey is still there, and no new staff have come on board. You repeat the survey. Would the answers be the same? Of course not. People's wants change as they age, and everyone in the market is five years older. Let's change the assumption. What if you have had normal turnover in the five-year interval since the first survey? If you readminister the identical survey, would the answers be the same? No, because the market has changed in composition. In both cases, you would need to change the benefits package to continue being market sensitive.

You cannot reasonably meet *every* want of *every* market. For example, if one potential customer for counseling services says that he or she can only come in between midnight and eight in the morning, it is probably not reasonable or cost-efficient to have a counselor on site overnight just for one customer. However, the information is important, because it may point out a previously hidden market—those who work second-shift jobs and are ready to seek services at night rather than during traditional hours. Is there enough of a market to support a reshaping of your services to accommodate this want?

You need to be sensitive to regular changes in market wants by making adjustments in the way you provide your services. However, you need to cushion your desire to fully meet every customer's want with prudent business assessments and financial planning to ensure that you meet the wants you can afford to and defer on those that you cannot do either efficiently, effectively, or with a high degree of quality.

4. Setting Your Price

A sensible price is one that: First, recovers all of your costs of providing a service or manufacturing a product; second, adds a profit to that price; and third, meets the realities of the market (Exhibit 5-5). The first and second parts increase the price. The third part usually reduces it.

Let me focus you for a moment on the first part: full cost recovery. I know far too many organizations that are convinced that they must underprice their competition at any cost; that cost is all that motivates a customer. Thus, they often juggle their costs around so that their sales price appears to be one that ensures full cost recovery but really doesn't. In this way they feel that they are assured of getting the work, of locking in the customer. What they are *really* doing is ensuring that each time they provide the service they *lose* money. Such a deal.

It is crucial in price setting to remember that people don't buy based on price—they buy based on *value*. Price is a variable component of value. For some people price is 99 percent of value, for others just a small amount.

Exhibit 5-5   Price Setting

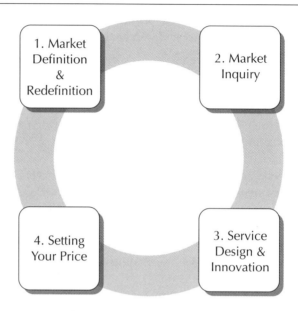

If price were the only issue, there would not be any luxury products or services, no first-class seats on airlines, no Ritz-Carlton hotels, no limousines clogging up the streets in our big cities. If price were everything, we would send all of our correspondence first class mail. Federal Express would be shut down in a day. So would Gucci, Saks, and most of the stores on Fifth Avenue in New York, or Rodeo Drive in Beverly Hills.

So don't just think about price. Think about value. And never tell people what they should value—that's giving them what they *need.* Ask them what they value, and then give them what they *want.* Do people highly value your service, or the way that you deliver it? If so, they will be willing to consider paying more for it. If they don't value your services, then even a lower price may not bring them on as customers.

❑ FOR EXAMPLE: An organization that I work with provides interpretive tours of historic districts in their city. They are devoted to historic preservation and use their net revenues to fund historic preservation efforts. Their problem was that their tours were too popular. They only had so many really good tour guide/interpreters, and they knew that they could not train more very quickly. So, to reduce demand, they raised the price. By doubling it. Their rationale was that if they could not train more excellent guides (and they couldn't in the short two-year term), they would do only what they could excellently. And, by raising prices, they would reduce demand naturally, instead of making people mad by having groups too large, or by turning people away completely.

It was a gutsy call, and one that most not-for-profits would not be comfortable making. Other organizations would have rationalized that since their costs had not risen, their prices should not. They would assume that their status as a not-for-profit did not enable them to make a profit, and would not react to the market demand. But this group did, and with very, very unpredictable results.

Demand went up. Way up. It doubled in the first six months. Why? Because people assumed that a tour that cost a lot would be good—and thus desirable. The tours *were* good, and got rave reviews. But the increase in price did not decrease demand. So what did the organization do? It limited the size of tours, set up a reservation system including advanced payment (so that it got to use people's money early), but did not do more tours per day *than it could do well.* Yes, that disappointed people, but five years later the tours are still sold out five months in advance, and, as another benefit, donations from tourists are way up, again based on the perceived value of the service and the quality of the organization.

Don't ever assume that price is everything. Recover your costs, add a profit, and then listen to the markets. This is another really important issue, and I have included a complete chapter on the subject in my book *Financial Empowerment.*

5. Promotion and Distribution

By now you know your market, You know what they want, you know what you are providing, and you know the price (Exhibit 5-6). Great. But does your market know about you? Do they know that you are in business, that you have this wonderful product or service that is shaped to meet their wants? This area is what is called advertising. It is cold calls, warm calls, direct mail, word of mouth, in-person sales, referrals, and public information. Don't just shotgun your information. Carefully gauge how and what you tell your markets. Track how they find you, and use only those methods that work. Experiment with new ones, but drop them if they are not delivering for you. A great example of this trial and error is the explosion in web sites on the Internet that has occurred since 1995. Have they resulted in more business? For some organizations, yes; for some, no. The net offers access to huge markets, but are they the people you want to seek? Many of my clients have come to the conclusion that they must have a web site, that

Exhibit 5-6   Promotion and Distribution

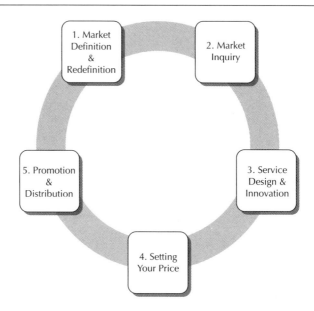

it is a cost of doing business, and that the most mission that they can do on the site is good public information and education. They are still experimenting, seeing what works.

You need to promote to customers, to people that you serve, as well as to people who send you customers; your referral sources. For a rehabilitation hospital this might be neurologists, for an ex-offender program it might be court adjudicators, for a wildlife preserve it might be travel agents or local hotels and restaurants. You need referral sources, and you need to give them information that helps them understand what you do and why they should send people to you.

Here again is a very important issue. You need excellent marketing materials, and you need to put them in the right hands at the right time. So, better marketing materials will be our entire focus in Chapter 9.

Distribution is a common marketing term, but it may be easier for you to think of it as service delivery with the following context: who, when, where, and how. Remember that all of these context items weigh heavily on market satisfaction. A simple example is day care. If the *who* is not people who relate well to children (and parents); if the *when* is not at hours that meet parents' work schedules; if the *where* is not in an accessible location perceived as open, airy, pleasing, and safe; and if the *how* is not seen as beneficial to the children, then the services will not be patronized well enough to do the community any good.

By asking your customers what they want you will learn a great deal about how they want the services provided. This cycle of asking and providing is yet another case of constant refinement. If there is a change in the wants for delivery, try to meet it if you can sensibly. To use the day care example, if your community's largest employer (a factory) suddenly went to a second or even a third shift, you might need to rethink the hours that you provide services. But if only one or two families out of 100 need the extended hours, you might offer them in-home sitting rather than keeping the entire facility open all night.

Just because the *what* of your services is excellent doesn't mean that you don't have to pay attention to the *who, where, when,* and *how.* They are also part of the marketing mix, and the constant cycle of asking and adjustment.

6. Evaluation, Evaluation, Evaluation

As you have already seen repeatedly, the markets and their wants change constantly (see Exhibit 5-7). You need to be evaluating the effectiveness of your efforts as well. Customer satisfaction surveys are one way, as are regular interviews with funders, service recipients, staff, and board members. But you also need to be watching competitors, and tracking where your customers come from. All of these evaluation tools are important. In later chapters, we'll cover how to choose and segment markets, follow the com-

Exhibit 5-7   Market Valuation

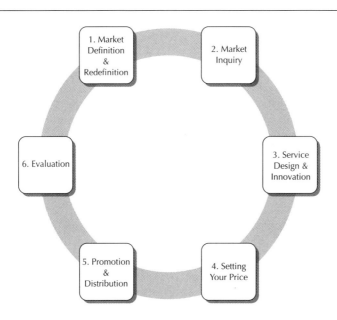

petition, and ask customers what they want, but the essential thing here is to remember that evaluation and improvement are critical parts of the competitive marketing cycle.

You can see that once you evaluate, you start over again; as I said earlier, the marketing cycle doesn't ever end, it just keeps going, helping you focus more resources on markets that want them.

Now let's look at two applications of this cycle in real not-for-profits. This should illustrate more fully the applications of the marketing cycle and its usefulness to you and to your organization in your marketing efforts.

❑ **FOR EXAMPLE:** A symphony wanted to expand its offerings to the local community, but found through surveys of ticket purchasers (particularly season ticket holders) that the current number of full symphony concerts was really all that the community could afford. However, the survey did produce some interesting comments (read: *wants*) from customers. They wanted concerts closer to downtown, and they wanted more intimate music, closer to the musicians. This was a result of the performance hall being a huge auditorium at a local university, 10 miles from the center of the city. People also noted that they would come earlier than the traditional 8:15 PM start. The symphony already had a chamber orchestra, but it played to small audiences at this admittedly too large auditorium. The board and staff identified their market: new ticket holders with children, as well as those who had responded to the survey. They had asked what this market wanted and the answer was clear: more small, intimate concerts closer to downtown, starting earlier. They took an existing service, chamber orchestra concerts, and adapted them to meet these wants. They changed the distribution—the where and the when. The next season they held four chamber orchestra concerts in a historic church (with excellent acoustics) in the downtown area. They started on Friday at 7:00 PM rather than Saturday at 8:15. The concert-goers in the first pews could be close enough to the performers to read the music as it was played!

The price was also lower than at the large auditorium (the symphony's costs were down due to fewer musicians to pay and lower rental fees). The symphony promoted the idea heavily through music teachers in the public schools ("Get your parents to take you to a concert"). The result was an immediate success, with each concert a sellout. The next season the organization provided eight such concerts and they not only sold out, but allowed the symphony to retire a burdensome debt.

The lesson? Even adapting existing services can be a winner when you ask your markets and listen to them.

❏ **FOR EXAMPLE:** The donations to a thrift store were down. And, the thrift store needed a continuing supply of quality donated goods to meet the constant demand from customers. (As an aside, thrift stores are excellent examples of organizations that work for two *widely* different markets: the donors of the goods and the purchasers of the goods.) The thrift store already had collection boxes, and would arrange to pick up goods if called. But still it wasn't enough. They decided to administer a survey in the local community, and found that what people wanted most was to simply get rid of excess "stuff," but only when they were (a) cleaning out their garage, attic, or basement, and (b) having a garage sale. A garage sale? It made sense, and the organization moved to adapt its existing pick-up service to meet the wants of the customer. Staff watched the papers and, every morning, people went to houses that advertised garage sales. They talked to the homeowners and left leaflets noting that instead of the owners packing up and retaining the household goods that remained after the sale, the thrift shop would stop by, do the packing, and take some, most, or all of the leftovers.

What had they done? Identified the market, asked for wants, adapted to meet those wants, and changed both their promotion and distribution to meet those wants. And it worked.

❏ **FOR EXAMPLE:** A midwest state government department, a funder of human services that we will call HHS, had decided to, yet again, change the way that it organized, planned for, and funded the provision of services throughout its state. Over a period of two years, HHS floated policy papers, researched what was going on in other similar states, met with legislators and the direct (not-for-profit) providers of service, and then announced its sweeping changes. No longer would providers be funded on grants, but rather based on outcomes and on the number of people served (a modified managed care approach). The providers who could come up with the most innovative, cost-effective ways to provide services and still reach desired outcomes would not only be allowed to provide the services, but would be encouraged to expand to other communities, even if that meant pushing out current, in-place organizations.

What response did the providers have? About 80 percent screamed that the new system would not work, would hurt people that were being served, and was unfair to the provider system as well. About 20 percent quietly tried to figure out how to do what the funder, the customer, wanted. First, they looked at whether HHS was still a customer that they wanted, and said yes, it was. Then they looked at what HHS wanted: innovation, cost-containment, and outcomes. Third, they asked themselves whether they could reshape their existing services to meet the wants of HHS and still meet their mission and values. It was not going to be easy, but they decided that they could. Fourth, they looked at their costs, and tried to reshape their services along with reducing their costs, again to meet a customer want. They looked at the way they delivered the services, the who, what, where, and when. Finally, they developed a promotion campaign for the funder, for HHS.

Which agencies were successful here? Did all of the 20 percent of the agencies succeed in making the changes? No. A number felt that they could not do what HHS wanted. And, some of the 80 percent stopped whining and followed the lead of the innovators. Many did not, and three years after the introduction of the new system, over half of those organizations were no longer eligible to provide service to HHS. Why? Because they didn't listen and respond to their market.

Use this marketing cycle to start up new services or adapt your existing ones. In either case, it will help you and your staff become and remain more market-oriented, and thus more competitive.

B. THE MARKETING DISABILITY OF MOST NOT-FOR-PROFITS

You now know that asking, listening, and responding to the wants of your many markets is the core of good marketing. Doesn't sound too hard, right? I agree, and while marketing is certainly work, it is not particularly difficult work, just disciplined work. However, in my years of training and consulting with not-for-profits, I have observed that it seems to be more difficult work for staff than it should be. Staff either don't ask, don't listen, or don't respond. Over time, I have come to understand why.

Most not-for-profit staff have a marketing disability. A real and severe disability. One that needs to be addressed and overcome for them to succeed in a competitive environment. Let me explain.

Most staff of not-for-profits come from what I call a service background. They are curators, teachers, social workers, nurses, ministers, scientists. They are trained to meet people, talk to them, and diagnose their *needs*. Or they are trained to assess a situation, or a community, and discover or reason out its *needs*. They are trained to know with confidence that they are "the professionals." They spent countless hours and lots of money in school learning this diagnostic skill. And, as valuable as that skill is, as necessary as it is in what the organization does, it becomes a disability as soon as the staff person says: "I know better than they (the customers) do what is *needed,* so I don't need to listen to what they *want.*"

Do you see the problem? By focusing on and reacting to their training, not-for-profit staff members negate the key transaction in good marketing: asking customers what they *want* and valuing the answer enough to respond. By centering solely on their own expertise, these staff discount or even ignore completely the value of their customers' opinions. Therefore, they don't *listen.* They often don't even ask! Thus, they *can't* respond to the wants of the customer, and they are *doomed* in a competitive market.

☞ **HANDS-ON:** Talk to your staff, particularly your highest-trained staff, about the importance of listening to the wants of the people you serve. Remind them that listening is not an inherited skill, it is a practiced one, and that listening, really listening, is not just waiting their turn to talk! Finally, work with them on how to see things from their customers', their clients', and their students' perspectives. The more they can do that, the more value they will attach to the opinions, the complaints, the concerns, the *wants* of the people that your organization serves.

To overcome this disability you need to constantly remind yourself and your staff that the people that you serve have the right to have wants, and that those wants are important. Your skills as a diagnostician should not be diminished by this attention to wants. In fact, training yourself to listen in a new way may actually enhance your sensitivity to what your service recipients are saying. As a result, you may be able to serve them in new and better ways.

Remember the marketing disability. It is with you always, and you need to overcome it if you are to be successful, competitive, and market-sensitive.

C. THE MARKETING CYCLE AND YOUR COMPETITORS

You have read the marketing cycle that I want you to use. You know that it starts with the target markets, asks for wants, and then shapes (and reshapes) both services and products to meet those wants, including market-sensitive pricing, distribution, and promotion.

So where in this mix are your competitors? What about those people who want to take away your customers and make them theirs? How do they fit? How can you adapt and respond to the competition?

As I said in the Overview, your competition is so important that we will spend the entirety of Chapter 7 on just that subject. Here I want to go over the parts of the marketing cycle and examine what your competition is doing. And, by doing that I hope to highlight a key point, and one of the characteristics of a market-driven organization:

Embrace competition: It will make you better at what you do.

Should you pay attention to your competitors? Certainly! Should you respect them? If they deserve respect. You certainly should respect the marketplace and its forces. Should you fear competition? No. If you do excellent work, if you ask your customers what they want and solve their problems, if you focus on customer service, and let the markets lead you, in most situations competition will not be life-threatening. Competition hones you, making you more efficient, effective, and focused on what you really do well. And that's good, for you, for your organization, and for the people you serve.

So, know your competitor, learn from the good ones, and be aware that new competition can show up at any time, but don't live in fear. Put your energy into constructive avenues. Let's start by seeing how your competition reacts to the marketing cycle.

1. Defining/Redefining Your Market

As we have seen, for you this means figuring out who you are going to serve (or who you already serve in a more defined way). For your competition, it means the same thing, but perhaps in a different way. They may look at who you serve and try to take away only the most lucrative segment, or only the one closest to them. For example, in the mid-1980s dozens of proprietary substance abuse centers sprang up throughout the nation, and took away the high-end customers from the traditional not-for-profits, the customers who either paid cash or had insurance. This is called "creaming" (as in skimming off the cream), and it happens in a lot of areas. Private schools may take only the best (or richest) students, museums seek to focus on kids (since parents will follow), environmental groups on people who want to buy "green" products.

☞ **HANDS-ON:** Sit down with your senior staff and ask them this: What do we do better than our main competition? Can we do more of this? How do we know we are better? Can we improve on our best? The idea is to reduce the fear of your competitors.

As I have said over and over, you have competition. Are you doing something for someone that your competition can do as well or better? Then watch out, because they are watching you! You may need to redefine your market to accommodate to the competition.

2. Market Inquiry

Ask, ask, ask, and listen! You've read that already. But you can also learn from your competition's asking, and play off of what they learn.

❑ **FOR EXAMPLE:** Perhaps 15 years ago, McDonald's, Showbiz Pizza, and many other for-profit enterprises started offering birthday parties for kids, where parents could go for a one-stop, full-service party, with favors, activities, food, and supervised play. This idea was the result of careful market research (asking) and focus groups (more asking), and was an immediate hit. Now it seems that everyone but your local gas station offers such services. Including not-for-profits. In our community the state museum, our local zoo, a not-for-profit nature refuge, our children's museum, and a number of churches have entered this market, some with a great deal of success. They observed an idea, asked their own customers if this was something that they wanted, and adapted the concept to meet their own resources.

While this may seem like a great, cheap way to find out things, do not fall victim to just being a copycat. You cannot always depend on the end product of others' marketing. What if they are making a mistake? What if their core clientele is fundamentally different than yours? Be a prudent observer, but make sure you do your own research.

Finally in this area, you can be sure that your competition is watching you, asking your customers, and perhaps your former employees, how you do what you do, how much you charge, what you do well or poorly. Depend on it. Little if anything in business is secret for long.

3. Service Design and Innovation

Your competition, in observing you, may "steal" your ideas (which, in nearly all cases, are fair game unless you can copyright or trademark them). Then they can improve or adapt them to meet their unique mix of customers and resources. Thus, you may look around one day and find that your best ideas have been improved on, taking away your best customers.

Of course, you can return the favor by doing what we reviewed above: observing, listening to your customers, and providing the best mix of responses to their wants that you can.

❏ **FOR EXAMPLE:** A few years ago, discount airlines were uniformly providing transportation but no food. The idea was to save not only the costs of the food, but also labor costs. But customers are used to some food, and surveys showed that they wanted both low cost and a meal. Then America West introduced low-cost bagged meals that were handed out *as passengers boarded the plane.* Good idea. Good enough that not only do most discount carriers now provide such service, but major lines do as well for short flights.

Your competition is watching, experimenting, trying new things. You need to as well. The market's gumbo of ideas, wants, and products and services is never static, never a sludge. Stay flexible and pay attention.

4. Setting Your Price

You've already heard me say that price is not the issue, that value is. That doesn't mean that your competitors won't try to attract customers from you by lowering prices, offering introductory discounts or coupons, or even "low-balling"—offering prices below cost to get customers to try them (and theoretically to be impressed enough to return).

The danger here for most not-for-profits is that a for-profit competitor probably has deeper pockets, and thus a much greater ability to price lower and for longer than the not-for-profit does. The temptation is to try to match price for price, and that can, in many cases, be deadly. If your competition offers a low price, evaluate it carefully. Does the price include everything that your price does? For example, does an introductory assessment at a competing mental health center for $49 include the same array of services, tests, and record review as yours? Does the lower-cost day care center have the same staff-to-child ratio as yours? Does the "cheaper" tuition at a competing school include all student fees?

Most organizations don't compete solely on price—they compete on a mix of price, quality, availability, service, speed, and comfort. This mix is known as value, as we have already discussed. If your service is truly more valuable to the customer (which you can find out by asking them), people will be willing to pay more. Not necessarily a lot more, but some. Don't get sucked into a price war that you can't win, especially if you can give more value to your customer.

5. Promotion and Distribution

Here is another part of the mix where you can learn from observation: advertising. Watch what your competition does. Particularly if you are being targeted by a for-profit, look at how they let people know that they are there. Do they truly advertise (billboards, in the newspaper, in magazines); do they have handouts, posters in grocery stores, ads on the radio and television? Think about what kind of customer they are trying to appeal to with such advertisements. It may give you a clue about their marketing and business plans. If, for example, the ads for a mental health center note "day care on site," it is pretty clear that they are interested in parents, and more probably in single moms, who may be most in need of such a service while they are using mental health counseling or group therapy services.

As in the caution I included in the service area, don't always assume that every kind of advertising and promotion that your competition uses is automatically for you. It probably isn't. And, with perhaps deeper pockets than you, they can probably chew you up in a competitive paid advertising campaign. So pick and choose your places to promote carefully, and don't let your competition draw you into a fight you can't win.

☞ **HANDS-ON:** Get a copy of every one of your marketing and promotional pieces. Look at each one and write down whether it is a broad-based piece or a piece that is targeted to a particular market. If you have more broad-based than targeted, you could be in real trouble if your competition is focused on one small (and usually lucrative) market.

Then there is distribution. Again, this is the how, where, and by whom part of the equation. Your competitors will, undoubtedly, try new things. They will need to to draw your customers away from you. Don't be too inflexible to try new things yourself. If what your competition is doing is working, consider if it will work for you. This area, more than any other, goes to the core of becoming and remaining responsive. Watch your competition (they are watching you) and learn from what you see.

❑ **FOR EXAMPLE:** There are more examples here than we have pages to print them on. How about affinity cards, the charge cards that allow you to get frequent flyer miles on a particular airline when you use the card? Many not-for-profits have watched this idea and said: "Why not for us?" Now you can get affinity cards that help many not-for-profits (as of this writing mostly environmental groups). Or first-time visit discounts (mental health centers), money-back guarantees (YMCAs), "free" gifts for membership (public radio and television). All of these concepts come directly from the for-profit sector, from not-for-profits' competitors. All appeal to the customer in special ways. All change the method of service or of enticement.

As I said above, the entirety of Chapter 7 will be on your competition, and many of these subjects will come up again in more detail. But suffice it to say here that your competition is doing the same basic things that you are. Be observant, open-minded, flexible, and prudent in your responses to their innovations, and you will improve your own set of services, benefit from your competitors' marketing expenses, and, perhaps, remain competitive yourself.

RECAP

In this chapter, we have had our first exposure to the classic marketing cycle. You need to chisel this sequence into your brain, as you will need it over and over as you go through the endless circle of asking, listening, adjusting, asking, listening, and adjusting.

Let's review it one more time. The marketing cycle is:

1. Market definition and redefinition
2. Market inquiry
3. Service design and innovation
4. Setting your price
5. Promotion and distribution
6. Evaluation, evaluation, evaluation

Then, we looked at the marketing disability of most not-for-profits. Remember that you are trained to diagnose needs, not ask for wants. You need to get over this disability if you are to succeed, and you need to warn your staff about their disability as well. Remember, everyone is on the marketing team, and everyone needs to ask, ask, ask, and then *listen.*

Finally, we looked at the marketing cycle through the filter of your competition, exploring what your competition does at each stage of the cycle and how you can and should react to it. Remember that you can easily get drawn into an escalating promotion or pricing war.

The marketing cycle will work if you follow it consistently. But it is not an event; it is a constant, endless process that will constantly and endlessly result in your improving your services and increasing the satisfaction of your customers. In short, your organization will do more and better mission. So use the process!

Discussion Questions for Chapter 5

1. Do we really know who our markets are? For all services and all funders?
2. How do we know what our markets want? When was the last time we asked funders, for example?
3. Do we recover all our costs in our pricing? Plus a profit? Is there a mission reason not to? When?
4. Does our promotion just scatter-shot, or is it targeted, and targeted at a target market?
5. Do we succumb to the marketing disability? How can we get staff and board past it?

6

Who Are Your Markets?

OVERVIEW

In Chapter 5, I showed you the marketing cycle that works, and works well, in a wide variety of situations, allowing you to improve your services, make the people that you serve happier, and produce efficiencies and effectiveness that your organization has not seen before. What was the first step in the cycle? Right! *Market definition and redefinition.* Good for you—you *were* paying attention! In this chapter we will go into that first step in detail.

CHAPTER THUMBNAIL

➤ **Market Identification and Quantification**
➤ **Market Segmenting**
➤ **Focusing on Target Markets**
➤ **Treating All Your Markets Like Customers**

I'll show you how to define your markets, and who those markets really are. I suspect you will be a bit surprised at some of the markets we list.

Then, I'll show you how to segment your most important markets into smaller parts. This will prove very valuable as you try to focus your efforts on your truly critical markets, and as you differentiate between the markets your organization really wants to serve and those that you would rather not be involved in.

Next, I'll show you some objective and subjective ways to focus on your most important and most desired markets. One of the most important rules in business is the *"80/20 Rule";* I'll explain what it is and how to take advantage of it. I'll also show you some ways to use your strategic plan to focus on the most important markets. By using both of these techniques you will be better prepared to make the most of your necessarily limited marketing funds and time; you can put your efforts where they will do the most good.

Finally, we'll get into detail on a crucial part of the marketing effort: treating each and every one of your markets (even those you may not especially care for) like a valued customer. If you, your staff, and all your volunteers learn this admittedly sometimes difficult skill, you will go a long way in both marketing and competitiveness. I'll show you some specific ideas on how to adapt to this new paradigm.

By the end of this chapter, you will have a thorough understanding of your markets, why they are all important to attend to, how sort through them and then focus on the most important.

A. MARKET IDENTIFICATION AND QUANTIFICATION

So, who are these markets we keep referring to? Let's look at a diagram that will help you focus on the many, many different markets you actually serve. As you look at Exhibit 6-1, note how many markets there are and keep in mind that this diagram probably does not include all of *your* organization's markets!

When I first suggested that you examine your markets, you probably immediately thought of the different groups of people you help through your services. That's understandable, but only a part of the whole picture. You *really* have, as you can see, four different and distinct main categories of markets: internal, payer, referral, and service, and probably 10, 20, or even 40 different markets contained within those four categories. Each category is important; you can't provide services without money, without a staff or a board, and nearly all organizations depend on referrals—someone sending people to them—for a significant percentage of their work. Each category bears further analysis.

NOTE: You can and should develop a form just like this for your organization. Draw one up on a flip chart, or have someone design one in your word processor. You'll have the same internal *markets as here, but you need to be as specific as possible about the* funders, services, *and* referral sources *you have. I'd suggest drawing up the form now, and then having it with you as you read the remainder of the chapter so that you can pencil in your markets as you see examples from other not-for-profits.*

Exhibit 6-1   The Markets of a Not-for-Profit

INTERNAL	• Board of Directors • Staff Members • Volunteers
PAYER	• Government • Membership • Foundations • United Way • Donations • Insurers • User Fees

SERVICE
(More than just the two
shown as examples)
	• Service A
	    Client Type 1
	    Client Type 2
	    Client Type 3
	    Client Type 4
	• Service B
	    Client Type 1
	    Client Type 2
	    Client Type 3
	    Client Type 4

REFERRAL SOURCES	• Many different sources, all with different wants

1. Internal Markets

There are three of these: your board, your staff, and your non-governing volunteers. All three are crucial, and all three deserve to be treated like markets, utilizing the same marketing process that we discussed in Chapter 5. All three groups deserve to have their wants met, to the extent you can. Unfortunately, most not-for-profits either ignore this issue, or drastically underestimate the importance of these markets. They treat their board as a necessary evil, their staff as a commodity, and their volunteers even worse. The management "knows" what the staff want (more money), so they never ask. The management doesn't really care what the board wants as long as they come to meetings and don't ask too many questions. Volunteers are to be put in whatever position is most in need, not matched with their skills, or oriented, or trained.

The downfall of these perceptions is that, in a competitive world, you need excellent board members, and to get and keep them, you need to treat them as a valuable resource. Likewise, you are going to need to attract and retain good staff, and it will be tough: You need good staff more than they need you. For many not-for-profits, volunteers are a huge payroll savings and provide a network into the community that no other force can. And, in a competitive world, board members, volunteers, and staff have lots of choices of where to put in their hours. It doesn't have to be at your place.

So, make a big mental note: In the process of becoming market-oriented and focusing on your external markets, don't forget your internal ones.

2. Payer Markets

These are the people who send you money for the services you provide. You may be offended that I consider these people a market. After all, you are here to do good works. Money is just a vehicle and an unseemly one at that. The people you really need to pay attention to are the people you serve. Right? Partially. In the old days of having a monopoly, you could afford to do this. No more. If, in a competitive market, you ignore the payers and the internal markets and direct your attentions solely to the people you serve, you are on a short road to oblivion. Remember, there are two primary rules of not-for-profits.

Rule One: *Mission, Mission, Mission.*
Rule Two: *No Money, No Mission.*

Ignore these at your peril.

As you can see, there are many payers, and we should examine their different wants. I do need to caution you here: Do *not* accept my listing of wants as gospel. Go ask them yourself. The following list generalizes the different wants of many payer markets, and almost certainly misses some important detail of the wants of one of yours. *Ask them what they want!*

➤ **Government.** For many readers, the government (federal, state, county, or city) is a key customer, one that may even form the backbone of your income structure. Too often, unfortunately, not-for-profit managers don't think of these important customers as *customers;* they consider them the *enemy.* While that attitude may have worked in the past, you can no longer afford to demonize government payers.

What do government purchasers want? Generally, they want a set of services (carefully defined) provided to a set of people (also carefully defined) in a set period of time, often in a set manner, with no audit exceptions and all paperwork in on time.

If you don't like having government as a key customer, develop a long-range marketing plan that reduces or eliminates them from your income stream. But while they are there, treat them with the respect that all your customers deserve. Ask them what they want and give it to them.

☞ **HANDS-ON:** If your organization has government income, consider this question carefully. When was the last time you asked your government project officer/funder, "How can I make your job easier?" Never? You are not alone, but that kind of question is essential to stabilize and improve relationships with all customers. When you read Chapter 11, "Incredible Customer Service," remember that it applies to this market as well.

Finally, don't fall into the trap of thinking of "government" as all one market, with identical and never-changing wants. You may well get funds from more than one government source, or even from different programs within a single agency or department. Each of these sources and programs has different legislation and regulations controlling them, and thus each has different wants from your organization. Each deserves your attention, at least if you want to continue to have them as a payment source.

➤ **Membership.** Many not-for-profits have a membership, which is an excellent way of developing important linkages with the community and a regular donation base—if, and only if, the membership benefits are worth the fee. Yes, environmental groups, museums, zoos, symphonies, and public broadcasters are all examples of organizations that have built large, long-standing membership bases.

What do members want? It depends on the organization and the sales pitch that it used to get the member. PBS members want quality programming, and often get a premium gift and a monthly program guide with their membership renewal. YMCA and YWCA members would not be satisfied just to know that the Y is open. For their fee, they want access to locker rooms, gyms, and pools, and reduced fees on Y programs. Museum members may get reduced admission fees or priority purchase on hard-to-get exhibit tickets.

You need to carefully and regularly assess the benefits that accrue to your members. You might want to make a list of the membership organizations in your community; that's the competition for this kind of funds. Are your members satisfied? You don't know until you ask, and in a competitive world, you can't afford not to know.

➤ **Foundations.** Foundations come in all shapes and sizes. There are huge ones like Gates, Ford, or Robert Wood Johnson, and hundreds of small local community, corporate, or family foundations spread through nearly every city and town in the nation. Their interests and funding procedures vary widely, as do the amounts of money awarded each year.

What do foundations want? While the breadth of interests is sweeping, within their areas of interest, most foundations want pretty much the same things: innovative projects that meet their criteria, organizations that can demonstrate strong community support, and projects that can be self-supporting, generally within three years.

Foundation funding is *extremely* competitive and, if you don't carefully research the wants of the foundation, you are wasting your time and theirs. Most foundations give you a good list of their wants right in their funding requirements, which can nearly always be found on their web site. If you can, go beyond that and, if the foundation has a staff, talk to a project officer or, better yet, go to meet with them (if that is allowed and encouraged) and dig a little deeper into what their "hot buttons" are. Ask what they like to see most and what they like to see least on applications. Then listen and do what they ask!

➤ **United Way.** Some United Ways are emerging from the dark ages of fund raising and dispersal by looking at not-for-profits as essential mission-based businesses and by funding worthy projects based on merit and community need. And, many are reducing their application requirements to make funding more efficient and less costly to everyone. Many others, unfortunately, are not and still fund based on how poor the organization is. "If your finances are not precarious, don't apply here. You've got to be broke to deserve our money." This has resulted in many, many of *my* clients dropping their United Way affiliations. Hopefully the innovators will become a trend.

If you are interested in United Way dollars, or get them now, pay attention to changes in funding priorities and methodologies. Talk to people (both staff and volunteers) involved with the organization in your community. Stay on top of any significant changes in wants. These dollars are also increasingly competitive.

➤ **Donations.** Still the bedrock of many small, community-based organizations, and certainly the case for all places of worship, donations (including bequests and corporate funding) are also highly competitive. Notwithstanding that, organizations that demur from seeking donations ignore one of their key resources: the ability to take tax-deductible gifts. What do donors want? Again, it depends, and lumping all donors together in one market basket is fraught with peril. The wants of annual givers vary widely from people who might want to give you a bequest. Some people want to support one program. Others prioritize giving to an endowment. Some want credit and visibility; most don't. Don't assume. Ask. And, if you are really serious about maximizing your donations, consider obtaining the services of a reputable professional fund raiser. Why? Can't you just do this yourself? Not necessarily. Way too many organizations try to do a little fund raising, or a little fund raising in a lot of areas (special events, direct mail, bequests) and wind up doing all of it badly. Here's the truth: *fund-raising does NO mission.* As a result, *it better make money.* In a competitive environment, you have to establish and maintain a core competence in one or more areas of fund raising before you start. That may mean training for your staff and volunteers, or it may mean hiring a professional, or both.

➤ **Insurers.** Some readers work for organizations that get funds through insurers. Insurers are, of course, financial intermediaries. As such, they are supposed to be obligated to pay for whatever condition or treatment is prescribed and covered through their policy. However, even though the insurer is supposed to be obligated by the policy of the insured to pay your organization, the speed and ease of that payment (and sometimes even whether the payment is ever received at all) depends in large part on your organization meeting the wants of the insurer. So whether your organization provides health care, home health services, mental health, substance abuse treatment, orthopedic devices, long-term care, or preventive services, meeting the wants of the fiscal intermediary, the insurer, is essential.

What are the insurer's wants? Usually these are heavily centered on process and paperwork. In the past few years, those wants have expanded to include technological competence: can you bill the insurer online, can they access your information online? More standard issues still are relevant, however. Was the insured medically required to seek services? Were they preapproved? Does your organization have the right licenses, certifications, and quality assurance? Do your staff? Are the forms complete? "Are you part of the managed care contract?" These questions are really wants.

If you are in any part of the human service field, you need to know how to "play the game," which is really just a cynical term for meeting the markets' wants. Pay attention to the process, the paperwork, and the fine print. You'll get paid sooner, and more fully.

➤ **User Fees.** These are admissions fees, ticket purchases, tuition, fees for counseling, or other payments received directly from the end user, the person that you serve. Like donations and membership, they represent a direct link between your organization and an individual payer who gets some benefit from the organization, either in service or self-esteem.

What do users want? They want what they pay for to be *high* quality, *high* value, and to meet their wants. Remember, price is not the issue—value is. If price were the only thing, no one would attend Harvard, Stanford, or the University of Chicago. They would all go to state colleges and universities. But all three of those institutions, like countless others of high cost, have thousands of applicants on their waiting list. Why? Because of the value of the education and the name associated with it.

How do you find out what users want? Again, you ask. And, you try hard not to fall victim to your marketing disability. It is particularly easy here, since you are so often providing services for a fee, and thus this, of all areas, is a function for which you have training and experience. Thus it is not difficult to fall victim to the trap of assuming that you know what the customer needs (and you probably do) and ignore what they want (which you don't know until you ask).

All of these markets are important, but later in this chapter, I'll give you some ideas about how to focus on the most important—the ones that hold the key to your future.

3. Service Markets

Just as in the payer markets, there are many, many service markets. These are the people that you serve, and they can be broken down by age, gender, education, income, zip code of residence, ethnicity, or the program or programs that they utilize. Most of you probably have thought that these were the people that you worked for, that this was the market you were serving. It is, but the internal and payer markets are essential as well.

As with the payer markets, it is crucial that you avoid lumping the people you serve together. The more discrete groups that you can identify, the more you can focus your asking and responding to them.

❑ **FOR EXAMPLE:** A mental health center provided numerous services. As it went through its marketing planning and market identification, it noted many, many markets within each service. Let's look at just one—outpatient counseling. The staff and board identified the following markets within this service:

One-to-one counseling:
—Chronically mentally ill
—Depression

—Post-trauma victims
—Veterans
—Teens in the high school
—Violent offenders

Small support groups:
—Grief and mourning
—Chronically mentally ill
—Veterans with post-traumatic stress syndrome
—Violent offenders
—AA

Of course, each of these groupings of people has different wants. To assume that all outpatient clients have the same wants would be ludicrous, but I see an awful lot of organizations that consider such a lumping appropriate. Don't follow their lead.

Although I cannot do your market analysis for you, I do urge you to break down your services by types of service and types of people. And, I also want to focus in on a critical service market that we haven't discussed yet.

➤ **Referrers.** We've already noted that your organization, like all others, has a limit on how much time and money you can spend on marketing. Wouldn't it be great to have people (who you don't pay) out there sending you members, clients, students, or parishioners? You can, and you may already. These are called referral sources. These may simply be informal recommendations from happy customers—someone who went to a play at your theater and was impressed, or a parent who loves how his or her child is developing in your preschool. Or they can be formal referrals from another professional, such as a surgeon referring a head trauma patient to a vocational rehabilitation facility, or a rabbi referring a troubled member of her congregation to a psychologist or psychiatrist.

What do these referrers want? Happy customers want to share their happiness, but it never hurts to thank them if you are aware of the recommendation. For the formal referral sources, though, it is a bit more complex. The first thing most referrers want is *capacity,* for you to have the ability to take the referral immediately and get it off of their desk. The second thing they want is *quality,* which is demonstrated by outcomes, by accreditation, or simply by having the same treatment philosophy that they have. The third thing most referrers want is to find out what happened. Most people want to know the outcomes, and more importantly, they are interested in the personal stories of success that come from interaction with your organization.

These wants are the ones that I see from my travels around the country. But as I cautioned you above, don't depend on my observations. As with any other market, you don't know what they want until you ask. Do you need referrals and recommendations? Absolutely! Find out what your referrers want and give it to them. Remember that, in a very real sense, the happy customer recommendations are the result of giving those customers what they want. The more you ask, the more you know. The more you know, the more you can respond. The more you respond, the happier your customers will be. The happier they are, the more of these referrals you will get!

All of your markets—internal, payer, referral, and service—deserve attention. Paying close attention to so many diverse groups is not always easy, especially since your organization, like all others, has only so much money and staff time to throw at even this critical activity. So what do you do? There are two more steps to take control of all this marketing identification. The first is to learn about market segmenting, where you turn the tables and think through who you *want* to serve and compare that to who you currently serve. Then you focus on your targets. I'll show you how to do both, and we'll start with segmenting.

B. MARKET SEGMENTING

We've already begun our discussion of market segmentation in the earlier example of the mental health center that identified in great detail all the different markets it served. While this kind of differentiation is important, market segmenting in a competitive environment is more complex, and more potentially rewarding than simply breaking down your current markets into the smallest possible divisions.

Market segmenting is the technique of looking at your larger markets in more finite parts, and then deciding which ones of those parts your organization can, should, and wants to serve. It is a technique that can really focus you on what you do best, and it is one that is relatively easy to learn.

You can view segmenting your markets from several angles. Perhaps you want to look at all the different kinds of people you serve with a particular service. By itself, this listing gives you the ability to focus on different wants, but it also arms you to make some important decisions about the people you serve. Do we want to continue to focus on this group? Does serving this constituency mesh with our strategic plan, our vision for our future? Is this market segment growing or shrinking, likely to buy more or less of what we are selling? Competitive managers, managers who are responsive to markets and their constant changes, are asking these questions. Unfortunately, many not-for-profit managers defer on such tough decisions because they are afraid of offending a traditional constituency by cutting back on a long-standing program, or because staff (or more often board) members resist abandoning a pet program.

☞ **HANDS-ON:** As you make lists of your markets and their segments, ask yourself, "Why are we providing this service?" and "Why are we serving this population?" If your immediate answer is solely, "Because we always have," you should stop and assess whether or not you should continue to. Think through issues such as: Do you have true expertise in the service or population? Is the service provided elsewhere as, or more, efficiently? Is this a core constituency for your organization? Is your organization identified primarily with this program or service population? Would reducing or ending this service dramatically affect your fund raising? And, of course, a crucial but not stand-alone indicator: Are you making or losing money in this area or with this group? Answers to these and many other questions will combine to help you make your decision, but never just continue to provide a service out of reverence for tradition. Make sure that it makes good mission sense.

Another way to use segmenting would be to look at a potential market for a new product or service and to see which areas, which segments, you want to pursue. With this use of segmenting you can pick and choose your target markets more efficiently and effectively.

❑ **FOR EXAMPLE:** An organization in the Pacific Northwest works with individuals with disabilities, finding and creating employment opportunities. The organization was presented with the chance to purchase a car wash, which potentially could provide excellent and steady jobs for its clientele. As it looked at the markets it didn't fall into the census trap I discussed earlier, and understood that its market was not the population that lived within 15 miles, but the people *with cars and trucks* that drove by regularly, whether they lived close or not. After making this initial cut, the organization looked at some segments that needed clean vehicles. These can be summarized as follows:

- *Retail:* People coming in to wash vehicles that they personally own. While this had advantages in terms of community visibility for people with disabilities, it also had the disadvantage of being seasonal, and very dependent on weather and day of the week. Thus the likelihood of steady employment was low.

- *Pre-Sale Cleaning for Auto Dealers:* Dealers need to clean cars prior to showing them. The organization looked at this as a real possibility for steadier work, but found that the liability of having to drive the cars and trucks to their site and the cyclical nature of auto and truck sales were two large barriers.
- *Cleaning of Fleets:* This market (which can consist of utility, postal, realtor, college and university, government, and other fleets) was a legitimate contender. The contracts would be large, steady, wholesale, and the drivers of the vehicles could simply stop in on a scheduled basis to have their vehicle cleaned.

The result was that the organization moved toward fleet cleaning, but only after trying retail. The initial try at retail was a mission consideration—more positive visibility in the community—but it was overwhelmed by the up-and-down nature of the business, resulting in long idle times for the staff. After this, they moved to the fleet cleaning.

You can use segmenting to affirmatively decide which markets you want to pursue, rather than simply reacting to all comers. But even with segmenting, you will still have many, many markets to monitor. And, as we have already said, only so much time and money to spend. You need to focus.

C. FOCUSING ON TARGET MARKETS

Now you know who your markets are, and you have segmented them to show you where market opportunities may lie. But where to focus your efforts? This is important to get the most out of your marketing, and there are two methods to utilize as you try to decide where your target markets lie. The first is empirical, while the second is more subjective. Using both is recommended, because by blending the results, you will make the best decisions on which markets to target.

1. The 80/20 Rule

The first assessment method you need to apply comes from the business canon called the 80/20 Rule. This tried and true maxim says that "80 percent of your income comes from 20 percent of your customers." When I first heard this spouted off at a business meeting 20 years ago, I thought to myself, "What drivel! How could something so pat and simplistic hold true across industries and businesses that vary so widely?" Perhaps you share my cynicism. Try it. I did, and the rule worked. I regularly apply it for clients that are in the depths of marketing planning to help them focus their efforts on the most financially important of their customers.

☞ **HANDS-ON:** Try this. Take out your income and expense statement for last month. Look at the income side of the ledger for the year to date. Take the total income and multiply it by .8 (80%). Then start with the largest customer, add that income to that of the second largest customer, then the third, etc., until your running income total reaches the 80 percent threshold. Now go back and count how many customers that took. If you now look at your entire customer base, you will find that the number of customers it took to reach 80 percent is very, very close to one-fifth, or 20 percent.

Using this method for your service markets is sometimes tougher, because of the difficulty of coming up with a common denominator of units of service, but it can be applied for most organizations with a little work.

The point of this methodology? Go with the flow. Focus on the largest one-fifth of your customers. I did not say, however, to ignore the smallest four-fifths. In a competitive environment, customers who get ignored tend to vote with their feet. And I don't think you would like to have 20 percent of your income stream vanish. But this methodology does help you rationalize spending the most time talking to, visiting, and asking your largest customers, both payer and service.

2. The Strategic Plan Method

Now that you have done the empirical approach, look at these same markets from a different point of view, through the lens of your strategic plan and your market research. Ask the question: "Which of these markets do I want to grow?" "Which parts of my community are the most important in terms of my mission?"

If, for example, you only get $5,000 a year in donations out of $750,000 total income, but your strategic plan calls for raising $200,000 per year in five years, you had better focus on figuring out this market, asking its wants, and attending to them, starting now. If you had only looked at the empirical analysis based on percentage of income, you wouldn't spend much time in this area, since it only represents six-tenths of 1 percent of your total income.

Another example of this has to do not with increasing the income from a certain market, but with decreasing your dependence on a current large customer. Many not-for-profits are intent upon reducing their dependence on a traditionally large purchaser, such as the government, United Way, or private donations. In this case, it may make sense to lessen what may have been a day-to-day focus on these markets to a reduced priority. But don't ignore them! They are still large payers and, for the time during which they remain large payers, treat them well.

Once you have done both of these assessments, pick your target markets and focus on them. And here is where you may have the most trouble, at least if your assessment results in a change in priorities. People, following the laws of physics, tend to move to the path of least resistance. In marketing that may mean talking to, helping, selling to, and asking the people you already know, are already familiar with, are already comfortable with—at the cost of not starting cold in a new, but high-priority market. Watch yourself to ensure that you are paying attention, and dividing your time appropriately, according to both your empirical and subjective analyses.

D. TREATING ALL YOUR MARKETS LIKE CUSTOMERS

In Chapter 2, we touched for the first time on this issue. Now that you have seen all the various markets you need to serve, perhaps this issue takes on a slightly different look. Let's go into this it a bit deeper.

1. Customers, Customers Everywhere

I hope that you and your staff already treat your service recipients as valued customers, greeting them warmly, offering assistance, solving their problems, listening to their concerns. While you may do this personally, it is critical that you and your senior management team both lead in this area and supervise closely, by regularly (and unpredictably) wandering around, watching and listening to the interactions of staff and your customers. Unfortunately, just as in the for-profit world, the not-for-profit world is divided into organizations that understand this and organizations that don't.

I am sure that if you and I met and I asked you to give me examples of businesses in your community that were committed to customer service and those that didn't have a clue, that you could give me a list of both immediately. Why? Because people pay attention and remember when they are treated well and when they are not. And, while your not-for-profit, like others, may have been given a break in the past by customers due to your status (and the perception that you really weren't a business), that slack has been tightened up, and you are now held to the standard of a proprietary business.

In fact, customer service is an important enough issue for you in your quest for competitiveness that the entirety of Chapter 11 will detail methods to provide "Incredible Customer Service," a level of attention that is rapidly becoming the benchmark for customer interaction throughout the nation. Here, I just want to continue the assault on the first obstacle to overcome: the idea that everyone—funder, staff, board, service consumer—is a customer.

2. Barriers to the Customer Service Mentality

There are a number of issues that get in most not-for-profit staff's way, and most of them we have already touched on. But I want to reiterate them in a slightly different light here to hopefully provide you additional insight to persuade you, and then give you ammunition to convince staff and board members. First, if people are not treated well, most will vote with their feet. Although you have traditionally had total or virtual monopolies on your kind of work and funding in your community, the coming wave of competition does not stop with your funders. Don't let your former status get in the way of dealing with your current condition.

Another barrier to developing a customer mentality has to do with the marketing disability we discussed earlier. If I know so much more than the people I serve, shouldn't they be simply grateful for my wisdom, my help, my beneficence? Hmmm. Sounds like a lot of doctors that I know. Doctors who don't get the fact that *I* am paying *them*, who make me sit on my heels for hours without apology, who treat me like a kindergartner, who always seem in a rush and don't see the person behind the patient. Doctors that I no longer, and will never again, consult. Remember, there are customers everywhere, and there are competitors everywhere. Don't send one to the other.

3. Internal Customers

One result of competition is that your community has or will have more organizations do what you do. A result of this is that your staff have new options for their employment. They no longer have only one place in a community to ply their trade. There are multiple opportunities. And to reinforce what I have said for years, you need your good staff more than they need you. Without good staff it is difficult to do good work.

I don't think anyone can argue that there are a fixed (and limited) number of qualified and engaged board members in any given community, and every organization would like to have them. Thus, if I as a board member want to serve, and I am not getting my wants met with you, I can easily resign and go help some other, more customer-oriented organization. An aside here is that many board members want to be associated with "winning" (also called businesslike, customer-oriented) organizations, and the ones that will win in a competitive market, are those that market aggressively and serve their customers—all their customers—well.

4. Funder Customers

Now to those pesky funders. This will be the longest stretch for many readers, as an awful lot of you have spent most, if not all, of your careers fighting with your funders rather than thinking of them as customers. Years of this kind of training and the resulting prejudice and difficult interpersonal relationships will be hard to overcome, what with our egos and pride getting in the way. And, even if you are the first one to stop fighting and start being attentive, the funder will (quite naturally) not trust you, or even be nice to you, for some time. Turning relationships around takes time, and you don't have much left, so start now.

Many readers are thinking, "But my funders are so unfair! They ask us to do more and more without an increase in funding. They want more paperwork done to account for every nickel, and they want it all done on unreasonable schedules when they themselves are virtually never on time. They are the customer from hell, and they really act more like they *own* us than like a *customer.*" I've heard this basic set of sentiments thousands of times. Here are two points: First, all businesses have customers from hell. Go to any airport during bad weather, and watch the gate agents deal with angry, irrational folks who are mad at the gate agent *personally* because it is snowing. They don't yell back. They have learned how to deal with them. You need to as well. Here is a preview of a key customer service rule we'll cover in Chapter 11:

The customer is NOT always right. But the customer is always the customer.

All of us, including customers, are wrong now and then. But that does not mean that the relationship changes because of the error. You are still selling something, and they are still buying. Act that way.

A couple of other notes on the new paradigm of funders as customers. If one or more of your funders are from state or local government, and if you are active in your state trade association, you may well be interacting with the same people in two roles: vendor and lobbyist/activist/advocate. Thus one day you work with the state department, wearing the hat of executive director, and ask, "How can I make your job easier?" and the next day you come in the same door as a member of the state association and object to a new regulation, rate, oversight clause, or piece of legislation. This schizophrenia can be trouble. One way to reduce the problem is to clearly and repeatedly identify yourself as a representative of the XYZ *association,* perhaps going to the level of even wearing a name tag with their logo on it when you are doing their business. However, even that does not guarantee that the state or local agency staff will differentiate between your differing hats. I am not suggesting that you need to give up lobbying. Just be aware of, and try to minimize, the potential cost.

Second, in many cases, I have seen organizations start to treat their funders like customers and, over the succeeding months, the funders have begun to respond by treating the organization more like a vendor, and less like a slave. In three cases, the funders started to let the not-for-profit be accountable for outcomes, not for process, reducing their paperwork load. In two other cases, the funder changed their funding method to allow the organizations to keep what they earned—the ultimate indicator of the vendor-customer relationship. Here is a case yet again of leading by example, and having people follow your lead.

5. Service Customers

Finally, your service recipients. Why wouldn't you treat them like customers? Because of the not-for-profit marketing disability. You know what they need. It is not a big leap from there to think that you know more than they do and thus devalue them, their ideas, their suggestions, their complaints, their wants. Don't. Each and every person you serve is ultimately a customer, and more and more a customer who can choose not to return. Here, as with the funders, your customers are not always right or reasonable or polite. But they are always customers.

I don't want you to think that I think this is easy. It's not, particularly at first. But you need to start now to think of all your customers as customers. In Chapter 11 I'll show you a number of tried and true techniques to empower your staff to fix problems, deal with complaints, and meet customers' wants. But for now, just start thinking of everyone as a customer and start practicing your refrain: "What more can I (we) do for you?"

RECAP

In this chapter, you have, perhaps for the first time, looked at your organization's many and diverse markets. You saw that you have *income markets, service markets,* and even *internal markets* of board and staff members. Next we looked at those markets and I gave you some broad generalizations about what each market wants, with the caution that you don't really know what any market wants until you ask. We moved on to market segmentation, and I showed you how to accomplish this task and how to use it to take a more assertive stance in choosing who you want to work for.

With so many markets identified, you needed a way to focus your efforts, to target the most important markets. I showed you how to do this important task, both empirically, with the 80/20 Rule, and subjectively, by integrating your strategic plan into the marketing mix.

Finally, we turned to the difficult and controversial subject of treating everyone (payers, board, staff, and service recipients) like customers. We covered each group and I hope that I convinced you of the problems you will face if you don't jump on this competitive bandwagon.

In a competitive environment, you have to be aware of who your markets are, and focus on the most important ones. You have to treat each like a customer. You have to ask their wants. Asking and customer service will be the subject of later chapters, but now it is time to move on to the other group identification process that is integral to successful marketing: identifying your competition.

Discussion Questions for Chapter 6

1. Let's make a list of all of our markets in each of the following categories: funders, internal, service, and referrer.
2. Now, do we **want** to be in all of these markets, or are we just here because we always have been?
3. Are there markets that we want to prioritize, to target? What are they by the 80/20 Rule? Or, based on our strategic plan?
4. Do we treat everyone like a customer? How can we be better at it?

7

Who Are Your Competitors?

OVERVIEW

I have said over and over that you are in an increasingly competitive world, and the facts surrounding that statement are irrefutable. Areas where you didn't compete five years or even five months ago are now open arenas. Things that you feel are secure from outside pressures will not be next year or perhaps even next month. Competition has become more and more the norm and less and less the remarkable exception.

So, for the first time for many readers, it is important to think of some people and some organizations as competitors. For many readers, anyone outside your own organization has always been "the community"—usually a friendly, welcoming term. In many, even most, cases this will still be true. But, as a mission-based manager, you need to learn the often obscure difference between a community member and a competitor, between a colleague and a competitor, between a peer and a partisan. Not an easy, nor, for many readers, particularly pleasant task. But it is an essential skill to learn if your organization is to compete at all.

CHAPTER THUMBNAIL

➤ Identifying Your Competition
➤ Studying the Competition
➤ Focusing on Your Core Competencies

This chapter will show you first how to identify who your competitors are and what they want that you have. We'll look at organizations that are after your clientele, your staff, your funding, your donated dollar. We'll review this competition from the perspectives of funders, the services you provide, the people you serve, and your referral sources.

Then, once we have identified who your competition is, we'll look into what they are doing. I'll show you a number of tried and true methods of smoking out your competitor's marketing methods, prices, and array of services. You will learn how to learn more about the competition and what makes it different, better, and often worse than your organization in the eyes of your clientele.

Once these two areas are covered, we'll look at your organization again and review the things that you have learned about yourself by learning about the competition: your core competencies. These core components of your identity are crucial to list and strengthen as you become more competitive. I'll show you how.

By the end of the chapter, you will know who your competition is, how to find out what they are doing, and which areas are your strengths and which are your weaknesses.

A. IDENTIFYING YOUR COMPETITION

Who are those pesky competitors anyway? To figure out who they are, let's review the array of markets that we covered in Chapter 6 and then compare those to your possible competition. You will see that you have competitors for each market, even those you may feel are sacrosanct. We'll start with your internal markets, and then move to payer, service, and referral markets (see Exhibit 7-1). Remember that the categories that I have included are both general and broad: That is, some of the categories that are listed may not be pertinent to your organization, and those that are, are undoubtedly broken into many smaller components by market type and by individual competitor.

As you can see, the internal markets are just as susceptible as the external markets to competition. You may consider the issue of someone from the outside competing for staff a nonstarter for your organization, particularly if you are in a rural area or in a geographic area with no other organization doing what you do. For example, if you are a children's museum and the only one for 100 miles in any direction, you cannot assume that no on else will come after your management or line staff: They may very well do so. Note that in Exhibit 7-1, I say that the possible competitors for staff are "Organizations . . . hiring people with the same skills as

Exhibit 7-1   Internal Assessment

INTERNAL Markets	Possible Competitors	How Do You Compete?
Board Members	Other not-nor-profits with board and volunteer positions available. A voracious competitor for the limited not-for-profit board "capital" in any community is the United Way, which is structured to use up thousands upon thousands of volunteer hours each year. Good organizations want good board members. Don't lose yours.	You ask the board members what they want, treat them as a valued resource, and give them important things to do.
Staff Members	Other organizations (both for-profit and not-for-profit) that are hiring people with the same skills as your staff.	You treat the staff with dignity and respect, involving them in management, budgeting, marketing, and planning. Like any other market, ask them what they want and give it to them when possible. Don't assume that just because you were once a staff person you know what all staff today want. You don't. Ask.

your staff," not "organizations providing the same services as yours." There is a big difference.

And, while many people who work in the not-for-profit environment want to stay there and not jump to the for-profit world, there are undoubtedly numerous organizations in your community that are not-for-profit and do good works. As the entire sector becomes more competitive, don't count on your friend from the United Way board to not "raid" your staff (or your board, for that matter).

One note on staff competition: There is a very positive trend in this area—people from the for-profit sector, mostly in their late 40s and early 50s, are moving to the not-for-profit sector. These baby boomers have, in many cases, done their 20 to 25 years at their employer, and qualify for retirement. They are of the age where many reassess their life, and remember the altruism of their youth. And then they act, by changing jobs and doing "something that matters." Don't forget to look in the for-profit arena for good staff, and also don't forget to emphasize what they want—that you do something "that matters."

Finally, on the subject of staff, while I have long contended that money is not *the* issue for most staff in most organizations, it certainly is *an* issue for every staff in every organization. If your organization is like most not-for-profits, you don't pay your staff what they could get elsewhere in the community, and there may not be a reasonable chance that you can in the near future. But you do need to try to pay a competitive wage, and to do other things that you can to be competitive. Some of those are listed in Exhibit 7-1. More are detailed in the staff management chapter in *Mission-Based Management*. It isn't always about money.

❑ **FOR EXAMPLE:** Consider this question: Have you ever met an *unhappy* Federal Express delivery person? Neither have I. Second question: Have you ever met an unhappy United States Postal Service worker? Me, too. Who gets the higher starting salary and benefits? The USPS. Similar to Federal Express are Cisco, Disney, Marriott, Lands' End, and many other superb firms, firms that, like all of us, lead with their line staff. Their compensation is fine, but not the best in the industry. To paraphrase J. W. Marriott, Jr., they take care of their people, and their people take care of them.

To be competitive for staff you need to take care of them, and that is not, repeat, not, always represented by dollar signs.

Now let's look at your external markets, starting with the PAYER market (see Exhibit 7-2). The people that send you money are *certainly* subjects of your competitor's interest. As you review the payer assessment chart, remember that your organization will have its own unique set of payers, and the ones you need to pay attention to will be the largest, the ones that have priority in your long-term plan, and the ones that are under the most competitive pressures, *in that order.* Don't wait to treat your target payer markets well until *after* there are competitors in the picture. Start now.

As you can see, you have a lot of potential competitors, and in each case I have suggested one or more of the basic components of our marketing cycle: select the target market, find out what they want, and modify (or create) a service to meet the wants.

Next is the set of external markets that you are probably most concerned about, the SERVICE Markets. These, most importantly, are subject to competition. And, since the number of people you serve is very often closely tied to the funding you receive, you need to attract and retain your clientele over a long period of time. Beware, though, your competition is doing the same thing. Let's examine the how and why, and start with you doing a little homework.

☞ **HANDS-ON:** Go to a copier, and make a copy of the table in Exhibit 7-3. If you can enlarge the copy to fill an 8 1/2 by 11 sheet of paper, so much the better. Then, fill in the table as best you can, either alone or with a

Exhibit 7-2   Payer Assessment

PAYER Market	Possible Competitors	How Do You Compete?
Government	Any organization or individual who can qualify for the funding under the government's regulations. More and more government agencies are going to true bidding for all services, and including for-profits in their vendor pool.	Know your funders' regulations cold. Make sure you meet all their "silly" regulatory and bureaucratic wants. Ask in advance what they want, and be consistent in keeping your promises.
Membership	All other not-for-profits that offer memberships are potential competitors, but mostly within certain fields, such as mental health, environment, the arts, animal rights, etc.	Make sure the benefits of membership are clear and tangible. Ask your members regularly what they want for their membership dollar. Add value—from the perspective of the member.
Foundations	Foundation funding is extremely competitive, and the competition comes more and more from organizations that have hired help to appeal to the foundations. Almost all of this competition is not-for-profit organizations; it may or may not be from your town, state, or area of service.	If you are planning to spend a lot of time in the foundation world, read the foundation press, get help from an experienced, successful grantwriter, and stick to the foundations that have an interest in what you do. Use the Internet to quickly learn what any particular found tion's expectations of you are.
United Way	Every other not-for-profit in your community who participates in the United Way, and many new not-for-profits that are starting up and applying to the United Way for funding.	Meet the United Way guidelines for funding precisely. If your United Way does community needs assessments, make sure that you participate so that you can ensure that your service area needs are included fairly and accurately.
Donations	Any and all not-for-profits who seek and accept charitable contributions. This broad category can be divided into corporate and individual, large and small, regular and bequest.	Focus on the kind of donor most likely to be interested in what you do. State who you are (your mission and values) clearly. Get professional help training if you plan to be competitive.
Insurers	Insurers, mostly as a result of managed care pressures, are looking for low-cost, high-quality providers of services. No longer limited to just health care, this can include any and all services covered under Medicaid.	Play by all the insurers' rules including their forms, any preadmission certifications, any licenses and accreditation you may need. Work with the people that you serve to meet the insurers' requirements as well.

Exhibit 7-2 *continued*

PAYER Market	Possible Competitors	How Do You Compete?
User Fees	Any not-for-profit that provides the same type of services that you do and makes the user directly pay through tuition, ticket fees, admission charges, office visit fees, etc.	You need to ask your users what they want, how happy they are with your services, and where you can improve—constantly.

team of management and line staff. I've provided an example that follows the blank table (see Exhibit 7-4).

As you do this, remember to be a*s specific as possible.*

Take this table and fill it in, making multiple copies of the blank table if you need to. If your copier has an enlargement capability, use it! The essential part of using this table is to begin the process of identifying who the competition is, and learning what you do well in that particular market. Additionally, I've divided the chart into two parts: THE SERVICES WE PROVIDE, and THE PEOPLE WE SERVE. This division is intended to focus you on the fact that competitors may come after people first (AARP goes after people over 55 and then focuses on the services that they need) or the service first (an arts organization advertising summer classes). Be thorough, and remember to look at the sample in Exhibit 7-4.

As you can see, the agency in Exhibit 7-4 is just starting its internal analysis, and is unsure of where its competition excels. Thus they definitely need to do more research. The things that they feel they excel at are mostly "friendly, experienced staff, sympathy, and training." That may be nice, but is it what people want? They need to carefully review and make sure that what they excel at is what people *want.*

Last, but definitely not least, let's examine your all important REFERRAL market and see who is competing with you there. Remember that your referral sources are the people who send you clients, students, parishioners, and members. For some readers, you may get referrals solely through word of mouth from currently happy customers. For many, particularly those in human service provision, referrals are a much more formalized part of your organization: A physician refers a patient to your organization for occupational therapy, a social worker refers a teenager to your program for counseling. In these cases it is important to find out the perception of the referral source about your organization and your competition.

If you don't have referral sources in the formal sense, remember this: a happy customer will sing your praises to 10 to 20 people over the next year.

Exhibit 7-3   Self Assessment

The Services We Provide	Competitors	Where They Excel	Where We Excel

The People We Serve	Competitors	Where They Excel	Where We Excel

Exhibit 7-4   Example of Self Assessment

The Services We Provide	Competitors	Where They Excel	Where We Excel
Short-term residential shelter	1. Salvation Army	Capacity	Friendly, accommodating staff
Job readiness training	1. Helping Hands 2. Veterans Administration 3. Local Job Corps 4. Welfare to Work providers	? ? ? ?	Staff with job experience
Counseling	1. Local Mental Health Association 2. Private Psychologists	? ?	Experienced counselors

The People We Serve	Competitors	Where They Excel	Where We Excel
People who are homeless	1. Salvation Army 2. Helping Hands Homeless Shelter	1. Capacity 2. Capacity, Counselling	Sympathetic, nonjudgmental
People with autism	1. St. Mary's Hospital 2. County Developmental Disabilities Association 3. School Districts	1. Marketing 2. Array of Services 3. Array of Services, Facilities	High level of training of staff

An unhappy customer will complain about you to 100 people within the next two weeks. Thus, you *do* have referrers, and when we cover customer service (Chapter 11), you will learn how to keep those referrers happy.

In Exhibit 7-5, you'll see a sample of a referral listing for an organization that provides rehabilitation services to persons with spinal cord and head trauma injuries. It includes headings: OUR REFERRERS, WHAT DO OUR REFERRERS WANT?, and WHO DO THEY REFER TO US? This categorization allows the organization to identify groups as well as individuals and focus on both the referrer and the market that they provide. For instance, if Dr. Jones sends only two patients per year, that may not make her a priority for the organization. But, if both of those patients are long-term, high-income patients, perhaps spending some time with Dr. Jones is advisable.

Looking at insurers, you will see that there are significant differences in what the referrers want, and thus in which referrers this organization should actively pursue. The same is true for the employers.

Exhibit 7-5   What Do Our Referrers Want?

Our Referrers	What Do the Referrers Want?	Who Do They Refer to Us?/Comments	Who is Our Competition?
PHYSICIANS			
Dr. Jones	Quick acceptance of patient, insurance coverage, accredited facility	Head Injuries (two 70-day patients last year).	St. Jude's Hanneman Rehab
Dr. Majeski	Insurance coverage, accredited facility specializing in spinal cord	25 Occupational Rehab patients last year— mostly spinal.	Unknown
Dr. Wheeler	Insurance coverage, medicaid certified, accredited facility	Various patients— mostly inpatient (40 last year).	Unknown
Dr. Foresta	Quick acceptance of patient, insurance coverage—all types, accredited facility	Only two patients two years ago but 20 last year. Mostly short-term assessment patients.	On staff at St. Jude's?
INSURERS			
Company A	Quick acceptance of patient, Medicare/ Medicaid certified, accredited facility	20 patients each and every year for the past 5 years.	Unknown
Company B	Quick acceptance of patient, Medicare/ Medicaid certified, accredited facility	Just starting to send us longer term. Only reimburse 80% of normal charges. 5 patients last year.	Unknown
Company C	Quick acceptance of patient, Medicare/ Medicaid certified, accredited facility, managed care capacity	Leader in managed care. Short stays mandatory. 50 patients last year.	Unknown, but talking with three rehab centers about inclusion in managed care network.
Company D	Quick acceptance of patient, Medicare/ Medicaid certified, accredited facility, managed care capacity	No history. A new player in the community. But covers almost 20% of the community due to three large employers.	Unknown
Company E	Quick acceptance of patient, Medicare/ Medicaid certified, accredited facility	Heinous oversight and paperwork. Only 10 patients per year.	Part of new managed care network?

Exhibit 7-5 *continued*

Our Referrers	What Do the Referrers Want?	Who Do They Refer to Us?/Comments	Who is Our Competition?
EMPLOYERS			
Meltdown Utilities	Lowest possible Workman's Comp results, deal directly with insurer, managed care capacity		Board President is on the board at Hanneman?!
Ace Manufacturing	Lowest possible Workman's Comp results, deal directly with insurer, managed care capacity	5 or so injuries per year. Ace is working on risk avoidance, and thus will be sending us less people in the future.	Unknown
Acme Automobiles	Lowest possible Workman's Comp results, deal directly with insurer, managed care capacity	Rapidly growing. Unionized. Sends us 20–30 people per year, but automating quickly.	No preferential arrangement yet.
Cellular Four	Lowest possible Workman's Comp results, deal directly with insurer, managed care capacity	Doubling the size of the workforce every three years. sent us 10 people last year, but all long-term patients.	Unknown.
Microhard Group	Lowest possible Workman's Comp results, deal directly with insurer, managed care capacity	Low accident rate for population.	No admissions in past two years.

Notice that, in this last analysis regarding the employers, the organization doing the analysis has not yet figured out who their competition is to any great extent. They obviously need to complete their inquiries. By using a chart such as this, the organization can be an aggressive market segmenter and choose the markets in which they want to compete, reducing their emphasis on other markets, and focusing their limited time and dollars on the market segments that best fit with their strategic plans.

You need to know who your competitors are, but this does not mean simply making a list. You need to look at them through various lenses: your funders, the people you serve, the services you provide, and the people that refer to you. Only by doing these different analyses can you hope to really get a good grasp of where to focus your greatest competitive efforts.

B. STUDYING THE COMPETITION

By applying the tools in the previous section, you can develop a list of your competitors and then prioritize the market segments to focus your efforts. Even with that focusing, you still have a list of priority competitors, ones that you need to find out more about. In using the tools I just provided you, you were asked to fill in what the competition does well and compare it to what you do well. I assume that your input on those charts was preliminary and based on word of mouth, or assumptions. If you are like most readers, it was probably not based on careful analysis.

1. What You Need to Know About Your Competition

With your competitors, you need to find out important information that you can then use to become a better competitor yourself. You need to learn the following four core things about your competitors:

➤ **What services do they provide?** Do they compete with you across the board, or only in certain areas? If they are a full-spectrum competitor, you probably need to investigate them more carefully than if they are only competing with you in one area, unless they are providing only your most profitable service.

➤ **What clientele are they seeking?** Do they target the same population that you do? Or, do they just take the most lucrative segment of your population, a technique known as creaming? On the other hand, do your target markets and theirs not really overlap? This is also important. If you are targeting people over 60, for example, and the competitor has that age cohort as a secondary or tertiary market, you may not have to worry as much.

➤ **What value do they give to the customer?** Remember, price is not the issue, value is. What does your competitor do that provides value to the customer? An added value at a museum might be a well-designed map, or a number of easily accessible benches or rest rooms. An added value for a counseling center might be a particularly friendly receptionist and free coffee in the receptionist area. Whatever the competition is doing, is it something that you can also provide, provide well, and that is within your mission statement?

➤ **What are their prices?** Is the price truly comparable to yours, or do you (or they) offer more service for the same price? While price is not *the* issue (value always is), it is an important issue for many customers. Make doubly sure you do your best to compare apples to apples when looking at price. Otherwise you may make bad decisions based on the assumptions that your price is lower (or higher) than the competition's.

❑ **FOR EXAMPLE:** I was recently working with two competing not-for-profit organizations who were considering a merger. These organizations provided sheltered employment to people with disabilities. They were reviewing each others' "daily rates" (prices) and one saw that their own rate was nearly twice that of their potential partner. They came to me upset, because they feared that this low rate indicated poor quality of service and they did not want to even consider joining up with a "poor-quality organization." I asked them why they felt the service was poor, and their answer was, "Look, our daily rate is $140 and theirs is only $82. They can't give good service for $82." "No," I agreed, "not unless they don't include the same costs in their rate as you do in yours."

And, in the end, we found out that that was the case. One daily rate included transportation, meals, and supervision after work. The other organization offered all of these same services, but billed them separately. Thus the comparison of prices with the name "daily rate" was invalid and misleading.

You need to find out about services, target markets, value, and prices—at a minimum. It would also be nice to know about other things, but these are the core issues to look at first. How do you find out? You do a little market research-aimed at your competition.

2. Where Do You Look?

Where do you start? What resources do you have? How much time do you spend on this? The answer to all three of these questions is the same: it depends. It depends on how actively you are competing. It depends on whether the competitor is retail (where a lot of information is in the public domain) or wholesale (where prices and services are more difficult to research). It depends on how much time and money you have to spend.

However, you need to start somewhere, so let's look through a list of resources that you can use to learn about your competition.

- *The Internet.* There is, of course, an enormous amount of information on the Internet. Here are some great places to start.

  ➤ Go to the competitor's web site. There is often a large amount of data on the firm, their services, and their prices right online.

You may also see their marketing strategy, be able to note what they are promoting, watch for sales or price discounts, and even get bids directly online. One caution: The data on the web site may well be out of date. Not everyone keeps their web site as current as they should.

➤ Look in the public record. If these competitors have bid for any public dollars, particularly against your organization, that bid is public information, and so is the background information on the firm that goes with it. Go to the funding source and ask for it by e-mail, or search the funding source's web site.

➤ If the firm is a not-for-profit, you can learn more about it at *www.guidestar.com,* which is a database of U.S. not-for-profits put together from their IRS 990 annual reports.

➤ If the firm is a for-profit, go to *www.ceoexpress.com* and look for the research area. There you will find the best and most up-to-date research sites and tools on the web.

- *The Public Record.* Of course, the phone is still an option! If your competitor is a not-for-profit, they need to file a report with both the IRS and with your state (either the Attorney General or the Secretary of State) each year. This financial information is available by calling the appropriate entity, or, in many cases, on the Internet. You will learn board names, total income, the organization's mission statement, etc. You can also call (or check online) with your state's department of commerce (or whatever your state calls it) to find out information on firms that do your kind of work. For example, you can ask the state department to do a search on every organization that provides child care services in a four-county area, and they will provide you with that information. It's your tax dollars at work! Use the public record.

☞ **HANDS-ON:** While you are at it, check your own records. You can enter and edit information on Guidestar.com. You can edit and update information at the Secretary of State and IRS. Make sure your information is up-to-date and accurate. When you run a search on a competitor, always run one on yourself—to find out what your competitor, and potential customers, are finding out about you.

If your competitor is a for-profit, you may be able to get information on them through a national database such as Dun & Bradstreet or a local information source, such as the Chamber of Commerce or the Better Business Bureau.

In either case, one of the first steps I would take is to call or e-mail the competitor, and ask for information on services and fees sent to you. There is no need to lie and pretend that you are a service recipient. Just ask for written material and have it sent to your home. If you think that they will recognize your name and not send it to you, ask one of your staff to make the same call.

Your referrers also usually have sets of information at their offices, or on their web site to provide to their clientele. For example, a social worker usually will keep information on all the programs he or she may suggest to a client; a minister may have the material from many resources in the community; a teacher may have sets of material on the many available tutoring organizations. (Note: they should have current copies of your marketing information as well.)

- *Customers.* Your customer base is an excellent source of information. When you do customer surveys, add in some questions on your competition. Ask such questions as: "Have you received this service from other organizations in the community? When? From whom? What did you like best about them? Worst? Why do you utilize our services rather than theirs?"

  Between surveys, you can ask customers informally when you see them in your organization. By doing this you will not only often learn important competitive information, but your customers will also feel that you care about their opinion of what is important. Don't ever discount the value of informal, regular asking. Your organization needs to have a culture of constantly asking.

- *Your state trade association, state association of non-profits, community foundation, or local management services organization.* These groups all should be tracking at least the issue of not-for-profit activity in their respective areas. Your state trade association (for whatever you do) is the best place to start, but the state nonprofit association that deals with all not-for-profits in your state, is also a good statewide resource. For a listing of state associations, go to *www.ncna.org.* Community foundations and management services organizations (MSOs, which are nonprofits set up to help other nonprofits manage better) are more local in interest and influence. For a list of MSOs, go to *www.allianceonline.org.* For a listing of community foundations, go to *www.tgci.com/resources/foundations/community.*

- *Board, Staff, and Volunteers.* The more ears and eyes out there, the better. After you make a list of your competitors and prioritize that list for the most pressing investigation, make copies, and provide them to your board, staff, and volunteers to let them know what kind of information you need, what questions you want answered, and that you would appreciate any help that they can give you in gathering the information. Now, suddenly, instead of just you and your circle of friends, acquaintances, and interactions, you have 20, 30, 50, or more people doing the same thing. The likelihood of getting information increases dramatically. One important side benefit of asking these people for help is that it reinforces the issue that competition is real and not just some figment of your imagination. Use your resources and, in this case, that means all of the other people inside your organization.

3. What Your Competition Is After

With these three important sources in mind, let's turn our examination of your competition to the people or things that your competition is trying to take away from you. Each group on the list below will have their own sources of information that may be of help to you. Opening up channels of communication early is important, so that you have established trust and access to information. Thus, even though not every one of the items or people on the list below will be a priority for you today, you may need access to information about that area in the future. I am not contending that you should give each area equal priority; just don't completely ignore any of them.

Remember, as you read the list, these categories are those in which competitors are trying to compete with you—for good board members, excellent staff, donations, bid work, volunteers, and direct services. In each, you need to find out how they are competing with you and try, if you can, to beat them.

☞ **HANDS-ON:** Think about the following issues related to your competition:

- *Board Members.* Ask board members (and friends and neighbors) who are serving or have served on other boards what they like most and least about their board *service.* Don't ask detailed and pointed questions about the other organization—you may not get good information. Focus your questions on the functions of the board that they liked and disliked. If there are board workshops run through your United Way, community foundation, local MSO, or local college or university nonprofit program, go to them and learn about the state of the art. You need to make your board service desirable.

- *Staff.* When staff come aboard, ask them what they liked most and least about their previous job. When they leave, ask them in an exit interview what attracted them to their new job (or drove them away from your organization). Read the want ads to check salaries and benefits. Take part in salary surveys run by local or state trade associations, or your state nonprofit association, to get a handle on competitiveness.

- *Donations.* Be a constant observer of how you personally are asked for money, and urge your board and staff to do the same. Do you like being "hit up" in the supermarket parking lot? By snail mail? By e-mail? By phone? In person? Within these groupings what approaches do you like and dislike? Do you give online? Does your staff or board? Look at the printed material other organizations are handing out, and how they pitch for donations on their web site. What appeals to you and what doesn't? The field of donations is incredibly competitive and sophisticated, and new innovations pop up all the time. Pay attention!

  ❑ **FOR EXAMPLE:** I recently received a letter from our mayor (on her letterhead) announcing that I had been selected for an annual honor associated with one of our human services not-for-profits. The mayor noted that I had been selected for my "numerous achievements," and that I would be feted at an awards dinner about six weeks later. I was a bit dubious at this point, since the letter said that my achievements were in the area of "financial consulting," which is not what I do.

  But then the other shoe dropped. The mayor was sure that I would appreciate the honor and that I would agree to commit to raise $1,000 for the not-for-profit! I've heard about a $1,000-a-plate dinner, but never a $1,000-a-plaque award! My reaction was, shall we say, not happy, but in a small town like ours, you really don't want to unnecessarily irritate the mayor. Fortunately, I had a conflict to be doing training out of town on the night of the awards banquet and sent my regrets.

  Overall, I give the organization an A for innovation, but the bait-and-switch approach really turned me off.

- *Bid Services.* When you participate in a bidding process, are the other bids, particularly the winning bid, made public? Can you find out who the other bidders were? As I mentioned above, if the bid was for public dollars, the information is public. Go get it. Find out what the winning bid offered (assuming that it wasn't your organization). Try to find out as much about the competition here as you can. I am involved in bidding for a project probably twice a year, and I always ask who else bid, what they offered that was different, and (if I didn't get the work) what was the deciding factor in selecting the other consultant. Sometimes it is something I can't control, such as that the other consultant was from the local community; sometimes it is something I could have done differently, such as the array or sequence of services offered. Sometimes, of course, it comes down to price. But each time I learn, and so can you. Never just walk away from a bidding process. Get as much information as you can.

- *Volunteers.* If your organization uses volunteers (other than the board of directors), then you know how important they are. As with board members and staff, ask your volunteers if they have done similar work in other not-for-profits, what they liked and disliked about their time there, and why they now help you.

☞ **HANDS-ON:** When you talk to your volunteers, use a group session rather than individual meetings. Volunteers tend, for the most part, to be a bit awed by the senior management staff, and putting them in a peer group will not only make them more at ease, but also generate more ideas and reactions for you. In addition, it saves you time.

- *Direct Service Ideas.* Here, your antennae need to be out for new services, service innovations, and ways that your competitors are adding value. Keep checking web sites, but remember my caution about assuming the currency of information. It may well be incomplete or out of date. Your other sources are the customers we discussed above, your staff (again, the more ears the better) and, in many cases, the people from whom you buy specialty products or services. Ask these vendors who else they sell to, and learn what you can from them about the organization. For example, if you buy physical therapy (PT) equipment from a large vendor, ask them who else in the area is buying similar equipment. They will give you a list of your potential competitors. Don't stop there. When the sales person comes in, ask, "How's business? Any big sales lately?" Suddenly, you find that your most important competitor is replacing all their PT equipment in the next three months. This is important information if you also know that customers value new equipment, or, as in the story in Chapter 2, your staff members want to work with the newest equipment. Ask your vendors as well as your customers.

In all of these cases, you are asking, asking, asking, and then trying to fit the often fragmented pieces of the puzzle together. The culture of asking is the root of your information, and you need to have a lot of people asking as well as a system to get the information back to you promptly. History is full of examples of organizations who had critical information but didn't communicate it to the person who most needed it at the crucial moment. Don't follow their path. If you just gather information but don't communicate it, you aren't doing your organization any good.

I'm sure that you have noticed that I did not give you one source or even a set of sources that will necessarily meet all your information needs. Finding out about competitors is often a haphazard quest, with incremental progress in some cases, and huge gains made in others. It will depend on the competitor, the situation, and your resources. But just because you don't think that you can get all the information you want immediately doesn't mean that what you *can* gather isn't important. It is. For your core competition, go after the information, keep it up to date, and use what you can to improve your own services and products.

C. FOCUSING ON YOUR CORE COMPETENCIES

By using the techniques discussed in this chapter, you now know how to identify your competitors, how to find out information about them, and how to focus on the most important of your competitors. Now what do you do? Do you try to compete on all fronts, with all types of organizations, in all services and for all groups of people?

Of course not. You don't have the resources, energy, or time to do all of that. What you need to do now is the third step in a three-part analysis. Let's review what you have done in the first two steps and then examine the third.

Step 1. Review the Markets

You have done this (as described in Chapter 6) already. You should know who your markets are, how many there are, which are your focus for the future, and which aren't. You have applied the 80/20 Rule and know its implications.

Step 2. Evaluate the Competition

You should have done this as well, as described earlier in this chapter. You know as much as you can gather about your competition, including an analysis of the competitor's strengths and weaknesses compared to yours.

Step 3. Look at Your Core Competencies

It is time for this third, crucial step. Since you can't compete on all fronts, where do you focus your actions? One place to do that is where you are already strong. Remember the SWOT (Strength, Weakness, Opportunity, Threat) analysis that you used to run when doing a plan? Do it again now with your board and staff, but stop after the Strength and Weakness parts. Identify the things you do well and the things you could work on. (*Note:* If you have never done a SWOT Analysis, they are terrific and worthwhile exercises. A good place to start on the web is *www.mindtools.com/swot.html.*) Now, compare those two lists to the things your markets want. Are the things they want the things that you do well? If so, fine. If not, do you need to invest in improvements? Or, should you focus on a market segment that wants the things that you do well?

❑ **FOR EXAMPLE:** A sheltered workshop in western New York State recently told me of a decision to get out of the business of packaging as a way of employing people with disabilities. The packaging industry had become too price-competitive, and too oriented to Just-In-Time, both areas where this organization did not feel it could compete well. Instead, it looked at what it *did* do well, and found that service—high-quality service—was its strength. Over a three-year period it changed its focus to work with customers who valued high levels of service.

❑ **FOR EXAMPLE:** A client organization of mine in Missouri decided that it could no longer provide residential services to mentally ill people because the regulations and expectations of their funder—the state of Missouri—were too high compared to the amount the state paid. This was a change in market wants that the agency could not meet; it could not do the service well for the amount it was being paid, and was dragging down other services by subsidizing the residential area of the organization. After a very difficult and emotional decision process, the board cut the residential services loose to a group of staff who left to form their own non-profit.

Now, look at the list of strengths and weaknesses again, in light of your competition's strengths and weaknesses. Do you compete strength to strength or weak to strong? Do you need to bolster some areas to meet a competitor's strength, or should you compete in an area where they are weaker? Remember, the key here is to consistently find ways to add value to your services, value from the perspective of your customer.

When you are done with this analysis, you should have a defined list of the things you, your staff, and your board feel that you do well, your core competencies. Focus on those, invest in keeping them state of the art. Buy the training, equipment, and staff that you need to keep these areas a focus on excellence for years to come.

Remember that you are not your competition, and that you don't want to be. Your organization is unique in its own right. Certainly, study and learn from your competition. But don't try to copy them in everything. Be yourself, focus on the markets you want to using your own core strengths.

RECAP

In this chapter, we have covered the important points that will help you identify and learn more about your competition. We looked at how to analyze your competitors through the lens of your services, the people you serve, your referrers, and your funders. I then showed you how to use staff, board, volunteers and friends, and even vendors to continually gather information on the four key questions you need to answer about your competition:

1. What services do they provide?
2. What clientele are they seeking?
3. What value do they give to the customer?
4. What are their prices?

We then turned to the issue of finding out about how the competition is coming at your board, staff, volunteers, and in direct bidding. Finally, I showed you how to analyze all of this information in light of your organization's core competencies. Focus on the things that you do well, and match those with what your target markets want.

One last word about the competition. Respect them, but don't fear them. They are organizations made up of people just like you, trying their best to provide a product or service in a chaotic and often confusing world. Don't ever assume that they can automatically do things better than you. Find out where they are good, and find out where they are weak. All organizations have some of both. The biggest mistake I see as not-for-profits realize that they are entering a competitive arena is fear. Fear closes your ears and eyes to information about your competitors. Fear incapacitates you, making you incapable of innovation and flexibility. Fear makes it impossible for you to take a risk on behalf of the people you serve. It will eat you up.

Embrace competition as a way of forcing you to do more mission, sooner and better. Respect your competition, and pay attention to them. Respect yourself as well, and be proud and at the same time realistic about your organization's capabilities. Compete head-to-head when you have to and when you can. Focus on your core strengths, build customer loyalty by giving them what they want, and you will be successful.

In order to give your customers what they want, I have told you that you need to ask, ask, and ask. And that is the subject of our next chapter.

Discussion Questions for Chapter 7

1. Do we really know who our competitors are? How can we keep better track of them? Should we focus on the top 10 or on the competition that is in our 80/20 markets?
2. Who competes for our referrers now? Are we doing enough for our referral sources? Can we do more?
3. What are our core competencies? Are we excellent in these? How can we maintain that excellence (improve our status)?
4. How can we keep up to date on all the techniques and knowledge that we need to maintain excellence?
5. In our target markets, do we need to worry about competition, or is there enough market for all of us?

8

Asking Your Markets
What They Want

OVERVIEW

Ask, ask, ask, and then listen! I hope you are beginning to repeat that as a marketing maxim, because it is the best one I know. Only by asking, asking regularly, and asking the correct people the correct questions can you find out that all-important piece of information: what your markets want. Only by asking regularly can you keep track of how those wants change with time. Only by asking and listening can you overcome the marketing disability that I described to you earlier. You need to ask.

But how do you ask? Whom do you ask? How often? In what format? What kind of outside help do you need? How much will it cost? Where do you start? Does the 80/20 Rule apply to asking? All of those questions will be covered in this important chapter.

CHAPTER THUMBNAIL

➤ **Surveys**
➤ **Focus Groups**
➤ **Informal Asking**
➤ **Asking Online**
➤ **Asking Mistakes**
➤ **After Asking**

First, we'll look at the most common way of asking: *surveys.* We'll go over survey methods, how to develop a survey, where to get help, and how many people you need to survey to be sure that your answers have meaning. We'll look at a couple of sample formats, review how many identifiers you should use, and examine ways to make tabulation and analysis easier.

Then we'll turn to *focus groups,* a favorite method of many market analysts. We will cover how to plan and run a focus group, what to ask, what not to ask, who to invite and where to get help. We'll look at how to analyze the data gathered and what to do after the focus group meets.

Next, we'll talk about informal interaction as an asking tool. We'll cover ways to ask, what to ask, training your staff to be constant askers, and some problems that other organizations have had with regular asking. Then, we'll look at some fatal mistakes people make surrounding their asking, ones that you want to avoid.

Then we'll turn to the increasingly popular area of asking online. I'll show you some ways to survey by e-mail and by your web site, and give you some do's and don'ts for using the web as your information gatherer.

Finally, we'll cover what you should do after you ask. This will include tabulating, analyzing and sharing the information, getting back to the people you asked, and integrating the information into your marketing plans. By the end of the chapter you should have a number of hands-on tools and ideas on how to proceed with this crucial part of the marketing cycle.

A. SURVEYS

We all know about surveys: They are expensive and complex, and get very little response. Right? Wrong, at least as a rule. Surveys can be expensive and complex and have undependable results. They can also be inexpensive, simple, and can garner a near 100 percent return. In this section we'll look at what surveys are and some rules for keeping them affordable, useful, and easy to add to your marketing efforts.

Surveys, when done properly, gather *objective* or *quantitative* data, that is, data that can have statistical significance. You can analyze this data over time, looking at the same questions every six or twelve months. For example, if you survey your staff, you can analyze the percentage who respond that they are "very satisfied" with their job, and see whether that number goes up or down each year. This is called *trend analysis.*

Alternatively, you can look at the same data and analyze it between groups in the same survey. Going back to our staff survey, you could examine whether the job satisfaction was higher in administration or in direct service, in one of your locations or another. This is called *cohort analysis.*

Another benefit of surveys is that, if done correctly, you can survey a small group of people and accurately transfer the findings of the small group to a much larger one.

❑ **FOR EXAMPLE:** I am sure that you see the results of survey data on television, or in advertisements regularly.

"Our most recent poll shows that Candidate X is ahead of Candidate Y by a 53 percent to 41 percent margin with 6 percent of the population undecided." *Then the announcer (or the graphic) adds,* "Survey of 2,045 American adults conducted June 15 to 16. Survey results accurate within three percentage points."

The surveyors looked at a tiny slice of all Americans and then made an extrapolation of those results to the population as a whole. This ability to survey a small group is very, very cost-effective if you need to know what a large group thinks of your organization, but only if the survey is done properly. You can't just ask 15 people on your block a question and have any confidence that the results represent your community as a whole (unless the block *is* the entire community!).

Thus, surveys have benefits that can really help your marketing. You can see how you are doing now, as opposed to last month. You can see which market segment is most in want of your services. You can find out who is happy and who is not. You can survey the *who,* the *what,* the *where,* the *when,* and the *how much.* What most surveys are not particularly good at is finding out the *why,* at least in any depth. For these you have focus groups, interviews, and informal asking. More on these later.

We will define a survey as a standardized, written sequence of questions given to a group of people to elicit information on a particular subject. The most important adjective here is *standardized.* You want to ask everyone the same questions, with the same tone, in the same sequence. Standardization is a crucial part of getting statistically reliable information from the survey.

Who could you survey? In theory, any market that you want to serve and in which you want to become or remain competitive. In practice, you would probably survey only your largest, your target, or your most crucial markets. You could survey consumers, donors, funders, staff, referral sources, even (though I don't suggest it) the community as a whole. You could focus your questions on need, on your competition, or on the satisfaction of the survey group with your organization.

So, there are a lot of people that you can survey, and a lot of information that you can get out of them. However, you only have so much money and time, so let's look at some suggestions for getting more out of your surveying. I want to ensure that all of your surveying dollars are well spent.

1. Have Instructions

At the beginning of the survey, have instructions for the reader. Keep them *simple* and *short.* Include the reason for the survey, any special instructions for how to fill it out, where to send it when it is completed, and the deadline for submission to have input considered. Also have a name and phone number for any questions that may arise.

2. Be Brief

You need to be as brief as you can be. When people fill in a survey, they are doing you a favor; giving you some of their time as well as their opinions. Help them by keeping the survey as short as possible. I see a lot of people who think that they are being smart by asking everything they possibly can on one survey to "save money on mailing." What happens is that the longer the survey, the less likely people are to fill it in. Thus the "savings" get eliminated since the return diminishes.

3. Be Focused

This is one way to accomplish point 2. Focus each survey on a particular issue: customer satisfaction, needs analysis, product testing, etc. Don't mix the questions; you will mix up the survey and its resulting data. Be focused, be brief.

☞ HANDS-ON: Warning, warning, warning! Your executive director or board president will ask you to make your survey longer, saying something like this: "Since we're sending out the survey anyway, let's save some money and throw in a few questions on one or two other subjects." Resist! Blame me! Why? Because not only does this soak up the limited time people will give you to fill out the survey, it causes you to lose the focus you have worked so hard to acquire in the survey. Fewer people return the survey, and it is less focused. Thus you don't save money, you waste it.

4. Don't Ask Too Often

If you send a board member or a staff member or a donor a questionnaire weekly, how many do you think they will fill out? I have already told you that you need to ask and ask regularly to track trends and keep up on new customer wants, but regularly does not mean daily. Again, value the time of the people you are surveying. Ask them, but only as often as you absolutely need to. Remember there is a thin line between being curious and inquiring and being a pest. Don't cross it.

5. Ask the Questions in the Correct Sequence and Wording

You can really mess up the data you get by asking questions in the wrong fashion, the wrong way, or even in the wrong order.

❏ **FOR EXAMPLE:** There is a wonderful story that I have heard repeated for years (and that I suspect is apocryphal) of graduate students in marketing who each year go down a busy street at noon, holding up a 8 by 10 inch glossy photograph of the current president of the United States. They ask the first 100 people they see the following question, "You know who this is, don't you?" and get a 95 percent correct response rate. Then they ask the next 100 persons, "Who is this person?" and only get a 79 percent correct response. According to the story, this experiment is repeated annually by each class to make the point: Be careful how you ask—it skews the answers.

You can really get valueless information by asking the wrong question the wrong way. My suggestion is that you should make a list of the information you want and then follow the suggestion in point 10 below.

6. Limit Your Identifiers

Identifiers are the things you usually fill out at the beginning of a survey. Are you male or female? What age group are you in? Married, single, divorced, widowed? Income bracket? These are all identifiers. You will almost certainly want to have these in your surveys as well, since it is the one way you can analyze the data by groups of people (called cohorts). For example, if you do a consumer satisfaction survey, you probably would like to identify people with the different programs you provide, or the different demographic categories you serve, or even the county (city, zip code) where they live. This lets you look at your data in more depth.

Identifiers are terrific, but they have a big drawback. The more you put on your survey, the less people will fill it in, for two reasons. First, it makes the survey longer, cutting down on the response level simply because the form looks too long to some people. Second, remember that most of the surveys you will do will deal with the happiness or satisfaction of your various customers. In these kinds of surveys what you really want is to find out all the bad news: You want to find out what's wrong so you can fix it and improve your services. But, the more identifiers you have, the more people feel that they will, indeed, be identified as an individual. Thus they will either not fill in the survey, or worse, they will fill it in but pull their punches, not being as frank with you as you would like. Then you have bad data, which is worse than no data. This second caution is, of course, moot in cases where you have people fill in their name. I suggest that for any survey where you ask for satisfaction levels, you keep the survey anonymous. My experience is that you will get much more useful information.

☞ **Hands-on:** When making a list of what you need to know on a survey, particularly in the area of identifiers, make a list of the breakouts you would like to see. This might be by gender, age group, ethnicity, location of service, or countless other "slices" of information. Then look at the list and for each item on it ask the question, "What am I going to do with this information? Am I collecting it from curiosity or need? Will I be able to use the information I collect?" Be brutal on yourself in this area. The strong tendency for people is to ask for too much information. I have read countless survey reports that are demographically loaded but light on real information. The reports nearly go into the shoe size of the respondents, but don't have much hard information that is of use. Make a list and ask "Why? Why? Why?" before including the identifier in the final survey.

This is not to say that identifiers are not important. Some are crucial analytical items for statistical significance, others speak to important program and service needs or concerns. For example, if 90 percent of your program recipients are women, but 55 percent of your consumer survey recipients are men, you have learned that extrapolating the survey data for all consumers may have problems. Thus having a gender identifier on that particular survey form was valuable. Similarly, for surveys that have questions that seek concerns with program hours, services, and other indicators of satisfaction, knowing which services the survey respondent uses most, or their location of service, may be very important. But their zip code may not be.

So be selective. Ask for some identifiers, but only as many as you *absolutely* need. Your outside help (see point 10) can give you some assistance in this area.

7. For Trend Data, Be Consistent

Trend data, as I mentioned earlier, looks at information over time: For example, how many of your staff are "very satisfied" with their job this year as opposed to last year and the year before? That is trend data, and watching the trends is a crucial part of good management, good marketing and being competitive. I have long said that, while data in isolation is *interesting,* data in context (compared to something) is *valuable.* The context here is the context of time. Are the trends positive or negative? Are you gaining ground or losing ground?

❏ **FOR EXAMPLE:** Let's look at a list of information gathered from surveys that you might be interested in tracking over time. Note that this is a generic list for not-for-profits and that you should add to (or delete from) this list to make it fit your unique circumstances.

- Customer/client satisfaction (may be more than one survey depending on the breadth of customers you serve)
- Staff job satisfaction
- Staff benefits preferences
- Community needs assessment
- Funder satisfaction
- Referrer awareness and satisfaction

Each item on the list could be a repeated survey (usually every 12 to 18 months) whose data could be compared with previous surveys. The trick in collecting trend data is avoiding the common pitfall of constantly amending (offenders in this area call it "fine-tuning") the questions so that the data is skewed, making it, at best, less accurate, and, at worst, worthless. You need to ask exactly the same questions over and over.

Having said that, if you have a question that is not giving you valuable information, definitely drop it. You save yourself and the survey respondent time. And, as circumstances change, you will need to add questions to accommodate those changes. But such amendments should be few and far between, and the wording of the questions that are repeated from survey to survey should hardly ever change at all.

☞ **HANDS-ON:** When you do change parts of your surveys, make sure that you note it in the report. For example, let's assume that your previous consumer surveys only had four choices in a question that asked, "Which of our programs do you use the most?" and the your current survey gives six choices, as you have added two new services since your last survey. This change, while valid and worthwhile, will skew the comparative data, and thus the change deserves a notation in the report. Always make such notations to be fair to the reader. And, if the only reader is going to be you, *still* make the notations, so that in future years, you can remember what changed!

Work for consistency in your data gathering. It allows the greater utilization of the information that you have spent so much time and money gathering.

NOTE: There are many, many other trends that you should be tracking within your management team, including financial ratios, donated dollars, days payable, staff turnover, customer complaints, salary comparisons, administrative percentages, etc. The list could take three pages, and, like any other, would need to be customized for your organization. Don't look at only survey trend data. There is a lot of information already inside your organization that you should be monitoring.

8. Include Closing Instructions

At the end of the survey, tell people what to do with the survey once it is completed. Even if you included instructions about where to send the survey and by when in the introductory page, do it again here, in large, bold typeface. If you are asking people to mail the survey to you, include a stamped, preaddressed envelope. Always include a fax number for their convenience.

9. Say Thank You

At the end of your survey, thank people for their time and effort in giving you information. It seems like a small thing. It's not. Let them know you appreciate their time and also tell them what will happen to their survey, when they might expect to see results, how the information will be used, by whom, and by when.

10. Get Help

As you have probably gathered, surveying is not just something you wake up one day and start doing. It takes time, financial commitment, and a fair amount of expertise. It is easy to do poorly, a challenge to do well. Doing it poorly results in that most dangerous of products: poor, inaccurate, and therefore misleading information. Doing it well can give your organization a true competitive advantage: good, accurate information on which you can set policy, develop programs, improve services, and do more effective mission.

All of which is to say you probably need help, at least to develop your initial surveys and learn the ropes. There is lots of help out there. There are professional marketing and surveying organizations, including a growing number that work solely in the not-for-profit sector. There are instructors and professors at your local colleges and universities who teach marketing, surveying, and similar courses. There are professionals who work for large corporations whose job it is to develop their internal and external surveying. There are staff at regional planning commissions, agricultural extension offices, economic development agencies, and in your local mayor's or county/parish commissioner's office who develop surveys. As I mentioned earlier, make sure you check your local MSO, your state association of nonprofits, your state trade association, and your local United Way and community foundation. All of these are resources you can tap.

What can this professional help do? A number of things. You should make sure that you get assistance in at least the following areas:

- *Selection of survey sample:* What is the best set of people to survey to get the information you want that is accurate while being affordable? This is a technical and statistically challenging area.
- *To pilot-test or not to pilot-test?* If you are surveying a huge group, or making a multiyear commitment to a survey instrument, it may be smart to pilot-test the survey with a small group to make sure that it is working the way you want it to.
- *Question development:* While you should absolutely be in charge of what information is sought, the way that it is asked is crucial. Should particular questions be open-ended or "forced choice"? If forced choice, how many options should there be and what wording should be used? In what sequence should the questions be placed? Should there be confirming questions included?
- *Survey administration:* Your survey consultant can help you with administering the survey. Should you mail or hand out the survey? Should it be anonymous? Should it be done in person? The consultant may even mail out, collect, and analyze the data for you.
- *Online asking:* Get some help in designing your online questions, and particularly your HTML input and survey collation information. I'll cover this more in a few pages, but many Internet Service Providers (ISPs) provide this add-on piece of technical assistance, and you may also find help here from your MSO or state association of nonprofits.

Don't scrimp here. If you go the cheap route, you may have correspondingly valuable data. Remember the old adage: You get what you pay for.

Sample Survey

In Appendix A, you will find a sample survey that I helped design for an East Coast organization that serves people with disabilities. As you review it, note that it is long, and deals with a variety of issues related to the satisfaction of the people that the organization serves. Since the survey was administered by trained surveyors in the home, the response rate was very high and the group could afford to have as many identifiers as it did. Also note the format, with numbers associated with each response. This design was to speed data entry for the survey as it was completed and analyzed in a database.

If you plan to do surveying, I would strongly urge you to order a copy of an excellent basic surveying text. One I really like is titled: *Designing and Conducting Survey Research: A Comprehensive Guide* (Jossey-Bass Public Administration Series) by Louis M. Rhea and Richard A. Parker. It is excellent and will arm you with the basic information you need to work with your outside expert.

B. FOCUS GROUPS

Focus groups are great. They allow you to easily do what surveys do not: to follow up on initial responses, accessing feelings, reactions, and emotions at a much deeper and more personal level. Focus groups at their core are facilitated sessions of 8 to 15 people that focus on a particular issue. They are often used to test the reactions of people to a new product, a potential commercial, or to compare reactions to two or three different potential advertising slogans or campaigns. Speaking of campaigns, politicians use focus groups regularly to test their messages prior to general distribution.

As a not-for-profit administrator, you have a number of potential uses for focus groups. These could include:

- Testing a potential new service with consumers, referrers, and funders.
- Following up on survey results that showed a problem (or an opportunity).
- Testing various themes and slogans for a capital campaign.

There are, of course, dozens of other uses for focus groups.

Focus groups gather what is called *subjective* information. They elicit immediate reactions, in-depth commentary, and emotive responses in ways that surveys cannot.

❏ **FOR EXAMPLE:** Let's say that you are surveying a core constituency and on one question you ask, "Overall, how would you rate your satisfaction with the services you receive from our organization?" You give the respondent a scale of 1 to 7 with a 7 being equivalent to "Terrific!" and a 1 being equal to "Awful." The responses are consistently 4s and 5s, where in previous years they have been mostly 6s and 7s. What's going on? Surveys are not the best way to find the answer. By the time you receive the data and analyze it, the respondents are on to other things. But you can ask the question in a focus group. "How do you like our services? Why? Is your level of satisfaction lower, higher, or about the same as last year? Why?" And, when someone in the group says something like, "Well, I'm not as happy because the staff just aren't as friendly," a set of follow-up questions can be asked right on the spot by the facilitator, honing in on what the problem may be. None of that can be done efficiently by survey.

As in surveying, there are some suggestions that I have to make your focus groups more valuable, less expensive, and more productive.

1. Get a Facilitator

This is absolutely crucial. You need to have a person *from outside your organization* who can plan and run your focus group. Focus group facilitation is a real skill, and it is much more important that your facilitator be strong in facilitation than an expert in your area of service. You can teach them about what you do.

Why have an outsider? Because the people in the focus group will be more frank with an outsider, and an outsider will be more objective about what she or he hears than you or anyone in your organization can be. Thus you get better, and more objectively viewed, information. Even if you are the best facilitator on the planet, the participants will see you as biased. Don't try to save money by doing the facilitation yourself. Find an outsider.

Facilitators are available in a number of places. Ask your Chamber. Call a marketing organization. Call or e-mail your MSO or community foundation. Check with your state association of nonprofits. Call your local college or university's program on nonprofit management. Talk to the marketing department of a large company or bank in your community. Get references, and check them. You want someone skilled in facilitation, who is willing to work with you, eliciting the information you need.

2. Focus Your Questions

After all, it is called a **focus** group. You need to focus your questions on a few key subjects. Your facilitator should help you with this, by turning your information needs into open-ended questions that lead people to open up and share their opinions, reactions, and emotions. You only have a limited amount of time (see point 4), and so you want to have your issues focused and in a priority order. Don't ask a group that is supposed to focus on a new service how they like your existing ones. It will get them off track and use up valuable time.

3. Have a Homogeneous Group

Here's another key ingredient to a focus group that succeeds: put like people around the table. For example, if your organization is a science museum, and you want to study the reactions of all your consumers to a potential new exhibit, don't have group that includes high school students, graduate scientists, and senior citizens. Inevitably, one portion of that group will dominate the discussion and the others will feel disenfranchised and not participate. Again, focus your efforts, in this case on one type of person, and you will have more responses, better information, and an increased value from your investment.

4. Don't Wear the Group Out

You have between 90 minutes and two hours. Then people's creative brains turn to mush. A good facilitator will keep track of the time and ask questions in priority order, but will also tell you that in the 90-minute to two-hour time range you should dismiss the group. No sense in keeping people when they are not going to be productive.

5. Compensate the Group

In the commercial world, people are often offered between $100 and $250 to participate in a two-hour focus group. You probably can't afford that, and, in fact, may insult people who are associated with your organization by offering them money. But do offer them something: coffee and doughnuts, lunch, transportation, a parking voucher. Get a restaurant in your community to donate gift certificates that you can hand out. Hold the group in a safe, comfortable space. After the session, thank each participant by letter, perhaps accompanied by a "token" of appreciation like a coffee mug, attractive paperweight, or other premium. Talk to your facilitator about what the community standard is for compensation, and don't be stingy. These people are providing you with literally invaluable information.

6. Analyze the Results Between Groups

After each session (which should be audiotaped), analyze the results. Are you hearing similar issues? Are there enough issues left incomplete that more sessions are merited? Do you want to add another group made up of the same type of people, or an additional one made up of a different category of people? Have your facilitator tell you about body language, inflections, and other things that he or she may have picked up. Have the facilitator give you his or her overall impressions of the group, and list where he or she thinks you have opportunities to improve.

Sample Focus Group Questions

In Appendix B, you will find the actual questions I asked at a focus group for a product to be developed by a sheltered workshop in the Midwest. Note how the questions are open-ended, and in the priority order that the organization wanted answered.

How many groups should you run? Like any other question of this sort, the answer is: It depends. Focus groups are expensive to administer, but many experts suggest that you run enough so that you begin to hear the same information repeated. Thus, if you are a school, you may run groups of parents, students, faculty, and alumni. You might run only two of all the types at first, and hear the same thing in each group except the parents, who might have so many different issues that you want to run three or four sessions. Again, you don't want to mix groups, and you don't want to work them to death, so plan your strategy carefully.

If you want to pursue focus groups, I again have a resource for you to read before you hire your facilitator. It is another good, basic guide to the subject: *The Wilder Nonprofit Field Guide to Conducting Successful Focus Groups,* by Judith Simon.

C. INFORMAL ASKING

Here we confront a major cultural change for many organizations. Developing that regular "culture of asking" that I have referred to earlier takes time and the belief of everyone in the organization that they are on the marketing team. Only a total team effort will gather all the information, elicit all the wants, pick up on all the problems and opportunities that are out there. Your staff and volunteers need to be urged, cajoled, and led to ask, and ask regularly. They also need to be trained to ask, because there is a lot of "bad asking" going on out there.

❏ **FOR EXAMPLE:** Here is an experience that most readers have shared. You go to a restaurant, eat, then get your check. You approach the cash register to pay, and you are asked by the person behind the register about your meal. This can happen in two ways:

OPTION ONE: The person looks down at the register, and, while keying in your bill asks, "Was everything okay?" To which most of us answer, "Yes." This person was told to ask every customer how things were, and they are complying with the letter of the training, but not the spirit. The question suggests that everything was okay. They are on what I call *asking autopilot.* I even had someone recently ask me whether "everything was okay" and I said "No." They finished up printing out the receipt, gave me my change, and said, "Well that's great. Have a nice day and come back soon!" Asking on autopilot.

OPTION TWO: The person behind the register stops, looks you in the eye, and says, "How was everything tonight?" Then he or she waits for your answer, and responds appropriately. This person was trained to ask the open-ended question that forces the customer to come up with their own answer. Even if most of us respond with the stock, "Just fine," we still are more likely to let the clerk or the manager know about problems with this question than in the question posed in Option One.

Train your people that asking is important and then give them the tools to ask correctly, and without skewing the answers.

Informal asking comes in many shapes and sizes. Different staff will be affected differently. Here are some ideas of where to start in developing some informal asking:

1. Have your staff trained to ask new customers where they heard about your organization. This might mean a receptionist, intake worker, someone sitting at an information booth, or any other person who would be the first point of entry.
2. When you interact in the community try to ask people regularly, "What do you hear about our organization? Do you know anyone who uses us? If you do, how have your experiences been? If it's a friend or family member, how have their experiences been?"
3. When you see your key vendors—your banker, insurance agent, auditor, office supply company, printer, and the like—ask them: "What do you hear about us on the street?" "Do you have ideas about things that are not being done now that we could do?"
4. Most importantly, whenever anyone in your organization interacts with anyone you serve, who donates or contracts for services, who is a member, or who in any way can be considered a market, the final interaction should be this question: *"Is there anything else we can do for you today?"* This question, consistently and politely asked,

will generate a constant stream of opportunities for service and improvement.

One danger in informal asking is that, since it is just that, informal, you don't have a formal path for the information gathered to flow to the correct place. For example, if a caseworker asks someone how their visit was, and the client answers: "Great. Oh, but the toilets really smell. That's a real turnoff to me," the information has *got* to get to the maintenance or janitorial staff. Otherwise, even though your people asked, the information was not put to good use. Make sure you train staff in *what to do with what they learn.*

More than any other kind of asking, consistent informal asking shows that you and your staff and volunteers care about the kind, quality, and level of service that your organization provides. It forces you to interact one-on-one, taking the chance of getting criticism or complaints face-to-face. People take note of that kind of risk-taking and appreciate it. Unless you don't follow up the asking and make one or more of the mistakes listed in the next section.

D. ASKING ONLINE

Using the net to ask is a very quick, very efficient, and very tempting way to gather information. You can ask five, five hundred, or five thousand people for information by e-mail very quickly and get back your information much faster than by personal interview or snail mail. But, predictably, there are some problems lurking in putting too much faith in online data collection. Let's run through some do's and don'ts about online asking.

First, the Do's

1. Do collect the e-mail addresses of staff, board members, volunteers, and as many of your clients, customers, donors, funders, former donors, former volunteers, and other community members as you can. Categorize them, and try to keep them up to date—not an easy task.

2. Do make sure that you have an easily accessible part of your web site for people to e-mail you asking for more information, or for making any suggestions that they might have about your services, or your web site itself. Part of developing a culture of inquiry is offering many venues for people to communicate with you. MAKE SURE YOU HAVE SOMEONE WHO CHECKS THE E-MAIL

ADDRESS GIVEN ON THE WEB SITE DAILY. Nothing is worse than offering information in an immediate environment like the web and then not getting back to people!

3. If you do an online survey, get some outside help the first time, and test any initial survey with your board members and staff. Send it to them, and then ask for their responses about how easy and intuitive the survey was. Use the board and staff as what the tech industry calls beta testers.

Now, the Don'ts

1. DON'T survey just with e-mail. By asking questions and requiring people to click "reply" and then type in answers, you increase dramatically the amount of bad data, or data that you simply cannot enter accurately. Instead, use the e-mail to explain WHY you are asking, to tell people that you appreciate their help, and then to direct them by a link to a part of your web site that allows them to enter the information you need into a check box, or data box. The benefit of this is twofold: You get more accurate data, and the software that helps you develop the Web page will also collate and analyze the data for you. And, you can change the information quickly and cheaply by simply editing the Web page.

2. DON'T fall victim to the ease of all this, and ask too much. Remember my caution about the line between inquiry and pestering being thin. Don't cross it.

3. DON'T assume that everyone, even in the twenty-first century, uses e-mail, or has access to the net. The number is much smaller every year, but make sure you factor that into your uses of the data you gather online.

There are a number of good places to go online to get started in this area, and some good software to use. As of the date of publication, these include:

www.statpac.com/online-surveys
http://free-online-surveys.co.uk
www.zoomerang.com

E. ASKING MISTAKES

Of course, things can go wrong. You can ask and ask and ask, and have problems. Let's take a minute and review the common mistakes that other organizations have made in the hopes that you can avoid them.

1. Not Expecting Criticism

If you ask, people will tell you. And it is naive to think that no one will ever have any problems with the way that you do business. They will. But I regularly see staff people wailing and gnashing their teeth about the criticism that their organization has received. I have literally seen organizations who send staff members to counseling to get over the shock of reading the survey responses that they have gathered.

Come *on.* No organization is perfect. People like to gripe. And, most importantly, you asked. What did you really expect?

The key here is to expect and even welcome criticism. I tell my clients all the time: *Criticism is an opportunity to improve.* If your organization is dedicated to continuous improvement, you have to ask and have problems pointed out to be able to make those improvements.

Just don't get gun-shy. If people take a shot at you, analyze what they said. Was it fair? Was it accurate? What want of theirs did it show you? Can you accommodate them? If the complaint was regularly repeated (in other words, not an aberration), then fix the problem!

2. Not Listening

This mistake is the logical endpoint of the marketing disability that I discussed earlier. You know it all, so why listen to what people want? You are the expert, so let's just appease people's sense of involvement by asking them, and then go on about our business. Chrysler did that in the early 1970s. They ignored what people were telling them about wanting small, fuel-efficient cars, and almost lost the company. Then they started to ask, and listen, and respond. In their responding they innovated. Not only did they save the company, but they invented new products, including a whole new (and highly successful) category of vehicle: the minivan.

You have to listen to what people tell you. That is not to say that you need to knee-jerk your responses and change your entire organization because two out of every 1,000 people are unhappy. But you do need to give each comment, each criticism, each idea a fair hearing. Otherwise you are wasting your asking dollars and missing significant competitive opportunities.

3. Not Responding

So you asked, you listened, but, heck, it's too much trouble to change, to respond. You don't have the time, or the money, and, anyway, you can't make all the people happy all the time. True, but you better darn well work to make your target markets happy nearly all the time. And you'll do that by being responsive to their wants.

❑ **FOR EXAMPLE:** Imagine that I come out to your organization to do a speech for your board and staff. I start off and am really moving along. At the intermission I ask you how you think that things are going. You tell me, "You are going too fast for some of our board members. Can you slow down and take some more time for questions? What you are saying is really good, and I want everyone to get a good grasp of it. We're in no hurry. Take your time."

What is my response? Do I tell you that I need to get through because your staff and board showed up half an hour late and I have a plane to catch? (The customer is not always right, but the customer is always the customer!) No, I tell you: "Thanks for the input, I'll pay more attention and take some time for questions. Let's get the people back in their seats and try to get back on schedule." When we reconvene, I ask for questions on the previous material and then proceed at a more leisurely pace, still paying attention to the clock.

Here, I made a reasonable response to a reasonable request. I asked, I got an answer that I really didn't want to hear but, if I had just gone on, my customer would have been justifiably upset.

You need to respond as well as you can, as promptly as you can, as reasonably as you can. And you need to empower your staff to do the same.

F. AFTER ASKING

Now that you have asked, what next? Asking again? Well, of course, but there are some things you should do after you have gathered the data. These include the following:

1. Analyze the Data

Look at your information critically and soon. Make sure that an interdisciplinary group of staff and board give the data close scrutiny. Was the survey sample significant? Are the results valid? If so, what did we learn? What can we apply? What trends pop out? What follow-up inquiries should we do?

You have taken time and paid good money to gather the information. Now, examine it carefully. I see too many groups that do a survey and either ignore what they learned, or don't examine it until the information is so out of date that it no longer is relevant.

Exhibit 8-1   Asking Feedback

WE LEARNED THE FOLLOWING THINGS AND HAVE TAKEN THE FOLLOWING ACTIONS:	
Items A, B, C, D	We have already implemented changes to respond to these excellent ideas.
Items E, F, H, J	We are budgeting these for the next fiscal year.
Items G, I, L	We cannot accommodate these suggestions because of regulatory restraints.
Items K, M	The board will discuss these policy change ideas at their next meeting.

2. Close the Information Loop

You have just imposed on the people who gave you valuable information. Do the right thing. Tell them what you learned. Send a memo to folks, or put a report in your newsletter, or just make an announcement at a staff meeting, but let people know that you asked and you appreciated their input. Be sure to list the key things that the most people said.

☞ **HANDS-ON:** Make a list of what you learned and then tell people what you are doing about it. It may look something like Exhibit 8-1.

By doing this, you not only allow people to learn from each other, you acknowledge their input and take credit for taking action—something that most people are pretty cynical about. They often assume that their ideas go into a large trash barrel. So don't do that. Instead, tell them what you heard and, equally importantly, what you have done about it. Show them that you are responsive.

3. Accommodate to the Wants of Your Markets

If you ask, people will tell you what they want. Now that you know, make the changes that you can to accommodate the wants. This, of course, is the other side of two of the errors people make that we just reviewed above: not listening, and not responding. While you should never make promises you cannot keep, you should always try to accommodate your markets as best you can. This means that you should review your survey or focus group information with the people that provide your services, and try to come up with ways to accommodate what your customers have told you. Don't just tell staff what to do. Have them become part of the marketing team by learning how to use the information that you are gathering to do a better job.

4. Incorporating Your Information into Your Marketing Plans

Later, in Chapter 12, I will show you how to put all of your marketing information into a cohesive plan. Just let it suffice here to say, don't ignore the data that you gather as you go about putting together your initial plan, and, more importantly, in adapting your marketing methods to changing circumstances. It is very easy to say: "Well, we've decided our goals for this year, and we'll review this new information that we've just gathered next year during our annual review." Next year? That may be too late. If you are confident of your data, use it. Good planning takes into account changes in the situation. If you have new information, even if it conflicts with the course you are on, use it! Imagine a ship captain whose vessel is set on a particular compass heading. He gets information from a satellite that there is a huge ice pack ahead. Does he stay on course (going with the plan), or does he use the new information, go around the danger, and eventually achieve his goal—reaching his destination safely?

RECAP

In this chapter, we have covered the crucial function of asking your markets what they want. You need to develop a culture as well as a system of asking to maintain your competitive edge. If you don't ask, how are you ever going to keep pace with the constantly changing wants of your target markets? Answer: You aren't.

First, we looked at surveys, and discussed the ways to and ways *not* to survey. I suggested 10 rules for surveying which, to review quickly, were:

1. Have instructions
2. Be brief
3. Be focused
4. Don't ask too often
5. Ask the questions in the correct sequence and wording
6. Limit your identifiers
7. For trend data, be consistent
8. Include closing instructions
9. Say thank you
10. Get help

We then moved on to focus groups, noting how they obtain qualitative data rather than the quantitative data that surveys can gather. Again, we went over some rules, this time the following six:

1. Get a facilitator
2. Focus your questions
3. Have a homogeneous group
4. Don't wear the group out
5. Compensate the group
6. Analyze the results between groups

We then turned our attention to how to get the most out of informal asking, noting that this kind of constant attention to customers really pays off in a variety of ways, but that it takes training and motivation, and everyone in the organization to do it well.

We looked into the area of asking online, and reviewed some do's and don'ts in this increasingly popular way of gathering data.

We next reviewed what *not* to do, by looking at some common mistakes people make in their asking. These included not anticipating criticism, not listening, and not responding to what you have learned. Finally, you were shown what to do after you ask, including analyzing your data, closing the loop, and making sure that you take appropriate actions to respond to your new knowledge base.

Asking, listening, and responding are parts of a constant cycle, a vital part of the marketing process. Now that you know how to ask, we can turn our attention to the next issue: letting people know what you do—making better marketing materials.

Discussion Questions for Chapter 8

1. How often do we formally survey our target markets? Is this often enough? How recently have we updated the surveys that we do? Do we look at trend analysis now?
2. What about focus groups? They are expensive. Are they a good tool for us? For what kind of customer?
3. Can we get survey data from our competition? Is any of it public information?
4. Do we close the loop after we survey now? Should we? How?
5. How can we get better at both asking and listening? What about making sure that ideas from the line staff get to us?
6. Which of our markets would use online inquiry best? How do we best make use of this?
7. Do we have a good method of encouraging feedback and inquiry on our web site? How can we improve this?
8. Can we try a questionnaire online with our board or staff to see how it works, and get their responses?

9

Better Marketing Materials

OVERVIEW

On to your marketing materials. You now know who you are trying to serve (your markets) and what their wants and needs are. You know about your competition and what they are offering to your markets. Now comes a critical part of *both* your marketing and competitive cycle: getting the word out. In Chapter 5, I referred to this step as "Promotion and Distribution." In this chapter, I'll show you how to do the promotion part of that step.

Marketing "material" covers a lot of ground. It can be the traditional three-fold brochure, or stacked handouts that come in a larger folder. It can be advertising in a local newspaper or magazine, or a flyer that is placed under a windshield wiper. It can be your business card, or your web site. It can be your promotional spot on local television or radio, the notices you send out in direct mail, or the educational materials you give free of charge to the people you serve in person or online. It can be information on memberships, donations, or even a promotional trinket such as a key chain, calendar, or coffee mug. For most readers, their organization will be promoted through a mix of these vehicles in addition to word of mouth, referrals, and straight sales.

But whatever it is, the mix has to address some similar issues. Many not-for-profits, like their for-profit peers, do a great job at developing and appropriately using their marketing materials. Many, however, do not. And, many not-for-profits are still doing that job as if they are living in the old, less competitive economy. They focus on *public relations* and *promotion* rather than *marketing*. There is an enormous difference.

And, there is an overarching rule for marketing material: It must connect with the targeted market, from the customer's point of view. This means that good marketing material grabs the customer and shows that person that you understand their wants, who they are, and can solve their problems. By reading your brochure, listening to your radio spot, or looking at your web site, can the customer quickly understand the benefit of using your organization's services? If not, you have not made the connection.

CHAPTER THUMBNAIL

➤ **The Problem with Most Not-for-Profits' Marketing Materials**
➤ **Solving Customers' Problems**
➤ **Things to Include in Your Materials**
➤ **Things to Avoid in Your Marketing Materials**
➤ **Developing Different Materials for Different Markets**

In this chapter, we'll talk about *marketing* materials as opposed to *promotional* tools. First, we'll cover this problem as well as a number of others that I regularly see in not-for-profit marketing materials. Then, we'll focus on the issue in sales: solving customers' problems. I'll show you how to tell if your current marketing material does this and, if not, how to improve it so that it does. Next we'll turn to a section on the seven things that you should *include* in your materials, and another on the seven things to *avoid.* Finally, I'll give you some ideas on developing different materials for different markets, which sounds like a very straightforward and no-brainer idea, but apparently isn't, because a lot of organizations ignore it.

By the end of the chapter you should be much better able to analyze your existing marketing materials and to create new ones that really speak to and excite your many markets. Remember, your marketing material is out there speaking for you every day. If it is speaking in some unknown tongue, you are losing opportunities to connect with people who you could serve.

A. THE PROBLEMS WITH MOST NOT-FOR-PROFITS' MARKETING MATERIALS

You have already read that the critical sequence in marketing is identifying your markets, asking those markets what they want, and then developing or amending services to meet those wants. This is called being *market-oriented,* and it is much preferable to being *service-oriented,* where an organization just pushes its available services with little regard to what the market wants.

And here is the problem. Most of the marketing material that I see is *service-oriented,* pushing the existing service array, usually in jargon, and hardly ever in a way that really appeals to the wants of the markets. It is dull, dense, and not of interest to too many people beyond the individual who wrote it. It is also often poorly written, unprofessional-looking, and out of date. It doesn't spell out the benefits of using the organization and makes no attempt to connect with the customer.

Why? Why, in an era of dirt-cheap, easy-to-use software and excellent low-cost color printers, do not-for-profits scrimp on marketing material? Why shoot yourself in the foot every time a potential customer, donor, referral source, banker, or board member sees an advertisement or promotional piece? The answer is multifaceted, and it has to do with the marketing disability, tradition, being penny-wise, and a misunderstanding of the true nature of marketing. Let me spend a minute on each of these.

1. The Marketing Disability

In Chapter 5, I spent a few pages exhorting you to overcome the marketing disability of not-for-profits. Remember that the disability springs from most not-for-profit staff's professional training in diagnostics, which results in an attitude of "we know what you need" and the corollary (but unspoken) attitude of "we don't care what you want." This shows up in marketing material that contains:

- A history of the organization (a self-congratulatory one at that)
- A list of services (usually in jargon)
- A description of hours and locations available
- A phone number, e-mail address, or web site

What have we here? Otherwise useful space taken up with old news (the history that no one outside the organization really cares about), a cold list of jargon-filled services that anyone without a master's degree *in your discipline* has trouble understanding, a "come and get it" listing of times and locations, and impersonal contact information.

Great first impression. Push your services, make no personal connection, confuse them with jargon. Often the marketing piece will add insult to injury by including a request for money!

❑ **FOR EXAMPLE:** I see marketing material like the one described above in all parts of the not-for-profit sector. In my work with organizations that provide vocational services to persons with disabilities, I often see brochures or pamphlets that list the services that the organization can provide to such persons and their families. Here is a sample list, taken from a real (unfortunately typical) brochure that came across my desk recently.

- Employment assessment
- Job placement
- Family respite
- Vocational transportation
- Work supports
- Work hardening
- Supported employment
- Employee enclaves
- Occupational therapy

All of these terms are legitimate technical descriptions of services in the field. But to anyone outside (like parents, funders, donors, and anyone else who is not intimately involved in the field), most of them are Greek. I once asked a group of management staff from an organization that provides services such as these what the term "work hardening" really meant, and whether they really expected people outside their organization to grasp its meaning. "Heck," said one, "90 percent *of our staff* don't know what it means, and I'm not sure that I could give you an accurate definition." I then asked why they included it in their marketing material. "Sounds impressive," was the answer. The marketing disability—in full swing.

☞ **HANDS-ON:** Try this jargon test. Hand your marketing material to a neighbor or friend who knows *nothing* about your services. Ask them to read it carefully, circling every word that they do not *fully* understand. Make sure that they know that this is not a test of their knowledge, but a way of helping you make your materials more understandable. Try this with two or three friends, and include your newsletters, if you print those. Don't overload individuals, just give them one or two things each to review. You will learn a lot about what is jargon and what isn't.

2. Tradition

"We have a grand tradition here at our organization. We have a great reputation. We want to build on that." I hear this regularly but, interestingly enough, most often from organizations that have really lousy marketing materials. They are so focused on their past that they can't even see their present, to say nothing of their future. Good marketing, competitive marketing, is interested in what the markets want today, and in predicting what they will want tomorrow. If your marketing materials are focused on the past and look like they were designed in 1965 (perhaps because they were?), you are not going to be appealing to today's markets.

Let's look at the quote above: first, the term *tradition*. As I said in the last chapter, traditions are great, as long as you build on them. When traditions appeal to a market, they really help an organization. An induction ceremony for a club, fraternity, or sorority, a dress code at a restaurant, a particular emphasis on customer service at a hotel, these are all traditions that *could* really appeal to customers. My family and I go to a family camp in New Hampshire every summer, and at that camp July 4th is celebrated with a "tradition" of a parade, picnic, and games. We return every summer in part because we enjoy this tradition.

But traditions can also be customer-aversive. Let's look at the same set I listed above: an induction ceremony ("demeaning"), a dress code ("stuffy") or customer service ("they weren't *that* nice"). So you need to build on your positive traditions and get over your negative ones, remembering that it is not your opinion that counts, it is that of your markets. If your marketing materials are lost in the past, you will look like you are out of date, which is right up there with out of touch.

3. Penny-Wise and Pound-Foolish

This is a problem that is a holdover from 10 years ago, and can be summed up in the statement, "We can't afford nice-looking materials. They are too expensive, and they are unseemly for a charity." Wrong on two counts.

> ***COUNT ONE:*** With inexpensive software and inkjet printers, anyone with a mouse can develop very high-quality marketing materials that can be updated easily, quickly, and inexpensively. Ten years ago, you might have spent $1,500 to $3,000 to design a brochure, letterhead, and business cards and get them printed. Today, half of that amount will buy you the computer, software, printer, and the predesigned stationary to do all of that yourself. And, of course, the hardware can be used for other things as well.

> ***COUNT TWO:*** Your material, if it looks good, doesn't look *unseemly*. It looks *professional*. Tacky material—outdated, cheaply produced— speaks of a cheap organization. That you cannot afford to be. At any price.

Spend a little money for a lot of return. This does *not* mean that you need to go out and put all your money in a 40-page, four-color glossy catalog when a three-fold brochure will do, but it does mean that you shouldn't be sending your information out on a hand-typed and then photocopied piece of paper. Raise your sights and your standards here. Look at what your competition is doing. Look at what your markets want. Show that you know their wants in the quality of the marketing materials.

☞ **HANDS-ON:** When was your marketing material last revised? Your web site? Your logo, slogan, letterhead, and other items? If you can't remember, or can't find the documents, it was too long ago. Refresh your materials now! As I said earlier, it's cheap, and we'll spend part of the next chapter giving you lots of specifics on how to take advantage of the benefits of low cost technology in this area.

4. Public Relations or Marketing?

I've lost track of the not-for-profit marketing material I have seen that tries to cover all the bases on one or two sides of an 8 1/2 by 11 sheet of paper. It includes the things I listed above (history, jargon, money requests, etc.) but never focuses on a core marketing sequence of targeting a market, asking that market what they want, and then providing it. Instead, the organization has hired a public relations staff person whose training is really in dealing with the media and giving your organization a good image in the community, but not in marketing.

I don't intend to denigrate public relations. A lot of organizations that I know could use some talented PR help. But PR alone is *not* marketing. Good public relations can supplement a marketing effort, raise positive image, let large numbers of people know that your organization is there, and give a positive opinion about you. But that still does not necessarily mean much to the marketing effort.

❏ **FOR EXAMPLE:** A few years ago, I was assisting an organization that provides rehabilitation to people with spinal cord injuries in the Northwest with the development of their marketing plan. During my first visit, the planning committee told me that they were going to spend $15,000 on a public relations firm to raise the image of the organization in the community. "*Why?*" I asked. "We did a survey, and only two percent of the community knows what we do. So we need to raise our visibility," they replied. "*Why?*" I repeated. "Because people need to know about us." "*Do you get a substantial amount in small donations, or are you planning on expanding your grassroots development efforts?*" "No." "*Do you get referrals from the general public?*" "No, from physicians, insurers, and hospital patient advocates." "*How many of them know about you?*" "We don't know." "*That is the group where your visibility needs to be highest.*"

The group had fallen prey to the PR ego bug. "*Everyone* needs to know about us!" But *everyone* wasn't their market, and the best way to focus your limited marketing resources is on the target markets that you have chosen.

Make sure that your board and staff understand the differences between marketing and public relations.

These four all-too-common problems lead to unfocused, service-based, poor-quality materials. Now that we know the reasons for poor material, let's look at what your marketing material *should* be doing and then at checklists of things to include and things to avoid.

B. SOLVING CUSTOMERS' PROBLEMS

All successful salespeople know that you develop a long-term relationship with a customer by repeatedly being there to connect with the customer and then solve his or her problems. As you watch television the next few weeks, notice how many advertisements talk about (or demonstrate) a problem first, and then state that their product has the solutions. Backed-up toilet? Hemorrhoids? Expensive long-distance? Flabby stomach? Have to get a package absolutely, positively, there overnight? All of these are the problems shown in one five-minute stretch of commercials on the evening news recently.

Note that I am focusing on the problems, *not* the solutions. That is because selling solutions without a problem is being service-based. Selling a solution to a market problem (want) is being market-based. Thus, your marketing material should demonstrate that you understand what your market wants, what their problems are, and that you can solve them.

❑ **FOR EXAMPLE:** I recently saw a brochure for an art museum that gave a great deal of information, but never really connected with me (or apparently many other people, as attendance was down). On the cover, you had the name of the museum, a picture of the building, and a lost-in-the-past slogan ("Providing Access to the Arts for Adams County since 1910"). Inside was a breathless description of the museum in very dry terms ("250,000 square feet of exhibit space, a permanent and rotating collection, lecture hall that is also used for small music performances and poetry readings, etc.). Then there was a listing of some of the artists whose work was displayed and a list of the collections on display. The back cover was a map, hours, and a place to call for more information.

All of this information (with the exception of the slogan) was factual and, to some people, important. But was it to a potential visitor? What about statements such as "Art comes alive at the Adams County Museum! If you are an art enthusiast, come see a local collection of the masters close to your own home. If you are an art teacher in need of exhibits to view and discuss, the Adams County Museum is a great field trip. If you are a parent who wants to expose their child to art, bring your child for a visit and then return for one of our art classes."

Each of these statements connects with a target market that the museum had identified but not addressed in the marketing information. They had assumed that parents, patrons, and teachers could glean what they needed from a generic brochure. In fact, what they needed was four brochures: one general one, one for art patrons, one for art teachers, and one for parents. Each of these focused brochures could be headlined in a focused manner such as "FREE RESOURCES FOR ART TEACHERS FROM THE ADAMS COUNTY MUSEUM." (Teachers are attracted to the words "free resources" like bees are to honey. Their problem: never enough resources to meet the needs of their students.) "ART ACTIVITIES FOR KIDS AT THE ADAMS COUNTY MUSEUM." (Parents have a problem: bored children. The word "activities" addresses that issue.) I'm sure you get the idea now. Figure out who your target markets are and write your material to speak to them.

☞ **HANDS-ON:** Never, ever, assume that a market will make the connection between your resources and their problem. They won't. And, in fairness, it's not their job. It's yours. In asking the market about what their wants are, you should be asking about their problems. This information comes best through the focus groups and informal asking that we discussed in Chapter 8, but also it comes through reading the general and business press. You will read, for example, about the problems of Americans feeling that their days are too short. Lesson? If you can save them time, you can attract them. You will read about their concerns about education, the breakup of the family. Can your organization make a connection here? Do you provide some kind of educational experience? Do you focus on the family unit in a definable way? If you do, these "buzzwords" should show up in your marketing material.

Solving people's problems puts the focus on them, not on you. It develops empathy for them, not emphasis on your services. It makes a connection, and avoids the hard sell. And it works. I should also point out that solving people's problems should be the process by which your staff connect with individuals in person or by phone. Your staff and board, in their informal asking, should be willing to listen to problems, and then be thinking of how your organization can solve that problem.

C. THINGS TO INCLUDE IN YOUR MARKETING MATERIALS

Now let's turn to a list of things that you should make sure are included in your marketing materials. I would suggest that your marketing committee review all of your materials, commercials, handouts, and presentations for the following seven components. And, remember, you have to *connect with your customer,* showing him or her the benefits of using your services.

1. Your Mission

If your mission statement (or charitable purpose) is succinct and not full of jargon, it is an excellent thing to include in most of your marketing material. If it is so long that it will take up 90 percent of your space, forget it. But your mission is the defining statement of what and who your organization is, and you should be able to lead with it.

2. Focus

Each piece of marketing material should be focused on a target market or a service component. The art museum in the example above could develop a piece for art lovers, another for parents, and one for art teachers. That would be an example of focus on a target market. A YMCA might have a piece on summer camp, one on its aerobics classes, and one on its basketball and soccer leagues. That would be an example of focus on a service. But, and this is very important, even within the "service pieces," it is critical that you use terms that connect to the market wants. If you just focus on the service, you are back to that service-oriented rather than market-oriented mentality. More on different materials for different markets in a few pages.

3. Brevity

Blessed is the person who can say it in the fewest, clearest words. Remember that no one is forcing the reader to spend the time reading your material. It needs to be *brief,* or they will get bored and stop reading. No lengthy sentences or minute detail. Give the essential information only. With all appropriate apologies to the English majors among you, your role model for your printed material (not your web site, which can be much more detailed) should be *USA Today,* which is heavy on bullets, and not too many sentences with commas! Keep it short, and keep people's attention.

4. Connection

Does the material clearly show that your organization understands the problems of the target market(s)? And, does it clearly state that you can help solve those problems? If not, you are trusting the reader to make those connections, and that is a mistake.

5. Appearance

As I mentioned earlier, there is no excuse for sloppy material, poor writing, and cheap-looking paper or graphics. They speak volumes about your organization. Word processing and printing are so inexpensive now that there is little impediment to developing professional-looking materials at a very reasonable cost.

6. References

In certain materials, it will be important to list well-known customers. For example, if you are a health care organization, it may be important to list the large employers with whose employee health plans you qualify, or the managed care plans. Other organizations need to make connections to state and national associations to show a level of quality ("Certified by the National Association of XYZ"), or to a community standard ("A United Way Agency"). As with your other text, be brief and put only those references that mean something to the target market for that particular marketing piece. For example, being accredited by the Joint Commission on the Accreditation of Hospitals may be important to a referring physician, but meaningless to a patient. Be selective and focused.

7. A Source for More Information

Always include a location where people can call for more information. Include a phone number, hours of availability, *and the name* (not the title) of the person to contact. I realize that this means that you will have to update the materials when that person changes jobs, but the personal listing is valuable in two ways. First, it is just that—personal—and gives a name to an otherwise impersonal organization. Second, it routes the questions to the right person immediately. One thing that nearly all of us despise is being put on hold or handed off endlessly from person to person trying to find out some simple fact, figure, time, or other answer to our question. By putting the name of the correct person on the brochure, you simplify the process and usually avoid the problem.

All of these things should show up in some fashion in your material. Now, let's look at the other side of the coin.

D. THINGS TO AVOID IN YOUR MARKETING MATERIALS

I assume that you have now gone through your materials to make sure that the items above are included. But there may well be things that are in your materials that you should pull out. There are certainly things to avoid. I've provided you with a list of seven common items to make sure that you keep out of your material.

1. Jargon

The worst offense in marketing material is to speak in a language people don't understand. You don't impress people by confusing them. Using jargon puts a big barrier between you and most audiences. I have long contended that if you can't explain or describe what you do in words that a fourth-grader can understand, you don't really understand what you do. Simplify. Clarify. And remember that the average American reads on a mid-high-school level.

Having said that, there is a time for jargon. If your marketing material is to professionals in the field, jargon is the language of the profession, and thus appropriate. If, for example, you were developing a brochure to advertise a continuing education program in computers the terms ASCII, PC, icons, Internet, and modem would probably be appropriate. If you were training on labor law, citing of the laws and using common labor law terms and issues would be important. Write for your audience.

2. Inappropriate Photos

Here is the sad truth. Most people don't care about how your building looks. You do, because you probably have put a great deal of blood, sweat, tears, energy, and money into the property. But most pictures of buildings are a waste of precious space in a marketing brochure. Pictures of people are usually much more effective, but even those can be counterproductive if they are grainy, unfocused, or so small as to be unrecognizable. Make sure each and every photo (or graphic) that you include is valuable and, like the text, simple, focused, and understandable. Also make sure that for any image of any person you use in any media (print or online) that you have a valid, current, signed photo release.

3. Lack of Focus

There is nothing wrong with a general-purpose brochure, but there is something definitely wrong with having *just* a general-purpose brochure, or with having a general-purpose brochure that tries to do everything for everyone. Focus is the heart of good marketing material. Ask yourself, "What is the purpose of this piece of paper?" If the piece goes much beyond that central purpose, it is almost certainly unfocused and too long.

4. Asking for Money

With the exception of fund-raising letters and brochures whose focus is explaining the various ways to give to your organization, asking for money is outside of the core purpose of the marketing material and thus out of focus. I know that it is tempting to just throw in a sentence or two about donations, particularly if you are desperate for money, but that desperation will come through, and some markets may well be turned off. Stick with your focus.

5. A History Lesson

Very few people care about your organization's history, or even how long you have been in existence. Having said that, some organizations need to validate their experience and stability by saying things like "Serving the Finger Lakes Region since 1965." But more often I see people who use 400 words to explain the origins of their organization in great (and agonizing) detail. They list the initial incorporators, the first few office addresses, and even give pictures of some of the sites that they have occupied, noting additional important dates in history.

There is nothing wrong with history, and we certainly can learn from it. But is a recitation of your organization's past (however laudable) "on-message" for the marketing piece you are developing? Probably not. But if it is, is your recounting of the development of your organization brief and readable? Stay focused.

6. Out of Date

I really love pictures of staff, board, and service recipients in bell-bottoms, with shag haircuts, or in leisure suits. They make me want to run right down to the disco. The problem is the disco is closed, a part of the past. Pictures that are from a bygone era will set you up for ridicule, not respect. They will disenchant people, who will wonder whether it is your programs or just your photos that are outdated. Again, in this era of quick and easy software that includes photos at the click of a mouse, there is no excuse for having your brochure look like a retrospective.

7. Boring

If you wrote the text in a particular piece, you probably won't be a good judge of this. Get it read by people inside and outside the organization. Ask hard questions: Is this boring? Does it run on? Can we say more in fewer words? Are we "on-message," focused, and keeping connected with the intended audience? Don't trust your own instincts here. Get a few outside opinions. I usually am pretty happy with my own writing, but it is *always* improved by the friends, coworkers, and (in the case of my books) the editors who read it. Get an outside opinion or three. It will help you avoid the dreaded B word.

☞ **HANDS-ON:** I have the best way to get a real-world, inexpensive read on two issues: boring and jargon. Do this. Get a group of five to seven high school sophomores (not juniors, not seniors, not freshmen), sit them down with a pizza, some soda, and your printed marketing materials. Ask them to read through your materials, and to circle any words that they don't understand, and to tell you in no uncertain terms what they feel is boring about your materials. Trust me, they will. Sophomores are 15 or 16 years old, and they are not worldly enough to have heard most of your jargon, but they are old enough to *love* telling an adult when they are wrong. Try this; lots of my clients have, and it really works!

E. DEVELOPING DIFFERENT MATERIALS FOR DIFFERENT MARKETS

I noted above the need to focus on different markets. Look now at the different markets that we discussed in Chapter 5. You may have donors, staff, volunteers, referrers, and board members, United Way, government, users, insurers, members, or other markets and you can't just get away (or adequately address all these wants) with one three- fold brochure. You need different materials for different markets. But you probably don't need 12,402 different pieces. Nor do you have unlimited resources or time to develop lots of materials, even accounting for the low cost of hardware, software, and color printers.

You want to have a focused set of materials, and you probably will have to develop them over time. Here are some tips for developing the best materials for the least money.

1. Plan Using a Committee

Don't try to do this alone. Get a group together and then plan your materials. Which markets are big enough and important enough to merit an individual piece or pieces? What are their wants? What should each piece address? What kind of look should it have? Brochure, 8 1/2 by 11 sheet, booklet? How much money do you want to spend and when?

2. Get a Common "Look"

You probably have a logo of some kind. If you haven't updated it for 20 years, now might be a good time to think about it. Whether you develop a new logo or keep your existing one, get a scanned, digitized version of it. You'll need that for your remaining work. Have a common paper color, typeface (font), and set-up to your materials. One excellent way to "jump start" this is to look through catalogs that sell paper in "look" sets. You can get 8 1/2 by 11 sheets, brochures, cards, even announcements all in the same look, and just add your text and graphics to them. But, however you approach this, you want to have an identifiable and consistent set of colors, text, and graphics in your material.

3. Meet the Wants of the Different Target Markets

"Well," you say. "I have identified 100 different markets. Do I need 100 different brochures?" Probably not. But you do you need to focus your marketing material on your target markets. Let's look at the types of materials that you might develop, and the target markets that they might address. Remember as you read Exhibit 9-1 to focus on your target markets.

These are just a quick set of ideas. You will undoubtedly have many more. The bottom line in this area is to remember to meet the wants of the markets, and to recognize the virtually impossible task of doing that in a single, general brochure. Focus, focus, focus.

RECAP

Now you know the way to improve your current marketing material, and to develop new or modified material as you enter new markets. You should realize that marketing material needs to solve problems and identify with

Exhibit 9-1   Target Markets and Associated Materials

MARKET	Want	Possible Marketing Material
Board	Initial information, ongoing information.	Board orientation manual, newsletter. Online newsletter. A special section of your web site.
Staff	Initial information, ongoing information about the organization.	Staff orientation materials. Online newsletter. A special section of your web site.
Donors	Information on ways to give and what happens to the donation. A number to call (with a name).	Specific piece designed for donors. Online newsletter.
Government	Information on program quality, program availability, meeting of regulations.	Specific piece designed with needs and keywords of government—emphasizing outcomes, quality, and certification levels. Online newsletter.
Foundations	Demonstration of expertise and experience in the field of the foundation's interest.	Probably a general informational piece, with a specific application for funds. Perhaps a piece on the mission statement, endorsements. Online newsletter.
Membership	Information on the benefits and costs of membership. A number to call (with a name).	Specific piece on the value of becoming a member—from the member's perspective. Online newsletter.
Service Recipients	Information on services and outcomes. A number to call (with a name).	Pieces designed with target groups in mind (parents, teens, seniors) or regarding specific services for larger groups (camps, congregations, tours). Online newsletter. Special section of your web site.
Referral Sources	Information about the quality of the program, and its array of services.	A piece that might be filled with jargon if designed for a professional referrer. Online newsletter. Special section of your web site.

its target audience, and not sell products and services. You should be able to recite the seven things to include in your marketing material:

1. Your mission
2. Focus
3. Brevity

4. Connection of problems and solutions
5. Appearance
6. References
7. A source for more information

And, you should know the list of things to avoid, including jargon, inappropriate or unnecessary photos, a lack of focus, asking for money, including a history lesson, being out of date, and being boring. Finally, you learned about how to make different materials for your different markets, and how to remained focused within that material on the markets' problems (their wants) rather than on your services, no matter how wonderful they are.

Remember, your marketing material speaks for you when you are not there. It is, in a very real sense, delegated the responsibility to be your salesperson, to answer questions, promote your services, and establish a rapport with a potential customer. All without any supervision, and often without the opportunity for follow-up or evaluation.

If your marketing materials are good, then you have hundreds or even thousands of "spokespersons" out in the community that are helping interest people in your organization. If your materials are not good, the best you have done is simply wasted some time, money, and paper. At worst, you are hurting your organization every time someone looks at your brochure, sees your web site or your ad, or hears your piece on the radio. Speaking of web sites, they are an integral part of the marketing mix, and we'll discuss them at some length in the next chapter, "Technology and Marketing."

Spend the time and the money to get it right. Follow the list of things to include and, remember, you aren't just in the promotional business any more. If you build it, not only will they *not* automatically come, but they won't even care. But if you build what the market wants, and then show them how it solves their problems, they will come in droves.

Discussion Questions for Chapter 9

1. Does our material include jargon? How do we know?
2. Does our marketing material sell services or solve problems?
3. How do we measure up to the list of things to include?
4. How do we do on the list of things to avoid?
5. Let's look at our target markets. Do we have marketing pieces that are developed specifically for them? How can we improve in this area?

10
Technology and Marketing

OVERVIEW

Since the publication of the first edition of *Mission-Based Marketing,* so much has changed in the interface of technology and marketing that the subject deserves its own chapter, and so here we are. Let's be clear at the start: Technology is not a substitute for following the marketing cycle I showed you in Chapter 5, nor can it take the place of good asking, good listening, and providing superior customer satisfaction services. It cannot choose your target markets, nor can it provide leadership in team marketing. That having been said, technology can enhance all of these important facets of good mission-based marketing. In this chapter, I'll show you how to use technology to its fullest in the pursuit of your organizational marketing improvements.

CHAPTER THUMBNAIL

➤ **Using Technology to Market in a Better, Faster, and More Focused Manner**
➤ **High-Tech Asking—High-Tech Listening**
➤ **Your Web Site(s)**
➤ **Better Marketing Materials**
➤ **Development**
➤ **Newsletters Online**

As we begin the chapter, we'll talk about the many ways that you can use technology to market better, including better marketing materials, online research, communication with users, funders, staff, and volunteers, better ways to ask online, improvements in your web site(s), ways to disperse regular information by e-newsletter, and much more. Then, we'll get down to specifics. We'll look at ways to do some of your asking online, by e-mail, and by Web page. We'll turn to ways to improve your web site(s) and give you a checklist to use in evaluating your site as well as others. Then, we'll look at ways to use the tech you have to develop better, more flexible, more focused printed marketing materials. You'll see how to use incredibly inexpensive methods to turn out great materials. Following that, we'll look at technology applications in development, including some software. We'll next examine a great way to do outreach with no printing costs at all: an online newsletter. And to close the chapter, I'll provide you with some online resources for better marketing.

By the end of the chapter you should be much better able to see how to use the best of technology to market the best of your services to the neediest of your service recipients.

A. USING TECHNOLOGY TO MARKET IN A BETTER, FASTER, AND MORE FOCUSED MANNER

So what are the things you can use technology for in your marketing efforts? There are tons, and the number and resulting benefits are growing every day. You can take donations online and track donors or manage special events with development software, you can e-mail your best customers, you can make your organization financially and programmatically transparent on your web site, you can update your marketing material weekly and print it yourself at lower cost, with more focus. You can keep in touch with your volunteers, staff, and board markets through targeted web sites, and you can stay on everyone in the community's mind with an electronic newsletter. All that and much, much more. But I am sure that some of you are thinking, "Yeah, yeah, yeah. But the people *we* serve don't have computers, don't have e-mail. What's the big deal?" Well, besides the fact that your staff and board almost certainly have some access to the net and to e-mail, tech still can help you do your promotional materials better and, you may be surprised about the people you serve:

❑ **FOR EXAMPLE:** The events in this story occurred in late 1999, which was the Dark Ages in terms of Internet access. A friend of mine who runs a huge homeless shelter on the East Coast and who, like me, is a bit of a tech-head, called me late one night to tell me about a person who had checked in earlier that evening. My friend does intake once a month to keep himself close to the people his organization serves, and a person who, according to my friend, "was a caricature of a homeless man, the person a group of fourth-graders would draw if asked to draw a homeless man," showed up at the intake desk. My friend checked him in and, since it was the first time this man had used this particular shelter, asked him how he heard about the shelter, and why he had chosen to come in. The man looked at him for a second, and said, "Well, I was, y'know, surfing the web, and I came across your web site, and it looked good, so I, like, came over."

Where does a homeless person surf the web? You know, don't you . . . at the library. I've told that story a hundred times in training sessions, and when I tell it *everyone* laughs, I assume with surprise, and yet *everyone* knows the answer to the question of where the homeless man got online. Nevertheless, we continue to believe that the net doesn't affect us. It does. And don't forget, this story occurred way back in 1999.

Remember too, that access to your organization online doesn't limit itself to just the people you serve. Go back to your list of markets. What about your funders? Your donors? Your volunteers? Your staff? Most if not all of them have the ability, even the desire to access you in a variety of right-now ways. The people you serve are a *vital* market. But they are not your *only* market.

So, technology can help us market better. But, as I said above, it should not be an excuse not to do the basics of marketing such as asking, listening, and responding. Worse, tech can and does get in the way of good service.

❏ **FOR EXAMPLE:** In my opinion one of the worst uses of technology in relation to marketing is the widespread use of automated telephone operators. Universally we *hate* having our call answered by some disembodied voice (or worse, a computer-generated one) saying, "For a directory of staff members, press 1, for a listing of services press 2." Yet many, if not most, organizations have these machines. They were sold to you as way of keeping up, of saving money, of being more efficient. Great. Except they tick people off and worse, are the first impression many people have of you. They may save *you* time, but they *delay* your customers. They may make you happy, but they don't make your customers happy. Now, you already know I am a big tech supporter, and I love voice mail, but my strong advice to you is to have a real live person answer the telephone during office hours. And, make your automated answer during non-office hours as short and understandable as possible. No one has a problem with leaving a message during off-hours, or if someone is not available, but think through your system from the customer's point of view. I recently called my accountant, and got the office receptionist. My accountant was out, and I asked to leave message on his voice mail. "Oh, we can't do that. You have to call back, and I'll let the machine answer," she said! Don't blindly accept all technology as a benefit. Think through every use of tech.

Okay, enough cautionary tales. Lets look at some specific areas where you can do more sooner, better, faster, and cheaper.

1. Data Gathering/Research

We have an encyclopedia at home, for our children, actually two sets—one upstairs and one down where our family computer is. But 99 percent of the time, our kids ignore these resources, as the net is faster, deeper, and, most importantly, a habit for them. I have to regularly remind them that there is good information in print resources. Yeah, how quaint, Dad.

Despite my old-fashioned love of printed things (like this book), for much of the information you want, the net *is* the place to go. Want to find out what the state of the art is in a certain kind of brochure or web site? Go online. Need to know about best practices or benchmarking in your area of service? You can find that on the web. Want to investigate which government or foundation funding is available for a program you want to provide? There are at least four web sites that do that for federal and state funding, and will even e-mail you alerts when your key words are "hit" by their software. Want to find out about your competitors? There are resources through your state economic development agency, your chamber of commerce, as well as commercial sites galore.

Using the net for research is one of the prime benefits of being online. Use the resources that are there, and that are improving every day.

☞ **HANDS-ON:** Spend some time learning how to search on the net, and getting a listing of the places you have available to look. Use your bookmarking function (in Netscape Navigator) and favorites function (in Internet Explorer) to keep a listing of good sites for funding, best practices, and competition research. If there is someone on your staff who is particularly adept at efficiently finding things for you, don't just delegate all your research work to them, do the searching with them, letting them mentor you in how to navigate the often confusing maze of web search options. And, good news: The next iteration of the net, called the "semantic web"—more user-friendly, and more responsive—is due to be up and running by 2006. So there is hope if you are not a tech-lover.

See Chapter 13 for some good research web sites. And, always remember to check my web site, *www.missionbased.com,* for the latest and most useful links.

2. Online Access

I assume that your organization has a web site, but how much time have you spent looking at it as your first point of access? You want to allow people to access some of the things you do online. Why? Because we live in a right-now society. More and more people are used to checking you out online. You need to not only have basic information on your services, locations, and the like, but think about ways you can add value with your web site. Here are some questions to consider:

- Can people find out about our locations, hours, and services easily on our web site (within two clicks of opening the main page)? Can they get directions, and print a map?
- Can people sign up for appointments, purchase tickets, check their grades (whatever is appropriate to your organization) online?
- Are there sources of information on your site for people to learn more about the issues that concern your organization? For instance, if your core service is foster care, is there a deep set of resources on becoming a foster parent, adoption, etc.?
- Is there information on staff, at least enough to let potential customers feel more at ease with the person who may help them? Do you include pictures and a short bio?
- Can volunteers (current or potential) explore options of things that they can do to help your organization?
- Can donors donate online? Can such donations be restricted by the donor?
- Can a funder see your current letters of accreditation, licenses, and any other quality assurances online (for example, as a scanned document)?

I'm sure as you read this you can think of many other things that could reach out to people who access you online, meet their wants, and impress them with your ability to solve their problems. And, of course, don't be afraid to ask people what they want from your web site. They'll give you great feedback, and useful improvements to consider.

3. Staff, Board, and Customer E-Mail

One of the few television shows I regularly watch is *Law & Order*, which over the past few years has been on, it seems, 24 hours a day in reruns. As I was writing this chapter, I saw an episode from 1998 where one of the younger detectives was using something new—"some electronic mail thingy" in the words of an older detective—in an effort to solve a crime. It reminded me how far we have come in a very, very short time. While not all of our board, staff, and customers have e-mail, most do, and for them, communication by e-mail is *expected and preferred.*

What can you do in terms of marketing and e-mail? Basically two things: Communicate quickly, inexpensively, and efficiently, and keep your organizational presence in front of people without printing and postage expenses. Here are a number of things to consider, most of which have been tried and found useful by a number of my client organizations.

Weekly e-mail updates on regular issues

This could go to board staff and volunteers, and could include a brief update on meetings for the week (perhaps split into staff, board, and volunteer areas), information on where minutes from last week's (or month's) meetings can be found on the organization's web site, announcements of new staff, retirements, certifications, awards, etc. This e-mail should be short, but could eventually transition into an online newsletter (see section F below).

Reminders of meetings

This can increase attendance, and preparation. A short e-mail reminding people of the place, time, subject, and agenda for a meeting, as well as what they should be bringing with them, and/or have prepared.

Requests for input/assistance

If you need resources from the community, ask your volunteers and staff for help. An e-mail is quick, and can be just the trick to get their attention and have them respond to you quickly.

Job postings

Again, letting all staff, board, and volunteers know you are looking to fill a position can help spread the net wider. You already have trouble finding and keeping good staff; why not use this method to jump-start the process?

Customer updates

I would guarantee that all of your paying customers (funders, foundations, state and local governments) both have and regularly use their e-mail. So why not use the medium to communicate the good things about your organization, such as certifications, awards, and new services?

☞ HANDS-ON: E-mail should be a *supplement,* not a *substitute* for communication. Always remember that there will, at least for the foreseeable future, be people who are involved with your organization who do not have access to e-mail, or do not have access to it 24 hours a day (for example, staff who use e-mail only at work). And, don't assume that people check their e-mail four times a day. I regularly get surprised by people who only check their e-mail once a week, or even once a month.

☞ HANDS-ON: If you don't have e-mail as an organization, let me be direct: Get it, get it now, and get an individual e-mail address for every staff member. It is not expensive, it is the expectation of your customers, and it is the best way to go to use this increasingly important tool.

4. Telecom

Now let's talk about phones, pagers, and automated telephone operators. You have already read my rant above about the automated operators (if you haven't already, go to the **FOR EXAMPLE** above). But phones, pagers, and voice mail help us have access to staff (on the management side) and give access to customers (on the marketing side). In order to provide customer satisfaction, you need to make sure you can quickly fix any problems that arise. In our current right-now environment, you have to be able to find out about the problem, get to the staff who can fix the problem, and let the customer know it has been fixed—soon. Telecom can help you to do that, but you can trip on a couple of speed bumps along the way.

☞ HANDS-ON: Don't fall victim to what I call ego tech: giving everyone on your staff a phone and a pager. While the cost of technology has fallen dramatically, it is not free. Good stewardship decisions require that we look and see who really needs the equipment, and regularly review that need. Look at the phone bills for all your organizational cell phones. How often are they being used? Who is calling who? Does the phone get used enough to merit its monthly fee? Same with pagers. Although not telecom, personal digital assistants (PDAs) also can fall into the ego-tech trap. Make sure you *need* the tools you are paying for.

☞ **HANDS-ON:** Check the available tech regularly—particularly in this area. Often the phones and pagers are free with a 12-month contract. For example, one client of mine with 10 different facilities in one community has changed the communications devices for their four maintenance staff from pagers, to cell phones, and finally to cell phones with two-way radio capability (think a phone/walkie-talkie combination) over the past five years. The cost for outfitting four staff with these immediate access tools is now less than it was for one pager five years ago.

☞ **HANDS-ON:** Speaking of price, check these too. Have your financial staffperson, or tech person, call your cell phone and pager provider every three to six months and ask for the best rate. I tell all my clients to do this, and they regularly e-mail me with thanks since their costs get reduced by 10 to 50 percent with an increase in minutes, free long distance, etc. If you haven't checked in the past half-year, do this *today.*

☞ **HANDS-ON:** Do you have voice mail on your phone system? You should. Now, how easy is it for people to access it? Try this: After hours call your system and time how long it is before you can actually leave a message. How long are the verbal instructions at each step? How long are the personal messages your staff leave? Shorten this time as much as possible. Voice mail is essential in customer satisfaction efforts, so try not to make your customers mad by making it inaccessible.

Telecom is a very, very important part of marketing and keeping close to your customers. Use it, but use it wisely.

That's quite a list, but only part of how technology can help you in doing better marketing. Now let's delve a bit deeper.

B. HIGH-TECH ASKING—HIGH-TECH LISTENING

Here again is an area where tech can help, supplementing your asking, and giving people new ways to tell you about what they want. But, as with other areas of marketing, tech can help but cannot substitute for hands-on asking. In this area, you can use surveying software, you can expand the use of your voice mail, you can survey by web and by e-mail, and you can use your web site as an access point for feedback. Let's look at each.

1. Surveying

One of the many things that computers do well is to collate, tabulate, and report on large amounts of data. Surveys are, in many cases, ideal sets of data to input into your computer system and have available. You can use standard spreadsheet programs such as Excel or Lotus 1-2-3, both of which have pretty good database functions (but need someone fluent with the program to really do a good job of setting them up) or database programs such as Lotus Approach or Filemaker, which nearly all have survey functions. You can also look at surveying programs such as Soft Survey or SurveyGold, which specialize in surveying work. As with all software, go to the vendor's site, download a sample program, ask for and follow up with references, and read reviews at sites like www.cnet.com. Only you can decide whether you have the money and the expertise to use these tools.

While software can really help you collect, analyze and track your information, you need to be careful of two things: survey design and data entry. In the area of survey design, try to have as many questions as possible rated on a scale, perhaps one to seven, so that you can have a numeric value assigned to an answer.

NOTE: Make sure you always leave a section on any survey for non-directed answers, with a question such as "Is there anything else you would like to tell us about your experience with us?" These answers are extremely valuable, even though they don't lend themselves to statistical analysis. The second area is data entry. Remember the old computer maxim, GIGO—Garbage In, Garbage Out. After you collect the survey and do the data entry, make sure you use a double entry mode in your software—that means that the data has to be entered identically twice to preclude entry errors. I know this is more work, but data entry is pretty boring after the 300th survey, and keying errors are common.

So what can using software do? Well, you can certainly get your results sooner, and sliced differently as you want to. (Just how many male respondents are "very happy" with your program as opposed to female respondents?) But more importantly, you can quickly develop both written and graphic reports, and put the data on the web so all your staff, board, and volunteers can see it; you can put graphics or summary information on your web site to show your community you are asking and listening; and, in terms of management benefits, you can quickly and easily track the same issues (employee satisfaction, the percentage of repeat donors, the happiness levels of your key customers) year after year—what is known as *trend analysis.*

Another area of high-tech asking is asking by e-mail. Once you put together your e-mail lists (of donors, volunteers, community contacts, vendors, etc.) you can quickly and cheaply survey them on any issue you want, as long as you don't pester them. This kind of survey can be as mundane as getting a head count for an upcoming board dinner, or as complex as doing a survey on perceived community needs. It is quick, cheap, and does not rely on the speed, or lack thereof, of the postal service.

☞ **HANDS-ON:** Do not, I repeat, do NOT just survey in an e-mail. If you list a series of questions in an e-mail, people get confused in their reply, and what you get back is also sometimes garbled or confusing. There may be carats (>>>>>) in front of each line, or you may **bold** your questions to make it easier to read, and then the reader's software doesn't support bold, or prints the HTML code, etc. So, here is the solution: Use the e-mail to ask for someone's input, and then, right in the e-mail, provide a link to a web site (usually a hidden part of yours) that is a page set up as a survey, with entry boxes, etc. This kind of site-based survey helps the person being surveyed enter data more easily, and, as an extra benefit, collates and tabulates the data automatically. There are sites that do this kind of surveying for you, such as *www.hostedsurvey.com* and *www.free-online-surveys.co.uk*, and software you can use as well, such as Soft Survey and SurveyGold. Also, if you are interested in this option, you may want to talk to your Internet service provider (ISP) to see if they offer surveying tabulation.

☞ **HANDS-ON:** Using high-tech surveying does *not* get you off the hook in regard to my rules on surveying that we discussed in Chapter 8. You still need to focus, you still only have about four minutes, you still need to consider not adding a ton of identifiers, and you still need to get some help in designing the survey questions.

2. Web Site

This is pretty straightforward: make sure there is a place on every page of your web site for customer feedback. Usually, this is just a link that initiates an e-mail to your organization. You want to offer the opportunity for input in every way possible, so make sure your online visitors can tell you how you can improve.

☞ **HANDS-ON:** Set up a special e-mail account for customer feedback. Most ISPs will let you route a special e-mail address, such as "feedback@(your address)" to a particular staff person's e-mail account. Using such an address alerts the staff person that this is customer input and should be dealt with quickly. It also removes the responsibility from the person giving you input from having to put a particular item in the subject line of the e-mail. Whoever has the responsibility to deal with feedback should check their e-mail at least twice a day, and route the input as appropriate to other staff.

3. Voice Mail

Voice mail is so common that no one pays a bit of attention to it—we all use it—nearly all of us love it, so what's the big deal? The big deal comes in two ways: First, how people get to it, and second, whether or not people check and follow up on their voice mail. First, let me reassure you: I love voice mail. Having the ability to talk to a voice mail system allows me (and everyone else) to quickly transmit their message, need, or complaint, to do it efficiently, and with whatever emphasis or emotion is appropriate for the message. It removes the potential for transcription error from a receptionist, and can be accessed 24 hours a day by both caller and recipient.

That having been said, there are pitfalls, and the biggest turnoff to a caller is a lengthy, confusing, or redundant system that takes too much time. We already know that you need to have a live person answer the phone during office hours, but let's look at the other issues a bit here.

❑ **FOR EXAMPLE:** A friend of mine, who works for a national insurance company and travels all the time, lives on his phone. He has seven zillion minutes on his cell phone, and a topic that comes up regularly when we eat breakfast together is the latest cell gadget. But when I call his pager number to either change an appointment or set one up, I get this sequence:

1. A 10-second message from my friend, telling me to leave a message.
2. A 20-second message from a computer telling me which button to push for various options—one I have to listen to completely before I can choose.
3. A *second* 14-second message from my friend telling me to leave a message.
4. A *second* 10-second message from the computer.

It's a good thing we're friends. This drives me nuts every time I call, and I'm sure it does for his customers. And, yes, I've told him about it.

☞ **HANDS-ON:** When was the last time you called in to your organization and tried to go through the entire process (no shortcuts, assume you are a new caller)? Do this today. Time yourself; how long does it take until you actually can start talking and leaving your message? Now, do the same thing again for someone who knows your extension. How long now? For new callers—no more than 30 seconds is acceptable; for people who know your extension, 10 seconds max. This may well mean that you have to change the greeting, both at the agency entry level and at your own mailbox. Remember, always have a live person answer the phone during office hours, but make the recorded part as easy as possible.

Now, the other issue here is checking your voice mail. This is the corollary of the problem we looked at with e-mail—people never checking it. I (and any customer, funder, donor, volunteer) expect that, when they leave a message, they will get called back. Soon. Very soon. So make sure to remind your very, very busy staff that part of their very, very busy jobs is checking and responding to their voice mail. How often? That depends on your organization. I have client organizations whose absolute rule on voice mail is four times every work day and at least once on weekends and holidays. Same for their e-mail. Why? Because they work with teens in crisis, and teens in crisis *cannot* wait. I've been in their staff meetings when everyone takes a voice mail break at once. What will work for you? Depends on how urgent your customer problems or service issues are. But err on the side of too often, and talk this through at a staff meeting.

C. YOUR WEB SITE(S)

One of the most visible outcomes of the tech revolution is your web site. Your web site is also something that brings with it increasingly high expectations from visitors (in terms of quality, breadth, and depth) and high opportunities for improving your marketing. I have visited literally thousands of not-for-profit web sites, and many are good, some are excellent, and some, well to put it plainly, are simply awful—and worse than no web site at all. You need to make sure that your web site is both deeper and wider than just a repeat of your printed marketing material. You need to make sure that there are many ways on the site for people to contact you—including snail mail addresses, phone, and direct e-mail. You need to check regularly to make sure all your links are active. (Use a free application for this like Link Sleuth—it can take way too much time to do it by hand!)

Lots of work, but lots of opportunity. And more and more people are using the web, and thus your web site, as a first place to contact you. How is that contact now? How does your site look compared to your peers'? And, are you making as much out of this resource as you can? Here are some ideas on ways to use the web better to appeal to your markets.

Board-Only and Staff-Only Areas

Such a site offers immediate access for your board and staff as well as op-portunities for them to learn more about what's going on in the organiza-tion. Here's what to do:

1. Set up the board site as a sub-area of your web site. Make sure to secure it, so that only approved people can get in. For most organ-izations a username and password are sufficient. One very useable format for this is to have a username that is the first letter of the first name and full last name (for me this would be pbrinckerhoff) and a password of the first name. That way, your web site administr-ator can set the access and, of course, remove access when a board or staff member leaves.

2. Set up an easily found link on the starting page of your web site for the board area and the staff area (I suggest two different areas, not one combined one—there will be overlap, but start with separate areas). Suggest that your board and staff bookmark the site in their browser for easier access. Hold an informational session at an up-coming meeting (for both board and staff), showing them the site, how to access it, and what is available for them to use.

3. On the site, you can include any of the following things that other not-for-profits have included:

   A list of staff (with pictures if possible), board members, board member e-mail addresses, a list of all committees, with the times and locations of meetings, access to all committee meeting min-utes, as well as minutes of board meetings, scheduling information for upcoming meetings and training opportunities, copies of all policies, printable copies of forms that board or staff members use, explanations of all program functions, other announcements for the organization. One organization I work with has an opening page for board members that lists all the meetings coming up for the next three weeks.

Consider doing the same thing for your other volunteers! This kind of deeper web site is exactly what the Internet provides—a customized com-munication tool that can enhance your mission, internal communications, and board satisfaction!

Public Education

One of the best things your web site can offer is public education on the issues that concern you. You can research and list books, tapes, CDs, videos, links to articles of interest or educational web sites, and other resources for further study by your web visitors. This is a community service, and it keeps your site visitors coming back. It can also tie in nicely with our next topic, affiliations.

Affiliations

You can affiliate with a commercial site as a way to raise funds. The easiest of these is Amazon.com. You can sign up as an affiliate at Amazon, post one of dozens of logos as a link on your web site and, when people go to Amazon through your web site, you get 5 percent of whatever they purchase there. There are two major applications of this. First, if you do public education as noted above, you can list specific books, videotapes, and other resources on your web site, and have links directly to those items on Amazon (you can even download the book cover graphics from Amazon). This is a lower-impact way of affiliating. Or, you can note your affiliation to Amazon (or any other affiliation you have) and place a link on your opening page, then e-mail all your supporters (particularly during the holiday shopping season), asking them to purchase their online gifts through your affiliation link. Again, free money, but not without controversy.

☞ HANDS-ON: This is, at its core, a political choice: Do you want to commercialize your web site? TALK TO YOUR BOARD about this before you just up and do it. I have dozens of client organizations who use this as a low-cost revenue stream, and dozens of others who do not. It is your choice, but one you want to make in coordination with your board.

There are many affiliation sites as of this writing, including Amazon, Barnes & Noble, Lands' End, and Nordstrom. Check the site out, see what the deal is, and after you decide whether or not you want to affiliate at all, affiliate only on a site-by-site basis.

☞ HANDS-ON: Remember that affiliation income will be treated by the IRS as unrelated business income, and you must report this in your annual 990-T filing. But, don't panic! You can offset the unrelated business income with some of your web site management and ISP costs. While I have dozens of client organizations that have affiliation income, I don't have any that have *net* unrelated business income (and thus pay taxes) after they deduct legitimate web site expenses.

D. BETTER MARKETING MATERIALS

One the greatest benefits of technology is the ability to produce better, cheaper, more focused printed marketing materials. Today's software and in-expensive printers provide you with the ability to quickly, easily, and cheaply develop excellent materials at the click of a mouse. We talked through a lot of this in Chapter 9, but let me hone in on how tech can help you here.

1. Focus

Throughout this book, I have told you to focus on specific target markets, and focus on specific services that you do best: Focus, focus, focus. Histor-ically one of the problems with developing and printing marketing materi-als for many not-for-profits has been cost. It was (note the past tense) so ex-pensive that many organizations developed only one or two marketing pieces and then printed four million of them (to get the unit cost down). This resulted in a one-size-fits-all design, as well as an inherent risk of be-coming quickly outdated. ("We won't reprint the brochure until we use up all the ones we have!") What changes? Service arrays, web site addresses, and telephone area codes for starters.

By developing your own materials using preformatted templates in Microsoft Word or WordPerfect, you can focus on individual markets and on individual services or service sets. For example, you might well have a brochure (I use the term loosely to mean any printed material) de-signed for foundations, one for government funders, one for just referral sources, and one for donors (or two or three for different kinds of donors). In terms of services, you might have brochures designed differently if you provide services to adults and children, or small children as opposed to teenagers.

And, you can do this quickly, since some of the material (logo, ad-dress, e-mail, phone, and even some text) can be used in more than one brochure. Focus, focus, focus in your marketing, and this means in your marketing materials, too.

2. Cost

Repeat after me: I can do it myself. I can do it myself. I can do it myself. And yes, you can. Even if you are not a tech wizard, or a gifted artist, and even if you are way too busy (who isn't in our sector?), you can do it your-self and save major money.

☞ **HANDS-ON:** Here's a money-saving tip: Want a free printer? A *good* free printer? Go to *www.colorfreeprinters.com* and fill out the form. If you qualify—you have to be doing enough printing per month—Xerox will send you the printer. You *do* have to buy the toner cartridges, so check this out carefully. You may find that buying a $100 to $200 inkjet is a better deal.

3. Flexibility

In Chapter 9, I told you to have specific names, phone numbers (with ex-tensions), and individual e-mail addresses for people to contact printed in your material. So what happens when that person leaves or changes phone numbers, or you get a toll-free number, or your e-mail addresses all change? If you have printed 10,000 copies of your brochure, you either doom people to try to contact you at an outdated number or e-mail address, or in the best case, you have someone, by hand, cross out the old information and write in the new, which looks, well, tacky and outdated.

The same holds true for changes in services, or in your mission state-ment, or for getting up-to-date pictures, etc. When you print your own ma-terials, you can change this information very quickly, and since you only need to print 10 or 100 at a time, you can avoid having out-of-date and thus misleading information be the first point of contact for your customers. Remember that—the first point of contact. What did your mother tell you? That's right, mine did too: "You can only make a first impression once." Our moms were right.

Here are some steps to take to begin working on your own materials.

1. Check your software. Whatever word processor you use, get the latest version, and make sure you have enough memory (RAM) and enough hard drive space to run the program. If you want to go for a higher-end look, you can buy specific graphics design pro-grams, but many of these are for professionals, and they are ex-pensive. For most, but not all, of my clients, the hundreds of pre-formatted templates in Microsoft Word and/or WordPerfect are plenty, and you can download lots of templates from the manu-facturers' web sites as well.

2. At whatever computer you will be doing the design work, get a larger screen (monitor), at least 15″. This will result in better work

and much, much less eyestrain for whoever is doing your design and layout work.

> ☞ HANDS-ON: Be smart here. By the time you buy a monitor and upgrade one of your computers, you may well be in the price range of buying a whole system, complete with a printer. At the time of this writing, there were many advertised systems with lots of RAM and excellent inkjet printers available for $700 to $1,000 and, of course, everything works with everything else, and you get the latest version of Word. Make sure you have enough RAM, a fast enough chip, a good quality (15″ minimum) screen, and a read/write (R/W) CD-ROM drive—your files will be big enough that you will want to store them on CDs—and perhaps take them out to be printed (see point 6 below). Do the math first!

3. Check your printer. Is it capable of printing at 1200 dpi (dots per inch)? Most new inkjet printers can. And they are cheap—under $200 for most, although cartridges can be expensive. Go to your local computer stores and print out samples from different printers, and compare them. Remember, you will be printing text, logos, and photos, so see examples of all three.

4. Go to an office store and look at the preprinted, predesigned stationery for posters, single sheet. You will be amazed at the selection, and you may want to get samples to discuss with your marketing team. Make sure that the paper is formatted to work with your software (most software has reference numbers for certain kinds of labels and stationery). At this point, you are just looking around to see your options. You don't need to decide right now. Look, make notes, take samples, and compare them to the preformatted templates in your software.

5. Check your expertise—board, in your volunteer group, on your staff. Find out who knows your software well, and who has good design or artistic skills. Then, go to a class, online or in town, on software use that focuses on brochure and printed materials development. (Also check the web sites listed in Chapter 13.)

6. Go to your quick-print shops (Kinko's, for example). At nearly all of these places, you can bring in a CD with your work and they can print it out faster, on higher-quality paper, and, of course, with very expensive printers. You should check out this option now, and save it for special needs. Again, most things you will print can be done fine on a good quality inkjet printer.

7. Now, get together with your marketing team and talk through how you are going to develop marketing materials, get the common look we discussed in the last chapter, and which printed pieces will be for which markets.

Finally, remember the do's and don'ts that we covered in Chapter 9. When you are doing your own materials, they are very important. I'll just list them here, and you can go back to the full discussion in Sections C and D in Chapter 9. Here they are, seven common items to make sure that you keep out of your material.

1. Jargon
2. Inappropriate photos
3. Lack of focus
4. Asking for money
5. A history lesson
6. Being out of date
7. Being boring

I won't mislead you and say that better materials are "just a click away," but you *can* do this better, cheaper, faster, and with more focus and flexibility.

E. DEVELOPMENT

If you are the person in charge of development for your organization and you are successful in the current environment, you are using technology, at least to some extent. Whether in printed media, your web site, software, e-mail, automated mailings, or just staying in touch with potential donors or long-time supporters by cell phone on the road, tech has changed the face of fund raising. Again here, there is no substitute for the basics of fund raising: a good mission, a good message, and, most important, a good "ask." But even organizations that do those basic things well can lose their competitive standing if they don't use tech well. Let's run through some of the key things of interest to the development professional in the area of technology.

Your Web Site

If you have a development function, you simply have to include the ability for people to donate to you online by credit card. If you don't do much fund raising, perhaps this can wait, but if more than $1,000 or 1 percent of your total income (whichever is smaller) comes from individual donations, do this now. Why? Because people are trying to donate to you online—perhaps even as you read this.

❑ **FOR EXAMPLE:** In our house, we have a coffee can by the door into which everyone drops his or her loose change. Once a month someone counts the change, and then at dinner the five of us talk through which charity will get the money. Sometimes people clip things from the paper to remind us about particular needs, other times we respond to things that are close to our particular interests. After this discussion, it falls to me to write the check and an accompanying letter to the recipient organization. In late 2000, our eldest son, Ben, who is the house techie, asked me why I bother with a check and a letter, when I can give online. Well, duh. So, since then, I have been trying (and often not succeeding) to give our donations online. I am appalled at how many national and even international organizations have either no capability to accept donations online, or a process that is so poorly designed that it is either hopelessly confusing, or incredibly time-consuming, or both. Actually, the best-designed donation options I have seen are developed (no pun intended) by local organizations. Think about it. If I am cruising to your site, after reading about a wonderful thing you have done in the paper with the intent of making a donation—what will I find?

☞ **HANDS-ON:** As of this writing, I am not impressed at all with the collective donation sites on the net. These are places where you can list your organization, and any donations will come to you, minus, of course, a small fee. The literature on this, although preliminary, is not good, and my anecdotal evidence from my client organizations and people who come to my training sessions is disappointing, to say the least. The rationale to join these groups, at least as far as I can tell, is to avoid having to pay credit card fees, and set up the donation capability on your web site. These costs are not that big, certainly not for an organization with a significant development component.

There are a number of web sites and firms that will help you with this, and it is a component of some (but not all) development software. Check with your peer groups (just go to their web sites and see what they are doing), and with your state and national association. They may well have printed, online, or live educational material on this issue. Check your own Internet service provider (ISP) to see if they provide this service (sometimes for free) for charitable organizations.

Make sure that the opportunity to give is prominent (but not overpowering) on your web site's opening page. Make sure to have an automatic e-mail acknowledgement of the donation sent to the donor. And, track your success in this area. Use your e-mail lists, your online and printed newsletter, and your printed development materials to let people know that they can donate online. Your cost for this will be mostly the cost of taking credit cards, and the individual transaction fees that the card companies charge. But it is a rapidly increasing method of donating, and it is one that serious development professionals cannot afford to neglect.

Web sites are also an excellent place to offer educational materials on ways to donate with bequests, trusts, stocks, your endowment, and other donation methods that need a more detailed explanation than a simple cash or check donation. You can also provide information on your organization's finances, administrative component, and the outcomes you achieve in the community in your development area, to help convince an online donor to make that gift! Remember, too, to have clearly listed names, phone number and e-mails of the person or people to call if a donor wants more information.

E-Mail

Donor lists, e-mail reminders of your big fund-raisers, reminders about bequests and trust development educational activities—these are just some of the benefits of having a good e-mail program that is tied to your development software. To make this work well, you need an individual e-mail address for whoever is in charge of your development office. People will respond more openly and confidently to a specific donation address. With many ISPs, multiple addresses can be forwarded to a single person, but the "TO" part of the e-mail alerts the recipient to the issue contained in the e-mail. For example, if you subscribe to my online newsletter, you send an e-mail to *subscribe@missionbased.com.* That e-mail is forwarded to my personal e-mail, which is *peter@missionbased.com,* but whenever I see an e-mail addressed to "subscribe," I know what it is about. My ISP does not charge me for this option. Again, talk to your peer organizations about how they are using e-mail to improve their development efforts.

Printed Materials

We covered this in detail in the previous section and in Chapter 9, but I just want to reiterate that you need to focus, focus, focus, including in the development area. Thus, you may well decide to have separate printed materials for separate areas of your development work, such as donated goods, annual giving, endowment, deferred giving, etc.

Software

Just get your hands on a copy of the *Chronicle of Philanthropy*, and look at the advertisements for software related to development. There is software to help you with direct mail, software to help you with special events (such as auctions, or charity golf outings), software to manage capital campaigns, and software that claims to do all of this and more. I am not an expert in this kind of software, nor do I do development work, but you don't have to be an expert to see the benefit of using this kind of technology to enhance your development efforts, improve your accounting and tracking, and ease the tedious record keeping workload. As with all software, download a demo, get references, see what your peers are using, and read the reviews. Go to meetings of your local Association of Fundraising Professionals chapter formerly the National Society of Fund Raising Executives and ask around about what software works best.

Development is certainly one of the areas of marketing that is most prone to a technology turbocharging. Tech may even make it feasible for your organization to ramp up its fund-raising efforts.

F. NEWSLETTERS ONLINE

One of the things I told you earlier when we discussed your web site(s) was the opportunity to use your site, in part, as a tool for continuing education of the people you serve. Newsletters also offer that opportunity; you can and should always have some educational information in your publications, combined with resources for further study. I have seen way too many print newsletters that just talk about the events of the past week or month, and pass up a great chance to inform their readers more about the issues of importance to the organization.

Online newsletters are a great inexpensive way to achieve the following marketing outcomes: keeping your organization's name, logo, and information in front of your best customers regularly; informing the reader about upcoming meetings, events, dates, and issues; and educating your reader on key issues of importance. Using an e-mail to announce the availability of the newsletter, and a Web page template to produce the publication every month, or every quarter, can be an excellent supplement to a printed newsletter. It may even replace it if your clientele is all online, saving you printing and postage costs. You can drop in digital pictures, add links to other sites of interest, and archive the newsletters for future reference.

Take a look at the newsletters at *zdnet.com* and *about.com* and my monthly publication, the *Mission-Based Management Newsletter.* When you subscribe, you get a monthly e-mail. The e-mail links you to the entire newsletter, or to a specific subject. You can make your own web site, or use dozens of newsletter templates included in Microsoft Word, Microsoft Publisher, WordPerfect, or any of dozens of other publishing programs.

Remember to give your readers the opportunity to subscribe and to get off your mailing list.

☞ **HANDS-ON:** Here's a quick hint for your e-mail mailing list, whether or not you use it for your newsletter. When you mail to a large list, *do not* simply cut and paste into either the **TO:** area or the **CC:** area. That results in those e-mails you get with way too many addresses in the header. What you do is send the e-mail to one person, perhaps even yourself, but have all your mailing list addresses in your **BCC:** area. That will keep your recipients much happier!

RECAP

In this chapter, we have armed you with the best that technology (at the time of our publication) has to offer your marketing effort. More importantly, I hope that we raised your awareness regarding all the good things that tech can help you with as you find your markets, ask them what they want, and try to meet those wants.

First, we ran through a list of marketing issues that are affected by new technology. Then we spent some time looking at the issue of asking online, through surveys, and through your web site. We moved to a closer study of how to improve your web site(s), including having specific areas for your board and staff, and making sure you can accept donations online. We spent the next few pages identifying ways that tech can help make your printed materials more focused, more timely, and less expensive. We looked at the tech/development interface, including software, e-mail, and web site issues, and finished with a quick examination of the opportunity for online newsletters.

Technology can be a marketing enhancer, but I cannot emphasize enough times that it can never be a substitute for a marketing orientation among the staff, a belief that asking and listening is a way to improve services, and a commitment to overall customer satisfaction for all your varied customers

---

Discussion Questions for Chapter 10

1. Do we use technology well in our pursuit of marketing?
2. Are there ways we can keep in touch with our markets better through e-mail?

3. Should we develop/expand an electronic newsletter?
4. What can we do better on our web site? Should we have dedicated areas of the site for staff, board, and volunteers?
5. Can and should we offer the opportunity for donations online? Why or why not?
6. Do we have the software, hardware, and knowledge to try doing our own marketing materials? Can we go to some workshops on this issue and give it a try? How much do we spend a year on printing now? Could we cut that significantly?
7. Are there better ways to survey and track the data we gather? Can we use off-the-shelf software, spreadsheets, or other tools to use the data better?
8. What regular research do we do on our competition? Can we do more online?

11

Incredible Customer Service

OVERVIEW

In a monopoly, you can treat your customers in whatever way you want, and they will still stay as customers. Why? Because they don't have any choice. If you are the only game in town, they have to use you. But in today's competitive environment you must appeal to customer wants and give exceptional, even incredible, customer service to stand out from your competition.

We can all rattle off organizations that do this. Why? Because, as customers, they are a positive experience that we don't soon forget. Nordstrom, Amazon, Lands' End, Dell, Marriott, and Federal Express are all

---

CHAPTER THUMBNAIL

- ➤ Three Customer Service Rules
- ➤ The Customer Is Not Always Right, but the Customer Is Always the Customer
- ➤ Customers Never Have Problems; They Always Have Crises, So Fix the Problem *Now*
- ➤ Never Settle for Good Customer Service—Seek Total Customer Satisfaction
- ➤ The Unhappy Customer
- ➤ Regular Customer Contact
- ➤ Turning Customers into Referral Sources

---

examples of organizations where exceptional customer service is the *minimal* standard from day to day and from employee to employee.

In this chapter I will show you many examples of incredible service and some tangible ways to make your organization a place where customers are more than just pleased with you. First, we'll look at the issue we touched on in Chapter 6, how to treat everyone, even your funders, like a valued customer. The attitude in your organization from top to bottom, from staff to volunteer, has to be that the people outside the organization are always customers. I'll show you how to instill that philosophy and the things that result when you do.

To treat people well and to solve their problems, you need to solve them *quickly*. Since you cannot be everywhere at once, and since problems can and do occur at any time, you need to empower your staff to make the problem right. For some readers this is a really scary idea, and I'll show you how to implement it with the least pain and risk. We'll go over the rules of customer service, and look at ways to use marketing and customer service to do more mission, using a concept I call *compassionate urgency.*

Compassionate urgency helps us when we look at our next issue: solving customers' problems, solving them promptly, and showing we care. I'll also show you here why it is important not to settle for customer service, but to seek total customer satisfaction. And, I'll show you six rules for how to deal with the inevitable unhappy customers that, like it or not, will show up on your door, or on the other end of a phone eventually—no matter how good your customer service is.

Next I'll show you how to make and maintain regular contact with your key markets and customers. These regular interactions are the foundation of the communications flow that you want to establish with your customers so that they will tell you their wants and problems.

Finally, I'll take you to the next level. Not only do I want you to have incredible service, not only do I want you to solve customers' problems with an empowered staff, but I also want you to take your good customers and turn them into referral sources—ones that continually send you new customers. Sound like fun? I'll show you how to play the game.

By the end of this chapter you should have a very good idea of how to improve the standards of customer service in your organization, the reasons why it is so important, and some techniques to apply right away to empower your staff and work toward a new level of incredible results for your markets.

A. THREE CUSTOMER SERVICE RULES

I've said this only about 20 times so far, but it can't be said enough: Your environment today requires that you, your staff, and your volunteers treat everyone well, everyone like a customer, even though you may have ever thought of them as anything but the enemy. You simply have to treat everyone—staff, board, volunteers, service recipients, and funders—like a customer if you are going to succeed as an organization in today's economic and political reality.

We discussed everyone as a customer a bit in Chapter 2 and at more length in Chapter 6, but it is so important (and so often ignored by not-for-profits) that I want to go through it again, this time with some ideas for how to bring your staff and board along for the ride. Let's review the three core rules of excellent services to all of your customers:

1. The customer is not always right, but the customer is always the customer—so fix the problem.
2. Customers never have problems; they always have crises, so fix the problem *now*.
3. Never settle for good customer service. You should always seek total customer *satisfaction*.

Success in the area of customer service (and customer satisfaction!) starts with those three statements. Not, of course, with just making the statements, but with believing them, and with structuring your organization to accommodate to them.

First, of course, you must look at *everyone* as a customer. I know that this is a real stretch for many readers, and a nearly insurmountable one for certain staff and board. For you, it may be difficult to think of your board as customers, when they have always seemed like a group of nice, but sometime meddlesome, burdens. It may be tough to equate staff, who you are supposed to monitor, supervise, and (sometimes) discipline, as customers. It may be a challenge to think of a funder as a customer at all, particularly if you have spent the past 15 years fighting with them over regulations, funding criteria, and oversight.

But they all *are* customers. That is why they made the list of key markets in Chapter 6. You can choose to treat them as such and have a much higher likelihood of success. Or, you can treat them like you always have and increase your troubles markedly. I will assume for the rest of the chapter, in fact for the rest of the book, that you will make the effort for the benefit of your organization and of the people you serve.

So, everyone is the customer, and the customer can make mistakes, but the customer is still and always the customer. Sometimes they are happy, sometimes not.

Let's look at each of the rules in much more detail:

B. THE CUSTOMER IS NOT ALWAYS RIGHT, BUT THE CUSTOMER IS ALWAYS THE CUSTOMER, SO FIX THE PROBLEM

Really, we get back to good management here. After nearly three decades in nonprofit management and consulting, I know the single most important thing managers need to do with their staff is to *always tell them the truth.* This does not mean that you need to tell your staff everything, but it does mean that *everything you tell them must be absolutely fact, no exceptions, no exaggerations, no talking the talk and not walking the walk.* What does that have to do with marketing? Lots, and here it impacts the way we motivate our staff. The old adage that "The customer is always right" is patently false, and we all know it. All of us know that we are not perfect. We all make mistakes. We also know that we are customers for many organizations and businesses. Thus, as customers, we are fallible. Your customers are the same: imperfect. In organizations that continue to tell their staff the old fable that the customer is always right, I have seen tremendous resentment against both management *and customers* build in employees. To say the least, this is counterproductive. A much more sensible way to look at it is that even though they may be wrong at times, their perspective is what counts. They *are* the customer, so make it right.

Taking this attitude with staff encourages them to overcome their natural resentment toward a customer who whines, or complains inappropriately, but it also lets *them* know that *you* understand what they are going through and dealing with.

C. CUSTOMERS NEVER HAVE PROBLEMS; THEY ALWAYS HAVE CRISES, SO FIX THE PROBLEM *NOW*

This can be the most mission-driven part of the three-part customer service maxim. From the customer's perspective, if they have a problem, it is not mundane, it is not run-of-the-mill, it is one-of-a-kind, it is theirs. If you or your staff, simply because you see this certain kind of problem all the time, treat it as no big deal, you will not address it quickly or with the empathy it deserves. We have all experienced this personally from the point of view of the customer.

❏ **FOR EXAMPLE:** You wake up feeling awful. You have a headache, fever, chills, achy joints, runny nose, and a cough. You make the decision to stay home, and then wait for 9 AM when your doctor's office staff gets in to call a nurse. At 9:02 you talk to the receptionist, give her your symptoms and say that you want to talk to a nurse. The receptionist assures you that one will call you as soon as possible. You hang up. And wait. And wait. And WAIT.

The receptionist and the nurse have had 300 calls for this kind of ailment in the past two days, and yours is just number 301. Your illness is not life-threatening, the treatment is what you are already doing (rest, fluids, pain reliever), so from their perspective it is not critical to call back immediately. They have bigger problems, such as the 10 people who just showed up unannounced asking to be seen as soon as possible (probably suffering from the same bug as you). Your call can wait.

Back at home, you are still feeling awful. You look at the clock every five minutes wondering: "Where the heck is that nurse?" By noon you are really angry, and by 1:00 PM you call back to find that the nurse is on her lunch break. Now you are both sick *and* really mad. It doesn't matter that the nurse is pleasant, sympathetic, and helpful when she does call at 4:30 PM. You are too angry to appreciate it.

❑ FOR EXAMPLE: Once you get well, you decide it is time to get a new clock. (You got sick of looking at it when you were waiting for the nurse to call.) You go to a local department store, find one that will look perfect in your home, and take it home. When you put the batteries in and put it on the wall, you find that it keeps double time, moving two hours for every 60 minutes. You take it down, get the receipt, box, and bag and return to the store, going up to the RETURN/CUSTOMER SERVICE counter. There is one person behind the counter and two people ahead of you. You wait. The counter staff person is friendly and helpful, but the first person is simply angry and wants to spout off for 10 minutes or so. You wait. You see another staff person on break in back of the counter and wonder why they can't help you. You wait. You finally are next in line, and the person waiting on you pushes a form in front of you to fill out that takes 10 full minutes to complete and seems more like an inquisition than simple information. You leave very frustrated at the 25-minute exchange. All you wanted was a working clock.

❑ FOR EXAMPLE: You pull in to a gas station with a car that is running rough. The service manager listens to the engine and says, "Yeah, you need a tune-up. Take about 45 minutes." Of course, it takes two hours, since they need a coffee break, there are customers for fuel, etc.

In all of these examples the problem (illness, a return, a broken car) were made worse by the attitude of the employee. In every case, their attitude was natural and understandable. And wrong. The nurse heard dozens of such calls every day, knew that there was no life-threatening issue, and made a professional judgment that medical professionals call triage. She ignored (or had never been trained about) the fact that you, from your perspective, were SICK. You didn't do this dozens of times every day, and you wanted a little assurance that you weren't going to die.

The entire methodology of returns when the clock was brought back was a mess. Many customer service counters in "customer-friendly" stores are now over-staffed, just so that people won't have to wait to get their refund or exchange. Why? Because someone finally figured out that the customer is already put out, so why make him or her madder by putting them through the third degree? I regularly go to customer service counters now to exchange something, and the service staff person will say, "Do you want another item like this? Do you want one of our people to get it, or do you want to select it yourself? Just bring it back up here, I'll stamp it and you will be on your way!" Or, if it is a return for cash, it takes 45 seconds. They recognize that I want to be on my way *now!*

The service station sees poorly tuned cars all the time. What the manager forgot was that not only is the customer's time important, so are promises. She promised 45 minutes and that became the "contract." Additionally, when your car is broken, or at least up on a lift, many of us feel truly stranded, thus aggravating the frustration and impotence that we have in the situation.

In all of these cases, the *perspective of the customer* that we discussed earlier had not been trained and regularly reinforced. You may see 50 sick people today, but their illness is their only one. You may have 150 irrational customers returning things, but what they want is to (a) gripe, and (b) get their money or a working product. Do both and soon. You may see cars like this all the time, but we need to get the customer on her way as soon as possible.

And here is the mission-driven part of this: For all the people that seek services we need to have that sense of *compassionate urgency* I talked about earlier. We can't let the fact that we've helped 500 or 50,000 people with the same problem before make us take any customer, patient, student, parent, parishioner, or other user of our services for granted.

❏ **FOR EXAMPLE:** The best single illustration of this that I have ever seen is a television commercial for our local hospital-based cardiac unit. The commercial is pretty standard, with a physician telling you why the unit is so good, a few visuals of the high-tech environment, etc. The cardiologist who does the commercial is a friend of mine and, after I saw the commercial the first time, I asked him whether the tag line I liked so much was his creation, or some marketing consultant's. "No," he said "that is something we say every day in our staff meeting." And the line? "We need to remember that *what we do every day* here is a *once-in-a-lifetime experience* for our patients."

I have never seen it put better. Good marketing is good mission. Your customers have to know you care, and that you care about them, their issue, their family, their problem. And if they do, they will return for more services, and send others as well.

Now you know that every customer problem is a crisis, not just a problem. You may feel that you solve customer concerns quickly and efficiently, but does everyone else? You may feel that they do, and here is the test. Ask yourself this: When I am out of town for two or three days, or on vacation for a week, things break, stuff goes wrong, customers have problems. What happens then? Do my staff fix the problems, or do they wait for me to come back?

If you have told staff to fix customers' problems, do you then upbraid them about their solution? If so, they won't take such a risk again, and your customer will be poorly served. Staff must be empowered to fix customers' problems. They must be coached, encouraged, shown how, and then entrusted to fix things when Mr. Murphy arrives, because he will.

❏ **FOR EXAMPLE:** All staff of Ritz-Carlton Hotels have the authority to spend up to $2,000 (as of this writing) on the spot to fix any problem that a guest brings to their attention. All staff: housekeeping, maintenance, front office, and security.

❏ **FOR EXAMPLE:** Lands' End Catalog is a business where 95 percent of the customers are never met in person by the staff. No chance to smile, to shake a hand, to look concerned. Yet whenever I call, I am always made to feel welcome, like an honored guest or even an old friend. And the staff will fix *any* problem I have with clothing, even after I have worn it and washed it a few times. "Send it back, Mr. Brinckerhoff, and we'll send you a replacement, credit your account, and we'll also pay for the shipping."

❏ **FOR EXAMPLE:** I once arrived at a Marriott Hotel at 2 AM with the mistaken idea that I had a reservation. The hotel was sold out, and it turned out that my reservation was at a Marriott on the other side of the same city. What did the clerk do? Did he say to himself, "This guy is an idiot. We're full. Let him take a cab to the other hotel"? He could have. But no, he saw a customer with a problem/crisis. It was 2 AM. His hotel was full, but he did have the Presidential Suite available. The president hadn't shown up yet, so he let me use an exorbitantly expensive room for $139. He solved my problem. At other hotel chains, he probably would have been reprimanded, if not fired. At Marriott he got commended for helping a customer who, by the way, has told that story to literally tens of thousands of people, since Marriott empowers its people.

The bottom line question here is: Do you really *empower* your staff to fix problems or just tell them to and then not support them? Empowerment means to delegate *and* support staff in their customer relations. It means that customer satisfaction is an organizational priority for everyone, and that you, as a supervisor, will go just as far to support a staff person in their customer relations as you will to actually satisfy the customer.

And let's face it. This is risky. All delegation is. But you need to have the attitude that you, as well as everyone else, learn from trying, and often learn best by making mistakes. Just the way competition is risky, so is letting staff fix problems in your absence. But if you encourage innovation, encourage initiative, coach and support your staff, and train them in the outcomes you want, then most people will rise to the occasion. You will find that some, perhaps many, of your staff have different ways of solving a problem, of meeting a want than you do. And often you will find that those solutions are *better* than yours. And that's okay.

Begin or expand your delegation with the understanding that the alternative is much, much more dangerous. If you don't delegate customer service, if you don't make sure that everyone is empowered to fix customer problems, if you make every issue wait for you to intervene personally, you will absolutely be losing customers. A competitive environment doesn't wait for you to personally get involved in every decision. It moves on. Empower your people to fix problems (oops, crises!) and fix them *now.*

D. NEVER SETTLE FOR GOOD CUSTOMER SERVICE—SEEK TOTAL CUSTOMER *SATISFACTION*

If I come up to you to sell my kitchen widget, and I just say, "Look at this widget! It is great! It is cool! It can do anything you need done in the kitchen!" you may buy it, you may not. In fact, I can probably be so obnoxious and persistent that you will give me money to go away. Now, how many times will you let me sell to you? That's right, just once.

But assume I come to you and ask you how you are doing, what's going on in your life, and you tell me you spend too much time in the kitchen. I then whip out my kitchen widget and show you how it saves you time. If you believe my demonstration, you may well buy it, if it shows you enough value. But more importantly, you will let me come back later and try to sell you something else. Why? Because I tried to *solve your problem.*

One of the great secrets of successful marketing is that it is really about how to make people happy with you because you solve a problem that is not of your making. If you ask a lot, ask regularly and *listen,* people will tell you their problems. And if you understand their problems, then you will be able to make the connection between your organization's services and those problems. You can solve those problems, or at least give it a good shot.

☞ **HANDS-ON:** NEVER, EVER, EVER assume that a customer—even one who has intimate knowledge of your organization, its core competencies, and all of its services—can or will connect their problem to your solution. They *may,* but more often, they won't. Don't sit back and wait for them to come to you. Go to them. Ask, listen, respond! This type of asking is best done informally or in focus groups, as we discussed in Chapter 8, and all of your staff need to be part of the culture of asking. I see too many organizations that are stunned when people go elsewhere for services, because "they know about us." Well, perhaps they do, but do they know (or remember) what you can do for them, for their problems? Obviously not.

Solving customer problems also means that you need to learn to look at things from your customers' perspective. How do they view you? How do they see your staff, your board, your buildings? If you only assume what they are thinking, if you say "I know what they need, because I've been here 25 years," you are not going to be getting to the issue: What is the customers' perspective on this?

Paying attention to the perspective of the customer is the corollary of listening to their wants. Incredible customer service starts with trying to be in the customer's shoes, showing that you pay attention to their wants, their issues, their problems. Not paying attention to their perspective is an outgrowth of the not-for-profit marketing disability. Recognizing that the problem is *always* a crisis and attending to it accordingly is essential. Having compassionate urgency is crucial. But looking at things from the customer's eyes will provide you with incredible insights. If you solve problems from your perspective rather than from the customer's perspective, you will solve the wrong problem, or solve the problem wrong.

❏ **FOR EXAMPLE:** In 1991, a good friend of mine became director of a large state child welfare agency, an agency that was under tremendous pressure to improve. Bad things were happening to the children in the agency's care regularly, it was in the paper every day, the federal courts demanded change, and morale was awful.

The new director asked a group of people, including me, to head out and see what was really happening in the field, and we took a number of trips to agency offices where we talked to line staff as well as the people the agency served. We found all kinds of things we could fix easily, and all kinds of problems that would take years to solve. On our first day on the road, we were in a large office in the state's largest city. We had seen staff for about an hour, and walked into the client waiting area. I was with the deputy director, Gary, a really great guy who became and has remained a good friend. As we walked into the waiting area, we saw that over the intake desk was a large set of numbers (think delicatessen) that changed as we approached from 234 to 235. A disembodied voice said "NUMBER 235 . . . NUMBER 235."

Gary went nuts, turned a bright shade of red, and said to me. "That is AWFUL! We are FIXING THAT! We are NOT calling people by number. How disrespectful. We are FIXING THAT!" I told him to calm down, and that I agreed; we needed to fix the problem. We sat down, talked to some people for about an hour, and left.

The next day, the edict went out from the state capitol to all offices: *The numbers come down. Call people by their names. Treat them with respect.* Good idea. Great improvement. Or not.

Four weeks later, I was assigned to go around the state and do what is called "sweep-up" in such change situations. Briefly, you try to find out if the things you tried to change actually happened. I wound up back in the same office, and talked to the staff, finding out that some things had improved, and some had not. Then I walked out, sat down with the clients and started to chat. Pretty soon a *huge* man (and I am not a small person) comes over, gets right up in my face, and says, "Are *you* the fool who took away the numbers?" I admitted as much, and the rest of the people in the waiting room then gathered around and piled on (verbally only, but I admit I wasn't sure that it was going to end there!), telling me that I was an idiot and worse. I told them that the idea was to call them by name to treat them with respect, and they got even more sarcastic about my intelligence. I finally got them calmed down and tried to get them to tell me what the real problem was. They said this:

"When we come in and the ticket we take says 278, and the sign at the end of the room says 134, we know we have time to leave and come back. When you call us by name, we're stuck here. Give us back our numbers."

Ooooh, that hurt. The change that we made—taking down the numbers—was the only one we instituted *without asking people what they wanted.* We *knew* what they needed: respect. What they wanted was freedom! By giving them what they "needed" *we reduced the value of the service.* You gotta ask, you gotta listen, and you gotta pay attention to the perspective of the customer!

Do you pay attention? I hope so. Let's look through some other areas of customer perspective. Do you think through the way you provide services from the customer's point of view? I hope so. Let's look at just a few of those perspectives.

1. Safety

Is the location that you ask a customer to come to safe? Can you make it more so? Do you provide adequate lighting, locks, security, escorts, supervision, or whatever else it takes to make your customers feel secure?

❑ **FOR EXAMPLE:** A number of years ago (under a previous director) my wife and I both had our lockers broken into and items stolen at our local YMCA. After these robberies, I discussed them with other members, and found a widespread concern with security, at least in the 20 or 30 people with whom I spoke. I took these concerns to the executive director, and offered to volunteer for any committee that might be reviewing security and suggesting improvements to the Board of Directors. I told him that other people were concerned, and that if unresolved, the concerns might well affect his membership numbers. The ED's response was, "We dealt with this issue two years ago. There are thieves everywhere. Whoever wants to leave can leave. They'll be back." Not exactly a customer-based perspective.

2. Parking

Is there low-cost (or, better yet, no-cost), easily accessible parking for patrons of your services? Ease of access is very important.

3. Cleanliness

Are your facility and grounds cleaned regularly (and I don't mean annually!). Do they pass the white glove test? Do the lights/HVAC/toilets/phones/vending machines all work? All of this weighs heavily on how people think of you and your organization. This is an investment and an obligation, but all it takes is one cockroach, one backed-up toilet to send some customers ballistic.

4. Ease of Finding Where They Go

Is your facility easy to find? Is it easy to navigate from one area to another? Are there clear signs, or helpful people nearby, or is a visit to your facility like a trek to darkest Africa without a compass?

5. Greetings

Do all of your staff greet all of your customers in a friendly, helpful manner every time they meet them? Are friendly greetings exchanged in the halls, lobby, galleries, or wherever and whenever they interact?

6. Bathrooms

Are they easy to find and easily accessible? Are they CLEAN? Are they safe?

There are many other ways that customers look at your organization, but if they are unhappy with these (or other issues) they will not want to return, or they will tell others about their bad experience. Just like this:

❏ FOR EXAMPLE: I was in Chicago making an all-day presentation at a large, well-known hotel. At the first break, I needed to use the rest room, and I went to the men's room near the conference rooms. I entered a toilet stall, did my business, and looked around for toilet paper. Not only was there no paper, there was no toilet paper holder. Nor was there any indication that there had ever *been* a toilet paper holder. No holes from a torn-out holder. Nothing.

Now what? I am in definite need (and severe want) of toilet paper. I decide to wait for everyone to leave and then scoot into the next stall. But, I guess that about this time another meeting took its break because about 30 men descended on this men's room. Now I'm really stuck, and to make matters worse, I have 75 people waiting for me to return to the podium!

Was I happy? No. Later that morning I went to the front desk to relate the problem, suggesting that they get it fixed immediately. They were, to say the least, unimpressed with my crisis, treating it like just another maintenance problem. This was a major mistake. Since that time, I have probably told 3,000 people that story.

Thus it is very, very important to look at your organization through the eyes of your markets, your customers. That is why you ask and ask and ask. But you also need to make sure here, as in other parts of your asking, that you are truly listening and not merely waiting your turn to talk. Listen and give them what they *want!*

☞ **HANDS-ON:** If you haven't yet used the hands-on suggestion I made earlier, now is a good time. Find a friend who is willing to come in to your organization as a potential customer. Ask them to come in at their convenience and to take notes of everything that they see that they like, and everything that they see that they dislike—even in the slightest way. Pick a friend who you feel will be tough on your organization, and emphasize to them that you want to improve things. After the visit, have your friend list the good and bad parts of the visit and, if he or she is willing, have them do the "debrief" with your marketing team or management team. It will be an eye-opener, I assure you.

E. THE UNHAPPY CUSTOMER

Fortunately, for many of your customers, simply asking regularly will suffice in terms of customer satisfaction, and problem identification and resolution. If you are in regular contact with them, they will tell you about their small problems while they are still small, and not have major issues with you. But about 1 in 10 customers will have a beef with you. And dealing with them, in a courteous, helpful, and ultimately successful manner is a skill that everyone on your staff needs to develop and to practice. Let's look at how to deal with this unhappy, ticked-off customer. Sometimes they are ticked for a valid reason (from your perspective), sometimes not. Remember, the customer is not *always* right. But they are *always* the customer. Thus, you and your staff need some guidance in how to deal with the customer who calls or presents themselves at your office door with a head of steam up. As you read these ideas, think about the last time such a customer vented their wrath on you. How many of these techniques did you use? What happened?

☞ **HANDS-ON:** When dealing with an unhappy customer, follow this checklist:

- *First, listen to their whole complaint.* Do not interrupt, cut them off, or in any way impede them from venting. If they are mad enough to complain, they want their whole say. Don't make them madder by correcting, interrupting, or explaining, at least not until they are through. Let them finish, *then* ask your clarification questions.

- *Second, acknowledge the customer's perspective.* Here there are two possibilities: The customer is correct, and you have messed up, or the customer is wrong, and you haven't. In either case it is crucial that you acknowledge their perspective. First, if the customer is correct, say, "Mr. Jones, it sounds like our mistake. I apologize, and I really appreciate the fact that you took the time to call." Or, the customer is not right, and you say: "Mr. Jones, I understand your frustration and I'm sorry you feel that way. I appreciate your letting us know about the situation." Acknowledge that you heard their problem and sympathize with their feelings. Make sure they know you heard them.

- *Third, ask them what they want.* Here is the place most of us mess up. We offer a solution to an unhappy person without asking *what they want*. Don't. Ask first, "Now, what can we do to make this right with you, Mr. Jones?" and if they don't know what they want, then offer a suggestion. More often that not, they really don't want anything other than to feel better and for the problem not to reoccur. Ask first.

- *Fourth, never make promises you cannot keep.* As helping people, we want to make our customers happy. One way we think we can do that is by giving them *anything* that they want. It makes them happy now, but really unhappy later when we can't deliver. When you say, "We'll have the material mailed to you today," "We'll be able to make your first appointment in a week," or "Check-in for a first-time client only takes 30 minutes," are all of these absolutely true? Can you do what you say, and to the letter? If not, don't say it, and make sure that all of your staff understand this. Here is an area where the person on the line of service can really make headaches for you. Tell your staff: Make only promises you can keep. And, here's a promise that's easy to make, but impossible to keep: "Mr. Jones, I promise this will *never happen again.*" Anyone ever heard of Murphy's Law?

- *Fifth, keep excellent notes.* Particularly if you have a customer problem, keep excellent notes about what was said, who promised whom what and by when, etc. Documentation like this not only protects you, it also *reminds* you of what your obligations are, making it more likely that you will keep your promises, and it provides a means by which you can share the complaint with other staff to ensure that the problem you just dealt with doesn't get repeated elsewhere.

- *Sixth, never assume a customer is happy.* Ask. Measure. Interview. If you do have complaints, call those who complain yourself. This action alone will defuse 90 percent of complaints. But don't wait for them to complain—only 10 percent of people do and the other 90 percent (that don't) tell 10 other people, and *exaggerate their problem.* So get out ahead of the customer problem. Ask, ask, ask.

F. REGULAR CUSTOMER CONTACT

Another crucial part of customer service is regularly checking in with them. By regular contact, particularly for the target group of customers, you will not only learn more about them, but will have the opportunity to see their problems, sometimes as they occur, allowing you to offer a solution, sometimes with just your presence.

❑ FOR EXAMPLE: I regularly touch in with my key customers, just to chat. I don't try to sell, I don't try to tell them about new training sessions I may have developed, or new publications that we may offer. I just call, drop them an e-mail, or drop in and chew the fat for five minutes, or sometimes 15. I ask them what is going on in their lives, in their industry, at their workplace. If they bring up a problem in an area where I have expertise, I will offer some ideas and suggestions on potential solutions.

I *never* sell on these calls. But I get lots of work from them, often on the spot. The reason? Because I am visible and available, and show that I care about them. Highly successful salespeople that I talk to all say the same thing: You have to stay in touch, you have to be visible, you have to be available, and that means the personal interaction.

❑ FOR EXAMPLE: Why do you think your insurance agent calls you on or around your birthday each year? To wish you a happy day? To remind you that you are getting older? No, it's to touch in, and to ask if there are any insurance needs that you might want to discuss.

❑ FOR EXAMPLE: Why do ministers greet their parishioners after services? Why do many make house calls, sometimes unannounced? To catch you being bad? No, to get to know you better, and to be available to help you if they can.

There are a number of parts to keeping in touch with your key customers that I would like you to consider. These are listed below. I do want to point out that I recognize that you don't have time to do all of these for every market, but you should focus on your most important markets, using the 80/20 Rule that we discussed in Chapter 6. Also, remember that a key customer group is your funders. Don't leave them out of your regular contact planning.

1. All Key Markets (Payers, Board, Staff, Volunteers, Clients, Contractors) Should Be Offered the Opportunity to Have Input into the Organization

For example, you can include customers in strategic planning by letting them review a draft of the plan. When you drop by to talk, ask them occasionally for ideas on how to solve one of your problems. Increase their ownership in your organization.

2. Keep Up on Customers' Important Issues

Read widely, and make notes of things that may affect your customers, whether an industry or a family issue. Ask them about it the next time you see them and let them know you understand their issues, their experiences.

3. Tell Them If Things Aren't Fixed Immediately to Call *You*

When there is a problem, let them know that if the normal solutions are not satisfactory, they can come back to you personally. Then, take the initiative and call them yourself to make sure that they are happy.

4. Send a Note Thanking Them for Each Payment

This is a small thing, but easily done. A small postcard can be preprinted to accomplish this.

5. If You Make Guarantees, Make *Sure* You Can Live with Them

Enough said.

6. Make Intermittent "Quality Checks"

Show up or call up and have just one issue: Is everything okay? Make sure that your staff know that you are doing this, and you will get two benefits: fewer mistakes and a customer who knows you are committed to quality.

7. Always Follow Up with a New Customer

For new large markets, a personal greeting and quality check is mandatory, and this is a senior manager's job.

8. Be Pleasant

Even when you are down, tired, frustrated, or sick, work as hard as you can to always be pleasant to others. Remember, you are always a member of the marketing team, and therefore always "on." Smiles, courtesy, and a pleasant attitude will buy you a lot of goodwill—goodwill that you may well need later. And here again is a place for our concept of compassionate urgency.

This is a lot of work, but you want customers to be customers forever. Invest in them and they will repay you tenfold. One of the ways that they will do that is by sending new customers, new clients, new students your way. That is the subject of our next section.

G. TURNING CUSTOMERS INTO REFERRAL SOURCES

How would you like a "free" source of customers? A source where you don't have to sell, make cold calls, send written material, or make a personal visit? Sound good? Well, you too can take advantage of this source: It is your current customer base.

In the previous sections I noted that unhappy customers go and tell people (a lot of people) how unhappy they are. The same is true for happy customers. And it is really true for customers who feel that you are giving them incredible customer service. Thus, if you implement the ideas in this chapter, you should wind up with customers who are happy enough to be willing to send you others. But do you just wait for it to happen, or are there some things you can and should do to move the process along? There are, and I have listed them below.

1. Referrals Are Not Truly "Free"

You need to work for them and work at them. But if you have done a good enough job at customer service, the happy customer is a resource that you should not waste.

2. Don't Be Too Eager with New Customers

One of the most common mistakes I see is people who have a new customer, and they immediately make him or her uncomfortable by asking for references or other referrals. Give a new customer time to experience your organization fully. Additionally, if I call a reference, I usually ask, "How long have you been a customer?" If the answer is "a week," I know that the referral, while perhaps sincere, is not based on such crucial issues as how the vendor solves problems. Be patient.

3. *Always* Ask for Permission to Use a Name as a Reference

Never, ever, use someone's name, or the name of their organization, without permission. Ninety-nine percent of people will happily agree to be a reference, but about half of them will be really ticked if they hear you are spreading their name around without their knowledge or approval. Do you really want to make half of your happiest customers mad? I don't think so.

You can ask for a lot of things in this area, including:

- Other organizations who are potential customers
- Permission to use their name as a referral/reference
- Mentioning your organization to peers
- Names of trade associations that they belong to

All of these things have use to you as you expand your marketing effort.

4. Remember to Meet Referrers' Wants

Your customers are giving you help. Do they want anything in return? Find out. For most people it may just be thanks, but make sure. Some people want their *title* always put with their name, some don't. Ask.

5. *Always* Call or Write a Note of Thanks

I assume that you are tracking where your customers come from. Whenever you find out that you received a referral, call or write a note of thanks. Every time.

Don't ignore the benefits of all the hard work you have put into improving your customer service. Ask for help from your customers in getting more work. Nearly all will be glad to help you. They want you to succeed so that you can be there to provide more services to them.

RECAP

Incredible customer service? Nothing incredible about it. It is an attitude and hard work, consistent application of a few basic rules, and a team effort. But incredible service is something that is achievable, and something that is very important to your marketing effort in a competitive economy. In this chapter I showed you why incredible service is the *minimum* standard to apply in a competitive environment, and that the customer-driven outcome you really want is *customer satisfaction.*

We discussed incredible service, and the issue of solving customers' problems. We reviewed the falsehood that the "customer is always right," but also reviewed the fact that "the customer is *always* the customer." Thus it is essential to fix the problem when it arises, but also to ascertain what the low-key problems in a customer's life are and try to make a connection with your services. We also talked about having all your staff take on an attitude of compassionate urgency when dealing with everyone who seeks services from your organization.

Third, I showed you why it is so essential to empower your staff and to have them able to fix what breaks immediately, not just when you are available to tell them what to do. Fourth, we looked at ways to make and then maintain regular customer contact as both a means of ferreting out small problems before they become big ones and, just as importantly, ways of learning about customers' wants on a regular basis so that you can propose solutions that you or your organization can provide. I noted that this is especially important to do with funders and gave you eight points to make your customer contact more fruitful.

Finally, we talked about how to reap the benefits of incredible customer service by turning your customers into referral sources. I walked you through six ideas on how to get more from your customers and have them have ownership in getting you additional work.

Incredible customer service is the way to keep your existing customer base in an ever more competitive world. It is a standard that more and more not-for-profits are aspiring to, and one that you need to strive for. It is a lot of work, and an investment, but one that will pay off very, very well.

Discussion Questions for Chapter 11

1. Are our staff empowered to fix customers' problems, or do they always rely on us? Do we encourage creativity and reward making customers happy, or do we punish our staff for not asking us?
2. Do we exude an aura of compassionate urgency with everyone who seeks services? How can we do that even better?
3. Do we sell services, or solve problems? Do we ask and then listen, or start with our hand out?
4. Do we regularly see all of our top and targeted customers? How can we

do better in this area? Are the right people visiting these markets in the right way at the best intervals?

5. How much of our work is referral? Do we know who we are getting referrals from? Do we thank them every time? Who else can we encourage to refer to us?

6. Think about the most recent experience with a business (restaurant, service, product, store) you had that was exceptional. What was it? Why was it exceptional? Do you think people go away from our organization feeling that way? How often?

12

A Marketing Planning Process

OVERVIEW

Now we need to put it all together. You have all the philosophical and technical information you need to move your organization toward becoming market-driven and mission-based. But to get from where you are to where you want to go, you need a plan.

Remember earlier, I said that you needed to improve, to change incrementally—1 percent at a time. In that section, I also noted that if those 1-percent changes were not directed by a plan, they could just result in going in circles. It has been said that, without a plan, the only way you get where you are going is by accident. I agree, and you certainly don't want to have the results of all your marketing efforts be haphazard or accidental. You don't want to have one part of your organization target one group of people and ignore another, especially if that second group is the target market for a different part of your organization. You don't want to have multiple "identities" to the public, nor do you want to survey one part of

CHAPTER THUMBNAIL

- ➤ **Developing Your Marketing Team**
- ➤ **An Asking Schedule**
- ➤ **Targeting Your Marketing Effort**
- ➤ **A Marketing Plan Outline**
- ➤ **Marketing Planning Software**

your markets five times, and another not at all. Good marketing planning will allow you to do all the things that you need to in a coordinated, efficient, and, hopefully, effective manner.

This chapter will show you how to begin the planning process. We will start at the beginning, putting together a winning marketing team. I'll make some suggestions on who to pick, how to put the group together, and what their job descriptions should be.

Next, we'll examine how to develop an asking schedule. You may remember that in Chapter 8 on asking, I noted that one of the mistakes people make is in asking too often—or too infrequently. This schedule will help avoid that. But how do you choose which market to ask when? I'll show you. And, it will lead nicely into the third part of this chapter, which will be some practical applications of targeting your marketing. You have already heard me say how you need to focus and target, focus and target. Here, I'll show you how.

Finally, I'll provide you with a fairly detailed outline for a marketing plan, showing you the content areas that I think are essential, as well as an example from a real marketing plan. We will also review how you can integrate your marketing planning into your organizational strategic plan. By the time you are finished with this chapter, you will have a good handle on how to get started with a coordinated, planned marketing effort.

A. DEVELOPING YOUR MARKETING TEAM

I said early in this book that marketing is everyone's job, not just the executive director's or the director of marketing's. Everyone is part of the marketing effort, but not everyone can sit on the committee, or team, that develops and implements your marketing plan.

You do need a team, however, and you need it to be broad-based and with a variety of experience and perspective. You need the team to develop the marketing plans, develop your asking, allocate the marketing portion of your budget, and do the lion's share of the regular customer contact. Let's look at the makeup of the marketing team, and then review its responsibilities. I think you will find that by developing such a team, you will greatly improve the results of your marketing efforts

1. Who Should Be on the Marketing Team?

I always like teams or committees that are broadly based. Thus I do not think that this group should be just board members, nor do I support teams that are only made up of senior management staff. Think of your organizational chart. It has vertical levels (senior management, midmanagement, line staff) and horizontal dimensions (varying programs or areas of service). I have found that a wide representation of your organization both vertically and horizontally benefits everyone the best. You get input from all areas, and grow your future leaders. If you believe me when I tell you that marketing is a team effort, and that everyone is on the marketing team, make sure you put those words into action when you develop the organization's marketing team. So who do I think needs to be involved? These people:

- *CEO.* The top staff person in the organization needs to be involved, at least in the selection of target markets, marketing planning, and other strategic issues. He or she probably shouldn't chair the committee, though.
- *Board Member.* You should ask one or two members of the board to be involved in this critical part of the organization, particularly if you have a board member who is involved in marketing in his or her regular job.
- *Marketing Director.* Whoever on your staff has the core responsibility for marketing should not only be on the committee, but he or she should most likely chair it.
- *Director(s) of Services.* Whether this is one or more staff, the people in charge of your core services need to be part of the asking and the listening!
- *Mid-Level and Line Staff.* You need people from throughout the organization. Many of these people have more direct contact with your customers than senior management, and thus their input is critical. It is also a great staff development experience for them.
- *Outside Expert.* Some organizations find it helpful to have one or two outsiders on the marketing team, almost always people who have specific expertise to offer.

The team should probably not be any larger than ten to twelve people, nor much smaller than five to six. That is the best size for a working group such as this.

2. What Are the Marketing Team's Responsibilities?

Once you gather your group, what do you have to do? The following is a list of outcomes that the marketing team should consider their responsibilities.

- Develop a marketing plan coordinated with the organization strategic plan. This plan should include strategic as well as one-year goals, objectives, and desired outcomes.

- Develop and administer a marketing budget.
- Develop a schedule of organizational asking.
- Develop and keep up-to-date all organizational marketing materials.
- Develop and keep up-to-date the organization "look" and logo.
- Monitor trends in the industry and advise the board and management team as appropriate.
- Implement adequate surveying, focus groups, and interviewing to stay in constant touch with the wants of the markets.
- Sponsor in-house training as appropriate on customer service, marketing, asking, and other related subjects for all staff.
- Keep in regular personal contact with key market segments.
- Regularly train to further their own marketing expertise. Get outside education for team members on surveying, interviewing, market analysis, and materials development. Develop internal expertise.

I know that this sounds like a lot to do, and it is. But if the group meets every two weeks (for two to three hours) for the first six months and then monthly on a permanent basis, there should be adequate time to get it all done. And, to get you jump started, I have broken out some crucial things you need to get accomplished in your first six months.

3. Outcomes for the First Six Months

The following are some suggestions of things that your marketing team can strive for in your first six months.

- *Attain Common Ground.* It is important that you come to common ground on definitions and methods on achieving common goals. I would suggest that you have all team members read this book. If you find it helpful, you can use the *Mission-Based Marketing Discussion Leader's Guide,* which is designed for groups just like your marketing team.
- *Identify Your Target Markets.* Go through the market identification process that you learned about in Chapter 6. Work toward a consensus on who your target markets are.
- *Identify a Contact for Each Target Market.* Where possible, identify an individual at each of your target markets with whom you will keep in regular contact. This is easier for a funder, and more difficult for a target market such as "teenagers" or "nursing home residents," but even within those broad markets there will be representatives, advocates, family members, or others who can fill that role.

- *Assign a Team Member to Each Target Market Segment.* Each member of the team will have at least one (and probably more than one) market to focus on. This will develop into an expertise over time, something you will really want to have.
- *Develop Benchmarks.* Where you can, look at the status of these markets now. In many cases you will already have internal data you can look at. How large is the market? How many customers return? Where are our referrals from? How happy are the markets with us? How many complaints do we get? How much staff or board turnover do we have? What are the levels of customer satisfaction now? All of this information goes into your benchmark setting. These benchmarks will be your starting point for improvement, because if you don't set them now, you won't be able to tell later how far you have come!
- *Develop an Asking Schedule.* See Section B in this chapter for more on how and why to develop an asking schedule. You need to coordinate your asking *now,* not later.
- *Develop a Rough Draft Marketing Plan.* See Section D for more on this. Suffice it to say that in six months you will be pressed to do all of the items above *and* develop a plan, but you can develop some goals and outcomes.

Your marketing team is a crucial component of your overall marketing effort. Choose the people carefully; give them the support and resources (including time away from their other duties) and make marketing a priority for them. Don't try to do this with one or two already overworked staff people. Get a group, motivate it, support it, and have high expectations of it.

B. AN ASKING SCHEDULE

In Chapter 8, I showed you the way to ask your markets regularly what they want. You will remember that there were interviews, surveys, focus groups, and, of course, informal and constant asking. So you know that asking is important, and you know how to do it. But asking, especially with focus groups (and to some extent in surveys) is expensive. How can you get the most out of limited dollars? Also, one of the mistakes some organizations make is asking too much, resulting in bothering (even pestering) their best customers for information that they could have gathered more efficiently in a planned, coordinated manner.

Thus, your marketing team needs to develop a well-coordinated asking schedule, one that includes the timing and content of all of your surveys, focus groups, interviews, and informal asking. It needs to reflect the market priorities established in the plan, as well as the budget realities that constrain you. Remember, you won't be able to ask everyone everything every year. Your budget won't let you, and you don't want to pester. Give your marketing team the authority to plan and approve all organizational asking and you will get more information for your money.

Remember to get information back to the people who need it most—direct providers of services.

❑ **FOR EXAMPLE:** A preschool for inner-city disadvantaged children had instituted a program where all staff (teachers, administrators, cafeteria staff, and receptionists) would constantly be asking everyone they could where they heard of the school and how they felt about the services and the education provided. In doing an assessment of their marketing efforts, I reviewed the data gathered by survey, focus group, and informal interviews. I noted that there was substantial and valuable information gathered by the surveys, the focus groups, and the interviews conducted by the administrators, but very little if any interview data from teachers or cafeteria staff. I asked the teachers whether they were doing the regular informal asking, and they said yes, and that they were taking parent suggestions and implementing them whenever they could. I asked if they were getting any complaints or suggestions about other parts of the organization. They said yes, but hadn't passed them on, since they assumed that the same information was gathered by the administration.

The same scenario was being played out by the receptionist and the food service staff. They all were asking and dealing with ideas, suggestions, or complaints in their work area. Each assumed that any problems brought up regarding other parts of the organization were being heard there as well. The information never was passed on, and it was critical that it should have been. Some serious concerns and some significant opportunities were missed because the information flow was not completed.

Make sure when you ask that the information gets to where it should be. This may mean that a copy of any and all information gathered should come to the marketing team. Or, you may be able to design a routing system that gets the ideas and concerns where they need to be. But, in any event, make sure that you are getting the information that you are paying for!

Now let me show you an example of an asking schedule that incorporates the key elements: who you are asking, when, how often, and in what manner. The example in Exhibit 12-1 is for a church that has extensive outreach, singles, and youth programs, which are their target markets.

Exhibit 12-1 An Asking Schedule

METHOD	MARKET	CYCLE	Deadline for this year
Survey	*Youth*	Every 18 months	February
	New Members	6 months after joining	As needed
	Singles	Every 18 months	June
	General Congregation	Every two years	None
E-mail Input	*20–40 year olds*	Every 6 months	February and August
Focus Group	*Youth*	Annual	One—after survey
	Youth Parents	Annual	One—after survey of youth
	New Members	Annual	Two per year
Interview (formal)			None this year
Interview (informal)	*All*	Ongoing	Ongoing

As you can see from the example, the church has decided to focus this year's work on youth and singles, with a second priority on new members. Even though the survey cycle for the general membership is two years, it won't even be done in the next 12 months. Note also the e-mail input: This is targeted at the parts of the church that are most likely to have and use e-mail. A simple e-mail survey, such as the one we discussed in Chapter 10, would suffice here.

☞ **HANDS-ON:** As I noted in Chapter 8, one of the advantages of asking regularly is that you can measure trends. But how often is often enough? There is a balance between surveying all the time and surveying once a millennium. My general guidelines are these:

- *Staff Surveys:* Every eighteen months—which gives you enough time to implement appropriate suggestions and have them take effect.
- *Consumer Surveys:* Some people survey annually, some every six months. It will depend on your type of services. A school might formally survey the parents and students semiannually, while a symphony might ask its patrons only once in a strategic planning cycle. Generally, I would say annually.
- *Funders:* Annually, or at the end of each funding cycle.

- *Donors:* Every two years, or at the point of the analysis of a large capital campaign.
- *Referrers:* Every six months.

☞ **HANDS-ON:** When you develop asking materials and reports (such as a report of a survey), put right on the cover of the report the date that it was administered *and the date of the next surveying.* For example, if I surveyed staff to ascertain their job satisfaction, I might put down that the survey was completed in June 2003, with a update of the survey due in two years, or June of 2005. By putting the deadline of the update on the report, you are more likely to remember to do the survey again.

An asking schedule will do much to take out unneeded duplication and unnecessary harassment of the people you should value most: your key markets.

C. TARGETING YOUR MARKETING EFFORT

Throughout this book, I have urged you to target many of your marketing efforts on your most crucial markets. We have reviewed the 80/20 Rule a number of times, and its application for your organization. But now you are going to put a plan together, one where you commit your inevitably limited resources to try to do everything for everyone. Some of your marketing team (and your board) will want you to interview everyone, or do focus groups on a certain market segment, or develop promotional material for every tiny niche. Everyone will have their pet idea, their personal priority. How can you do all of this with only so much time and only so much money?

You can't, and thus you need to prioritize and target the most crucial markets and the big-ticket items to get the most for your money and time. Let's look first at what I mean by crucial markets and then at the all-important and all-expensive "big ticket" items.

1. Your Most Crucial Markets

Let's make sure that you and I are on the same wavelength about your most important markets. In Chapter 6 we talked about focusing on the target markets and how the 80/20 method and strategic plan linkage are both important. They still are, and we will review them and add a political consideration for your marketing team to evaluate.

- *80/20 Rule Based on Current Income:* To review, the 80/20 Rule states that 80 percent of your income comes from 20 percent of your customers. Thus it makes excellent empirical sense to focus your marketing efforts on your biggest customers. And, as we learned in Chapter 6, this applies not only to income, but also to your services: 80 percent of your client/student/patient/member/parishioner encounters almost certainly come from just 20 percent of those market groups. So make sure some of your focus goes to that 20 percent.

- *Crucial Future Markets:* On the other hand, many readers feel that they are too dependent on one group, often government, for their ongoing financial well-being. You may be among them, and intent on reducing the percentage of your total income or service encounters from this one group. To do that, you will hopefully not shrink overall, but increase the income and encounters from other groups, groups of customers that may not currently be in your 20 percent club. That means that you should focus a portion of your marketing efforts outside the 20 percent as dictated by your strategic plan. Where do you see opportunities to serve? If you find them outside of your 20 percent, fine! Just remember to allocate your marketing budget accordingly.

- *Markets That Identify with You:* For most not-for-profit organizations, there are customer groups that are a crucial part of their identity. Most parochial schools, for example, take non-Catholic students, but even as the percentage of non-Catholics in the student body grows, the staff would be naive not to continue to market the educational opportunities that the school affords within the Catholic community. Are there markets that truly identify with your organization? For example, in many communities, blood donations are closely related to the American Red Cross. The YMCA is closely associated with swimming safety, and summer camps for youth; the American Cancer Society with cancer awareness, screening, and research. Do you have core markets, ones that are critical to your community image as well as your internal self-image? Even if they are small markets, can you afford not to market to them?

2. Big-Ticket Marketing Items

Big-ticket items are the ones that use up the most time or the most money. They are the ones that you cannot realistically apply to each and every market evenly.

- *Surveys:* Surveys, while they do not have to be exorbitantly expensive, do cost money and really take a lot time. It will be worse for the first cycle of surveying, as you learn to ask the questions in the correct manner and order. If you are surveying regularly (and I hope that you are), repeat cycles should take much less time, but not much less money.

- *Focus Groups:* These are flat-out expensive, costing between $2,000 and $10,000 each, depending on your facilitator, the setting, and the size of the group. This is why most organizations survey first, and then hone in on only the most crucial issues in their focus groups.
- *Personal Contact:* Time, time, time is the cost here. If you follow the ideas that I gave you in Chapter 11, you will see how much of your week this can absorb. Even though you will be spreading the personal contact part of marketing throughout the entire marketing team, this is still a time-costly part of the mix.
- *Marketing Material:* I hope that I made my point in Chapter 9 that marketing materials do not have to be inordinately expensive. But they do cost something, and it probably does not make sense to have specialty items for even the smallest market (unless you expect that segment to grow). But do not just develop a single general-interest piece. Have different material for your different target markets.
- *Your Web Site:* There is, of course, expense involved in maintaining and regularly improving your web site. Let me step back: There *better* be expenses associated with this crucial contact point. Don't accept a free, minimal web site that is just a front page and no more. Today, you need to use your web site as outreach, as an educational forum, as a staff and volunteer recruitment location, and as a place for people to donate funds. You can get volunteer help for some of this (as I told you in Chapter 10), but web sites are far too important to do on the cheap.

As you go about the development of your marketing plan, remember to focus, focus, focus. You and the rest of the team will want to do everything for everyone. You can't, so learn the discipline of focusing.

Speaking of the marketing plan itself, that is our next subject.

D. A MARKETING PLAN OUTLINE

I want to provide you with an outline of a marketing plan that you can use tomorrow as you begin the development of your marketing plan. However, I have seen a lot of plans and I have seen too many that share some common faults. Therefore, before we get into the actual plan contents, I am compelled to provide you with some planning definitions, and my suggestions on what the best marketing plan cycle is. Then I'll show you my suggested outline.

1. Definitions

If you have been in management more than about two hours, you have probably been to a planning workshop or seen an article on planning. That's good. What's *not* good is the 5,578 different definitions that people seem to use for the four core components of a plan; goals, objectives, action steps, and outcome measures. At the risk of becoming number #5,579, here are my stabs at the semantics of planning.

- *Goal:* A goal is a long-term statement of intended outcome. It may or may not be quantified. It may or may not have a deadline. The adjective "long-term" is the most crucial part of the description.

  GOAL EXAMPLE: *The Carter County Ballet will regularly revise its marketing material to demonstrate its ability to meet the wants of its target markets.*

- *Objective:* A shorter-term statement of outcome that supports the goal, has a deadline, has a measurable outcome, and has a person assigned the responsibility for that outcome.

  OBJECTIVE EXAMPLE: *The director of marketing will review, revise, and refresh all printed and electronic marketing material every two years, completing the initial review no later than September 30, 2003.*

- *Action Step:* A short statement of work with a measurable outcome, deadline, and responsible person listed. It must support an objective. These statements are most likely to show up in one-year plans. To most readers they would sound like work plan statements.

  ACTION STEP EXAMPLE: *In June, 2003, the director of marketing will review the target markets and compare the array of marketing materials to ensure that all target markets have material specializing in their wants and needs.*

- *Outcome Measure:* A measurable statement of *real* outcome. Both objectives and action steps need them, but far too many "outcome" measures that I see in plans are really process measures. An example of a process measure as opposed to an outcome measure would be: "Meet with 40 potential donors each month" as opposed to "Secure two donations of at least $1,000 each month." The first measures activity, and while that activity may eventually lead to donations, it doesn't mandate it. It is a process measure. The second statement mandates a real outcome. Don't get caught in the process trap. It will deflate the value of your plan immediately.

These definitions are what I have in mind when I see a plan. The need for deadlines should be obvious: Work expands to fill the time allowed for it. If you don't have a deadline, it will take forever. The need for a person assigned the responsibility is also crucial to a plan that will be actually implemented. If you name a person (as opposed to a committee, or even no one), and if that person has had a chance to review the plan before it is finalized, you have, in essence, a contract that the objective or action step will be achieved. And, in naming the person, they can (and definitely should) be held accountable for the implementation of the objective or action step.

2. The Planning Cycle

One question that is sure to come up with your marketing team as you begin the planning process is this: How long a horizon should the plan have? In other words, what time frame should the plan be written for? There are a lot of different opinions on this, and let me review the advantages and disadvantages of the most common choices organizations make.

- *A Five-Year Plan Written Every Five Years.* I think that five years is far too long to wait to rewrite any plan. Too much changes too fast to wait this long. I agree with a five-year horizon for a strategic plan, however, because I have found that forcing people to think out five years for their goals tears them away from the temptation of the immediate crisis. But for a marketing plan, five years is a bit long.
- *A Three-Year Plan Written Every Three Years.* About right on both the horizon and the rewrite, but is trouble to get detailed enough to give staff and board members guidance week to week or month to month.
- *A One-Year Plan.* We already have work plans. We need a longer-term vision.
- *A Three-Year Plan Written Every Three Years with One-Year Components Done Annually.* Now we're talking. This has the best of both the three-year plan—the long-term view—and the one-year plan—the immediacy of the work. Additionally, by writing the annual portion every 12 months, you can stay up with rapidly changing trends while still being guided by a longer-term view.

Remember as well that you should always coordinate your marketing planning with your organization's strategic plan. If your strategic planning cycle is five years, you may have a challenge getting on a three-year cycle for marketing. But overall, I think that the three-year period for marketing is best.

3. A Marketing Plan Outline

The following outline is intended to give you guidance as your marketing team attacks the planning process. It should ensure that you include all the important parts of a comprehensive marketing plan. The sections noted are in the order that I think is the most effective, but if you feel the need to switch or combine some, fine.

a. Mission statement

I always like to lead with the mission. It reminds both you and your reader who you are and what you are all about. We are talking, after all, about mission-based marketing. If your organization's board of directors has not reviewed your mission statement in the past few years, now is a good time to make sure that it is up-to-date and still relevant to the services you provide and the markets that you serve.

b. Executive summary

This section (which goes first, but should be written last) should *summarize,* not simply repeat the remainder of the plan. Included here should be a *short* description of your organization's markets, services, target markets, a *brief* listing of the core wants of your markets, and a reiteration of at least the goals, and perhaps even the objectives, of the plan. No more. A summary should be just that, a summary.

c. Introduction: Purpose of the plan

Tell the reader why this plan was written, who its intended audience is, how the plan is to be used, what body developed it, and when your board adopted it.

d. Description of markets

Who is it you serve? Where are they? Are they growing or shrinking? What changes are there in your markets? What trends? What is happening in the macroeconomy, on a state or national level, that will affect your markets?

Who is your competition? What do they do better or worse than you do? Put your information in text, tables, charts, or graphs—however you feel you can best communicate your situation.

e. Description of services

What services do you provide now? To what market segments? How many clients/students/customers do you have in each as opposed to five or ten years ago? What growth do you project? What new services are you planning to initiate during the term of the plan?

f. Analysis of market wants

First and foremost, demonstrate that you asked people what they wanted. Did you survey, interview, run focus groups, or ask informally? Then tell the reader what you learned. Finally, discuss how you meet the wants that you identified.

g. Target markets and rationales

From all the markets you described in section d, you have to focus on a few target markets. Tell the reader what those markets are, and provide the rationales for why you chose those markets as opposed to others.

h. Marketing goals and objectives

Goals and objectives should be included in a three-year plan. For the one-year plan, you need to get down to the action step level.

i. Appendices

Whatever "dense" data you feel that you need to support your rationales goes here, as should copies of your marketing surveys and other items that don't need to be in the body of the document. Don't make this part of the plan the thickness of the Los Angeles telephone directory, however. Be reasonable. The vast majority of the people who will read this plan either work for you or are on your board. Thus, if one or two of them want a copy of a survey, focus group report, marketing piece, or market analysis, they can ask for it. Don't burden (literally) every reader with all the arcane documentation you can think of. People don't measure the value of the plan by its weight. If it is too big, they may not read it at all.

4. Examples of Goals and Objectives

The following goals and objectives are actual ones from a rehabilitation center that works with individuals with disabilities in the Midwest. The goal actually comes from their strategic plan, and it proved the core of their eventual marketing plan. What you see below is just part of the plan, and they did an excellent job.

You can see the flow of activity from goal to objective to action step. You can see an assigned agent, a deadline, and a measurable outcome. Use these to compare to your draft goals and objectives. Do they measure up?

GOAL 4: Become a market-driven organization.

   Objective 4-1: Identify and quantify 10 key markets that The Center serves by 10/1/20__ (Director of Communications and Marketing.)

   Action Step 4-1-1: Develop a list of key markets and determine the top 10 markets (4/17/20__ – 6/30/20__; Director of Communications and Marketing).

   Action Step 4-1-2: Research each of the 10 markets to determine how large each market is in our primary service area, how many we serve, and how many need services (1/2/20__ – 3/29/20__; Director of C&M).

   Objective 4-2: Investigate systematically the needs, wants, and preferences of our markets with initial assessment completed no later than June 20__ (Director of Communications and Marketing).

   Action Step 4-2-1: Spend time finding out as much about each of our market's needs, wants, and preferences by conducting focus groups, looking at previously gathered information, talking with individuals, sending questionnaires, and using any other forms of information gathering that we can afford or tap into. This will be done on the following schedule:

   1) Adult consumers—April & May 20__
   2) Vocational rehabilitation counselors & VA referrers—June & July 20__
   3) Parents—August & September 20__
   4) Employers—October & November 20__
   5) Schools—December 20__, January 20__
   6) Doctors—February & March 20__
   7) Other rehab. providers—April & May 20__
   8) Case managers/Health care networks—June & July 20__

9) Influencers/Advocates—August & September 20__
10) Persons with barriers to employment—October & November 20__
(April 20__ – November 20__; Director of C&M, Marketing Manager).

Objective 4-3: Identify 10 key competitors and assess their strengths and weaknesses (1/2/20__ – 3/29/20__; Director of C&M, Marketing Manager, President, Vice President, Vocational & Children's Programs Coordinators).

Action Step 4-3-1: The Center staff make a list of 10 key competitors and what we think are their strengths & weaknesses (1/2/20__ – 1/22/20__; staff named above in objective).

Action Step 4-3-2: Question consumers, referrers, community leaders, board members, and any other appropriate sources to receive their opinions about specific competitors (1/22/20__ – 2/29/20__; Director of C&M, Marketing Manager).

Action Step 4-3-3: Compile information gathered in above two steps in a report which will provide a comprehensive look at The Center's competition which can be used in future marketing decisions (3/1/20__ – 3/22/20__ ;Director of C&M).

As you write your plan, keep in mind the need for outcomes, deadlines, and assigned responsibility. When the goals and objectives are in draft stage, circulate the work and let people comment. Then, complete the entire plan (using the outline provided above) and get the entire board to review, comment, and adopt it.

E. MARKETING PLANNING SOFTWARE

Before you begin your planning you may want to explore the current crop of strategic and marketing planning software. As this book goes the press, the best, most flexible of these is MarketPlan Pro, from PaloAlto software: *www.paloalto.com.* This software walks you through the key questions, and gives you the prompts you need to research the answers you need. It is a business tool, and does have more financial input than you may need, but you can skip that if you like.

However, like all software, what's available, and its features, change and improve regularly. Do a Web search, go to the vendor sites, and download a trial version. Ask for references. See what your peer organizations use. And, check my web site for latest as well: *www.missionbased.com.* Planning software can help, but it doesn't substitute for the hard work and thinking that the plan requires.

RECAP

In this chapter you have learned how to get marketing ideas put into reality: by developing a marketing plan. This plan will be the tool you use to ensure that your organization truly utilizes all the new marketing skills that you have obtained by reading this book. Without the plan, you may or may not.

First, we went over how to assemble your marketing team, including who should be on the team and what their responsibilities should be. I even gave you a list of the things that team should attempt to accomplish in the first six months, although for many groups the list may be a stretch. But you need to set your goals high so that you accomplish more than the minimum.

Then we turned to the development of an asking schedule, and I provided you with a sample template as well as some general guidelines for how often to ask groups such as staff, funders, customers, and referral sources. Next I showed you how to apply the skill that I have repeatedly discussed: focusing on your target markets. This is crucial now that you are about to develop your marketing plan, and I gave you three criteria: the 80/20 Rule, your strategic plan, and markets that identify you, on which to base your prioritization.

Finally, we got to the plan itself. I provided you with definitions of goals, objectives, action plans, and outcomes, as well as an annotated outline that you can use in your planning efforts.

You have learned a lot in reading this book. Now is the time to put that knowledge into action in a coordinated, effective manner. Develop your team and write your plan. It is a lot of work, but the rewards for your organization and for the people you serve will be great. Don't skip the planning. You will regret it if you do.

Discussion Questions for Chapter 12

1. Do we have the right people on our marketing team? Should we add or delete anyone?
2. How can we develop an asking schedule? Should we survey and do focus groups? How can we train staff to ask, ask, ask?
3. What about an information loop? How do we ensure that what the staff hears gets to where it needs to be?
4. Should we develop (update) our marketing plan? By when? Who should be responsible for this?

13

Resources for Marketing

In this final chapter, I have gathered the best resources I can find for you to support your marketing efforts. Here, I have included books, workbooks, web sites, software, and organizations that can help you with surveying, development, your marketing materials and the like.

I have organized the chapter into the following sections:

- Books, Workbooks, Periodicals
- Organizations
- Software
- Web Resources

Each of these areas is further divided by topics appropriate to the area.

ONE OTHER NOTE

The resources for market-driven, mission-based organizations are improving every day. With so many programs in higher education focused on our sector, and so many new publications debuting every month, this list will be outdated the day I submit it to my publisher for the final time. And, web site URLs are notoriously temporary. So, check my web site, *www.mission based.com,* when you get through with this chapter to see what's new since this was written. If you find your own excellent resources, send me an e-mail at peter@missionbased.com and I'll check it out and include it in my links section for others to use.

A. BOOKS, WORKBOOKS, PERIODICALS

Books/Workbooks

Adkins, Val. *Creating Brochures & Booklets.* (Graphic Design Basics). Cincinnati: North Light Books, 1994. ISBN: 0891345175.

Dillman, Don A. *Mail and Internet Surveys: The Tailored Design Method.* 2d ed. New York: John Wiley & Sons, 1999. ISBN: 0471323543.

Fink, Arlene, and Jacqueline B. Kosecoff. *How to Conduct Surveys: A Step by Step Guide.* 2d ed. Thousand Oaks, Calif.: Sage Publications, 1998. ISBN: 0761914099.

Greenbaum, Thomas L. *Moderating Focus Groups: A Practical Guide for Group Facilitation.* Thousand Oaks, Calif.: Sage Publications, 1999. ISBN: 0761920447.

Krueger, Richard A. *Developing Questions for Focus Groups.* Focus Group Kit, vol. 3. Thousand Oaks, Calif.: Sage Publications, 1997. ISBN: 0761908196.

Krueger, Richard A., and Mary Anne Casey. *Focus Groups: A Practical Guide for Applied Research.* 3d ed. Thousand Oaks, Calif.: Sage Publications, 2000. ISBN: 0761920714.

McLeish, Barry L. *Successful Marketing Strategies for Nonprofit Organizations.* Nonprofit Law, Finance, and Management. New York: John Wiley & Sons, 1995. ISBN: 0471105678.

Radtke, Janel M. *Strategic Communications for Nonprofit Organizations: Seven Steps to Creating a Successful Plan.* Nonprofit Law, Finance, and Management Series. New York: John Wiley & Sons, 1998. ISBN: 0471174645.

Schonlau, Matthias, Ronald D. Fricker, and Marc N. Elliott. *Conducting Research Surveys via E-mail and the Web.* Santa Monica, Calif.: Rand Corporation, 2002. ISBN: 0833031104.

Stern, Gary J., and Elana Centor. *Marketing Workbook for Nonprofit Organizations: Develop the Plan.* 2d ed. Vol. 1. Saint Paul, Minn.: Amherst H. Wilder Foundation, 2001. ISBN: 0940069253.

Periodicals

All of these are periodicals about the not-for-profit sector, and have some segment in each issue about marketing or development. You can view them and subscribe to them at the URLs listed below.

www.nptimes.com

www.boardcafe.org
www.philanthropy.com

You can also subscribe to my free monthly e-newsletter that includes a marketing tip each issue. Send an e-mail to subscribe@missionbased.com.

B. ORGANIZATIONS

The Alliance for Nonprofit Management: *www.allianceonline.org*

The trade group of management support organizations and consultants (including marketing) to nonprofits. You can subscribe to the free e-mail newsletter "Pulse" and read the FAQ.

Association of Fundraising Professionals (formerly The National Society of Fund Raising Executives): *www.nsfre.org*

A huge catalog of resources on fund raising is available here. Also a list of courses throughout the country.

The Council on Foundations: *www.cof.org*

There are more than 130 publications on grantmaking and grantseeking available at this site. Info on conferences and workshops is also provided.

The Foundation Center: *www.fdncenter.org*

You'll find information for grantmakers and grantseekers, information on proposal writing, and an online librarian available for e-mail questions. Also a great links page.

Independent Sector: *www.indepsec.org*

A host of information on IS's programs in philanthropy, communications, and the like can be found here.

Management Support Organizations: *www.idealist.org/support_states.html*

Management support organizations (MSOs) are nonprofits that can help you through technical assistance and training, helping you in a wide variety of areas. Some use their own staff, some use volunteer experts. You can find a list of MSOs in your area at the site.

The National Council of Nonprofit Associations: *www.ncna.org*

A network of nearly 40 statewide associations. You can find links to the associations in your state, read some case studies, and subscribe to a tax newsletter.

Society for Nonprofits: *www.danenet.wicip.org/snpo/index.html*

Publisher of *Nonprofit World.* The society page has access to past stories, an FAQ, and links to the Learning Institute for Nonprofit Organizations.

C. SOFTWARE

Marketing Planning Software

Market Plan Pro, Palo Alto Software, *www.paloalto.com*

Development Software

Here's a couple of links to listings of fund-raising software with reviews!

> *www.techsoup.org/articles.cfm?topicid=2&topic=Software*
> *http://nonprofit.about.com/cs/npofrsoftware/index.htm?terms= fundraising+software*

D. WEB RESOURCES

Desktop Publishing

A really good resource on how to do desktop brochure development.

> *http://desktoppub.about.com/cs/brochures*

Free Management Library

An incredibly deep and wide resource. I have highlighted just the link on marketing, but make sure to look around when you are there.

www.mapnp.org/library/mrktng/mrktng.htm

Fund-Raising Resources on the Web

A very thorough site that includes information on software, consultants, organizations, and other resources.

www.agrm.org/dev-trak/links.html

Marketing and Competitor Research

CEO Express is a great start for lots of sites. Scroll down to Marketing and Competitor Research.

www.ceoexpress.com

Nonprofit Marketing

These two links are great places to learn more about marketing ideas and applications on the web.

http://nonprofit.about.com/cs/npomarketing
www.nonprofits.org/npofaq/keywords/2n.html

Printers

This site, run by Xerox, gives high-end printers to organizations who qualify—not by being a not-for-profit, but by having enough volume of copies—and there is always a catch—you have to buy the toner cartridges.

www.freecolorprinters.com

Final Words

You are ready to move ahead. You have the tools, the motivation, the capability to make the journey to becoming a market-based and, yes, still mission-based organization. While the outcome is not assured, the need to do so is unarguable. And, a great number of people are depending on you to take the lead.

As you go through the process, you will meet barriers, and I have tried to give you the ways to avoid, and if unavoidable, surmount them. You will tire; you'll be frustrated and unsure at times. That is completely natural, and, I am sure, part of your daily and weekly work cycle now. I hope that this book has given you not just the tools, but also the motivation to get back up and keep at it. That was my goal in writing it.

The next 10 years will bring unimaginable change to every part of our economy, and our little corner, the not-for-profit world, will be no exception. The not-for-profit players in your community will change drastically year after year, as new organizations spring up and some of the oldest and most tradition-bound fall by the wayside or into mission-impotence from stubborn refusal to see what the community wants and then respond to it. "We've always done things this way" will be the clarion call of the doomed organization, even when what they have done is good, well-intentioned, and charitable.

The people your organization serves depend on you to be there to provide those services to them. You need to depend on them to guide you with their wants, to show you where the opportunities to serve are, and together to move your organization, your mission, and your community to new heights of effectiveness, well-being, and success.

Our country will always need our not-for-profits. It depends on the special kind of people who work and volunteer for such organizations to be the philanthropic cement in our society—the positive role models, the keepers of the faith, the hope, and the charity that have made us a great nation. In 10 years, however, we won't need not-for-profits that look like the ones we count on today. We will need organizations that respond to us as we will be then. Your organization can be such a not-for-profit if you ask, listen, and respond. In doing so, you will do much to ensure your ability to continue doing your mission. Best of luck on your journey. A lot of people are depending on you to make it a successful one.

Appendix A:
Survey Sample

This is a survey that was used by an East Coast rehabilitation center to assess the satisfaction of their clients with services. It was administered by interview in the client's home, so they could get away with having it longer than usual.

Note that the numbers to the left of each question's answers are there to facilitate data entry. This was essentially a closed-choice survey. As you read it you will see that in some cases there is a mixed choice for identifying the respondents. This is because in some cases the person with the disability was the respondent and, in some cases, it was the person's advocate.

Also note that this survey does not have (nor does it need) instructions in the beginning and at the end of the survey. The reason for this is that the survey was administered by interview. If you send out surveys by mail, you *need* the instructions.

Date_____
Client name_____
Parent/guardian name_____
Client's age_____

1. **Who is responding to this questionnaire? (Please circle the number.)**
   4 Consumer
   3 Family member
   2 Guardian
   1 Advocate
   0 Other: _____

2. **Sex of respondent.**
   2 Female
   1 Male

3. Indicate this person's primary disability.
   5 Mental retardation
   4 Cerebral palsy
   3 Epilepsy
   2 Autism
   1 Other: _____
   0 Don't know

4. Where does this person live?
   6 Residential facility   Please describe: _____
   5 Parent's home
   4 Guardian's home
   3 Conservator's home
   2 On his/her own (with residential support)
   1 On his/her own (no support)
   0 Other

5. Do you know what The Center is?
   2 Yes
   1 No
   0 Not sure

6. When did you/_____ (insert name of client) first come in contact with The Center?
   5 Less than 6 months
   4 6 months to 2 years
   3 2 to 5 years
   2 5 to 10 years
   1 More than 10 years
   0 Don't know

7. Do you know your client program coordinator's name?
   2 Yes
   1 No
   0 Don't know

8. How well did your coordinator explain your/_____'s rights and the services available to you?
   4 Explained very well
   3 Explained somewhat
   2 Not well explained
   1 Not explained at all
   0 Don't know

9. **How satisfied are you with the assessment and the services that were recommended for you/_____?**
   5 Very satisfied
   4 Somewhat satisfied
   3 Neutral/It's OK.
   2 Somewhat dissatisfied
   1 Very dissatisfied
   0 Not sure

10. **Do you feel your coordinator is acting on your/_____'s behalf in obtaining services for you?**
    4 Yes, very much
    3 Yes, somewhat
    2 No, not very much
    1 No, not at all
    0 Not sure

11. **What services are you/is _____ receiving as a result of The Center's assessment and referrals?**

    _____

    _____

12. **What providers are currently bringing these services to you/_____?**

    _____

    _____

13. **Does The Center contact you regularly to discuss your/_____'s progress?**
    3 Yes
    2 No
    1 Sometimes
    0 Don't know

14. **Have you contacted The Center about any questions or problems you have had?**
    2 Yes
    1 No
    0 Don't know/Don't remember

15. If YES, how helpful was the coordinator in solving your problems?
5 Very helpful
4 Somewhat helpful
3 Not very helpful
2 Not helpful at all
1 I have not contacted The Center concerning a problem.
0 Don't know/Don't remember

16. When you call The Center with a problem or question, how soon does the client program coordinator respond?
5 Within 24 hours
4 Within 1 week
3 Within 2 weeks
2 More than 2 weeks
1 I have not contacted The Center concerning a problem.
0 Don't know

17. Did you feel this action was fast enough to address your situation?
3 No
2 Yes
1 I have not contacted The Center concerning a problem.
0 Don't know

18. Are you satisfied with the amount of time your case manager spends with you/_____?
5 Very satisfied
4 Somewhat satisfied
3 Neutral/It's OK.
2 Somewhat dissatisfied
1 Very dissatisfied
0 Not sure

19. Have you/has _____ received the assistance you hoped for since you/he/she began working with The Center?
4 Yes, definitely
3 Probably
2 Probably not
1 Definitely not
0 Not sure

20. **Would you refer another person with a disability to The Center?**
    2 Yes
    1 No
    0 Don't know

21. **What 3 things do you think The Center does best?**

    _____

    _____

    _____

22. **What 3 things do you think The Center could do better?**

    _____

    _____

    _____

Appendix B
Focus Group Questions

This set of focus group questions was used by a Midwest rehabilitation organization to assess a potential product that it was planning to manufacture in its sheltered workshop to employ people with disabilities. The people in the focus group were furniture buyers from major stores within a 100-mile radius of the workshop. Included in this focus group was a product demonstration.

Note how the questions are open-ended, and how they move from one subject to the next. Also note that the executive director of the organization was present—which is unusual for most focus groups. He was needed to demonstrate the product and, as he was intimately involved in the product development, to hear ideas from buyers.

1. **Introduction**
   a. Purpose of this session
   b. Thank attendees
   c. Introduce participants
   d. Introduce Executive Director
   e. Introduce facilitator

2. **Futon Demonstration and Observation**

3. **Questions—THE PRODUCT**
   a. What is your overall impression of the product? Will it sell against the competition if competitively priced?
   b. What would you change in this product? How does it compare to others you have seen?
   c. What additional products or accessories might go well with the product?

d. How important are the following product features to gain competitive advantage?

FEATURE	HIGH	MED	LOW
• Quality/species of wood	____	____	____
• Quality, strength, durability of construction	____	____	____
• Fit and finish, appearance	____	____	____
• Ease of assembly and disassembly	____	____	____
• Easy folding mechanism	____	____	____
• Choice of styles	____	____	____
• Choice of stain/color/finish	____	____	____
• Price	____	____	____
• Warranty	____	____	____
• Other _____	____	____	____
• Other _____	____	____	____

4. Questions—THE MARKET

a. What are the trends in your market area over the past 18–24 months?

- Sales levels of futon products?

- Futon styles?

- Number of suppliers?

- Price?

- Quality levels?

- Choices for the consumer?

- Price?

- Types of consumers?

- Changes in distribution methods?

b. Do you have current suppliers of futons?

c. Are you happy with their service, quality, and product options?

Any other suggestions?

Would you consider carrying this product?

<u>THANK YOU FOR COMING!</u>

Index

abortion, 31
access ease, 205, 206
action steps, 225, 229
adaptation, 41–42, 52. *See also* flexibility
advertising, 67, 69, 83–85, 94. *See also*
    sales
  acceptance of, 1
  community visibility, 106, 107
  competitors and, 92–93
  copying, 93
  methods, 83
  targeting, 93
affiliations, 185
affinity cards, 93
agreement, 64
airlines, 57
Alliance for Nonprofit Management, 233
annual cycles, 70
appearance, 62, 71
  of marketing materials, 160–161, 165,
    187
  of wealth, 71–72
arts, 3
asking about wants. *See* market inquiry
assets, 61
Association of Fundraising Professionals,
    192, 233
associations, 4, 111, 127, 143
AT&T, 41–42
attention span, 68
automobiles, 57
availability, 71

bathrooms, 206–207
benchmarks, 219
bidding
  competitive, 4, 70
  information from, 130
board of directors
  changes in, 58
  competition education for, 43–44
  competition for members, 115–116
  competitiveness re, 128–129
  culture change and, 5, 21
  as customers, 110–111
  discussion of change with, 43–46, 50
  e-mail, 177–178
  evaluation interviews with, 85
  informal market inquiry by, 147
  as information source, 128
  as internal market, 98–99
  marketing involvement, 7
  marketing materials for, 170
  marketing team members, 26, 217
  motivating, 8, 30, 46
  need for good members, 98
  web-site areas for, 184
brand loyalty, 56
brochures, 167
  development of, 235
  focused, 163, 186
budgets, 70, 218, 223
buildings, 59–60
business assessments, 81
business skills, 1, 40, 43

capability, 104. *See also* competencies
  checkpoints, 32
  good service, 33
car wash operation, 106–107
cash flow, 61
CEO (chief executive officer), 217
change, 237. *See also* adaptation; flexibility
  ability for, 52
  acceleration of, 1, 52, 59, 67
  behavioral, 67
  costs of, 34
  cultural. *See* culture change
  direction for, 215. *See also* marketing planning process
  effort needed for, 53
  in environment, 62–63
  high impact, 63
  implementing, 64
  incremental, 54, 58, 66, 72, 215
  inevitability of, 45, 53
  large, 66, 72
  leading, 64–67. *See also* change agent
  low impact, 62–63
  to market-driven basis, 40–46
  mission and, 33
  names for, 63–64, 72
  need for, 66
  nonsupporters, 64
  outside organization, 66, 72
  pace of, 67, 73
  plan for, 58, 64
  problems of, 34, 49
  reasons for, 63
  resistance to, 43, 52–54, 58, 65
  in response to customers' wants, 16–17, 153
  reviewing, 58–59, 62
  for sake of change, 63, 71
  small, 54, 58, 62
  steady, 54, 58, 66
  successful, 59
  support for transition, 45–46
  threat from, 61
change agent, 53, 64–67, 72
chief executive officer (CEO), 217
child welfare, 46–47
children's parties, 91

choice, 41–42, 55
  availability of, 73. *See also* monopolies
churches, 22, 26. *See also* religion
civil liberties, 48
cleanliness, 205–206
coaching, 67
  for change, 5, 72
cohort analysis, 136
cohorts, 139
committees, 63, 216
communication, 178, 196
  customer contact, 2, 209–211
community, 114
  as information source, 148
  perception of organization, 39
compassionate urgency, 10, 14, 196, 200–201
  goodwill and, 211
  need for, 203
  in staff, 213
competencies
  core. *See* core competencies
  evaluating, 119. *See also* self-assessment
  in fund-raising, 102
competition, 14, 20–21, 27. *See also* competitors
  areas of, 1, 128–131
  bases of, 92
  benefits from, 90, 94, 134
  choices available, 41–42
  choosing markets for, 123
  discussing, 66, 72
  with for-profits, 4, 92, 93
  for funding, 1, 5, 45, 101
  increase in, 1, 39, 110, 114
  linkage to marketing, 2, 50
  reality of, 43–44
  successful, 45
  trend toward, 3
  underpricing, 81
competitive environment, 67–68, 73
  customer loss in, 108
  customer service in, 195
competitiveness
  characteristics of, 8, 13–15, 27
  financial, 4
  marketing's role in, 6
  need for, 20

perception of, 71
staff buy-in, 21
competitors
  attitude toward, 133–134
  being better than, 19–20, 27, 90
  distinguishing oneself from, 195
  evaluation of, 132, 133
  failed, 44
  for-profits as, 92, 93
  identifying, 2, 9, 114–115, 115–124
  knowing, 19
  learning from, 90–94, 133
  listing, 45
  marketing cycle and, 75, 89–94
  monitoring, 2, 85
  perspectives on, 75, 115
  research by, 126–127
  researching, 119, 124–128, 133, 236
  responding to, 89–90
  studying, 115, 124–131
complaints, 207–209
computers, 71–72. See also software
  ease of use, 57
  hardware, 187–188
consensus, 64
consultants, 43
Continuous Quality Improvement
  (CQI), 54
copyrights, 91
core competencies, 9, 38, 115
  comparison to competitors', 132–133
  focusing on, 40, 131–133
  matching to market wants, 132, 133
cost recovery, 81
costs, comparison of, 125
Council on Foundations, 233
CQI (Continuous Quality Improvement), 54
creaming, 90, 124
credit cards, 189, 190, 191
crises, 198–202, 203
criticism, 66, 72, 149
  expectations re, 151, 155
culture change, 5
  for competitiveness, 21
  flexibility and, 62
  for market inquiry, 16, 131, 135, 147,
    149, 203

from monopoly, 42
outside organization, 68–72
customer orientation, 8
customer satisfaction, 2, 14, 213
  assumptions about, 209
  evaluating, 85
  impact on, 23
  improving, 30, 38–39, 50
  membership, 100
  surveys re. See surveys
  total, 196, 197, 202–205
  voice mail in, 179
customer service, 10, 109–112. See also
  customer satisfaction
  to all markets, 100
  customer contact, 2, 209–211, 213, 224
  customer perspective on, 205–207
  employee attitude toward, 198–200, 213
  excellent, 7, 195–213
  pleasantness in, 211
  problem solving in. See problem
    solving
  promises, 210
  response time, 196, 198–202
  rules, 111, 197–205
  staff empowerment, 201–202, 213
  standards, 109, 213
  telephone answering, 174–175
  testing, 25, 207
  unhappy customers, 207–209
customers. See also markets; needs; wants
  attitude toward, 13. See also customer
    service
  contact with, 2, 209–211, 213, 224
  creaming, 90, 124
  dependence on, 108–109, 237
  devaluing opinions of, 89
  financially important, 108
  follow-up, 210, 211
  governments as, 99–100
  identifying, 2, 18–19
  ignorance of, 25
  internal, 110–111
  issues, 210
  labcls/names for, 19
  listening to, 27
  as market, 97
  as marketing cycle focus, 74

customers (*continued*)
  perceptions, 25, 75, 160
  perspective of, 198–200, 203, 205–207
  pleasing. *See* customer satisfaction
  as referrers, 121, 196, 211–212, 213
  as research sources, 127
  service. *See* service recipients
  sources of, 85
  targeting, 56
  types of, 104
  unhappy, 207–209, 211
customers, treating everyone as, 2, 6, 9,
      109–112. *See also* customer satisfac-
      tion; customer service
  belief in concept, 19, 27, 110, 113, 196
  competitive advantage in, 14, 97, 197
  funders, 18–19
  market identification and, 44
customer/vendor relationship, 70

data, quantitative, 136
day care, 84
deadlines, 229, 230
demand, reducing, 82–83
DePree, Max, 64
*Designing and Conducting Survey Re-
      search: A Comprehensive Guide,* 144
development, organizational, 189–192
distribution, 84, 93, 94
documentation
  of outcomes, 55
  of problem solving, 208
donations, 101–102. *See also* funding
  competition for, 1
  competitiveness re, 129
  online, 176, 189–191
  targeted, 55
donors. *See also* funders
  marketing materials for, 170
  as payer market, 98, 101–102, 118
  power, 55
  repeat, 39
  surveys of, 222
duplication of service, 3, 22

edifice complex, 59–60
education, 4
  re donating, 191
  governments' role in, 4

in-house training, 218
  re not-for-profit sector, 232
  part-time students, 55–56
  road shows, 16–17
  web sites for, 185, 192
efficiency, 38, 39, 50
  incentives for, 54
  in market inquiry, 219
80/20 rule, 96, 107–108, 113, 222
  customer contact, 210
  implications of, 131
  in marketing focus, 222–223
electric power utilities, 42
e-mail, 6, 177–178, 221
  for customer feedback, 181–182
  development program and, 191
  for information gathering, 149–150,
      173, 180–181
  newsletters, 192–193
  for surveys, 136, 150
endowments, 60
entrepreneurship, social, 1, 61
environment, 4
ethics, 31–32. *See also* values
evaluation, 85, 85–86, 94
  of competitors, 132
  of marketing materials, 168
  of web sites, 176
executive summary, 227
expectancy, pace of, 1

failure, 61
family activities, 16
fears, 45, 90, 133–134
financial competitiveness, 4
financial planning, 81
flexibility, 8–9, 14
  financial, 60–61, 72
  limits on, 49
  in marketing materials, 187–189
  mental, 59
  need for, 53, 53–58, 72
  organizational, 59–60, 72
  in response to competition, 91–92
  retaining, 53, 59–64, 73
focus groups, 7, 136, 144–147, 154–155
  analysis of results, 146–147
  compensation for, 146
  cost of, 224

facilitator for, 145
  information best gathered by, 144–145,
    203
  length, 146
  number of, 147
  participant mix, 146
  question focus, 145–146
  question sample, 147, 244–245
  recording, 146
for-profits
  as competitors, 4, 92, 93
  research on, 126, 127
Foundation Center, 233
foundations
  marketing materials for, 170
  as payer market, 98, 100–101, 118
  as research sources, 127, 128
  survey help from, 143
free market, 1, 3–4
funders. *See also* donors; payer markets
  changes in, 58–59
  as customers, 18–19, 27, 111, 197
  evaluation interviews with, 85
  new, 40
  perceptions of organization, 38
  refusing money from, 31
  relationship improvement, 38–39, 50,
    70, 111
  surveys of, 141, 221. *See also* surveys
  wants, 31
funding
  capitated, 77
  competition for, 1, 5, 45, 101
  donations, 101–102
  new, 50
fund-raising, 5
  letters, 167
  marketing's role in, 7
  professional, 102
  software, 235
  technology for, 189–192
  Web resources, 236

goals, 225, 228, 229–230
Gore, Albert, 79
governments
  competition and, 3–4
  dual roles as to, 111–112
  funding bases, 87–88

marketing materials for, 170
  nonunitary nature of, 100
  as payer market, 98, 99–100, 118
grants, competition for, 1
greetings, 206
guarantees, 210
Guidestar.com, 126

health care, 41. *See also* hospitals; managed care
historic preservation, 82
hospitals, 41, 48, 79
hotel industry, 56–57
human services, 4, 54, 87–88
  federal government bidding for, 4
  insurance and, 102
  referral sources, 119, 121

identity, 38. *See also* mission
  maintaining, 29, 35–36
  market groups and, 223
  multiple, 215
  transition, 36
identity drift, 36
image, 39, 50, 161. *See also* appearance
improvements. *See also* change
  from market inquiry results, 151
  as part of marketing cycle, 86
Independent Sector, 233
inertia, overcoming, 53
information, asking for. *See* market
  inquiry
innovation, 14, 61. *See also* flexibility
  in donation requests, 129
  encouraging, 202
insubordination, 64
insurers, 98, 102, 119, 123
internal markets, 97, 98–99, 112
  competition in, 115–117
Internet. *See also* technology; web sites
  access to, 173–174
  for information gathering, 175–176
  for research on competitors, 126

jargon, 158–159, 166
job postings, 177

letterhead, 62
lobbying, 111–112

location, 58, 60, 205
Lockheed Martin, 4
logo, 169

managed care, 34–35, 41, 54–55
management, 64, 198
  library, 235
  tools, 2
management support/service organiza-
    tions (MSOs), 127–128, 143, 233
market analysis, 104, 108–109
market definition, 7, 76–78, 94, 96–113
  census trap, 77, 106
  competitors and, 90
  form for, 97
  funders in, 44
  groups within markets, 103–104
  information from, 131
  by marketing team, 218
  process, 9
  segmenting markets, 96, 105–107,
    112–113
market inquiry, 9–10, 14, 78–79, 94
  analysis of results, 152
  competitors' work, 91
  continuous, 16, 52, 78–79, 127
  culture for, 16, 131, 135, 147, 149, 203
  customer satisfaction from, 38–39
  feedback on, 153
  focus groups. See focus groups
  frequency, 221–222
  ignoring, 88–89
  implementing, 218
  informal asking, 136, 147–149, 155,
    203
  information sharing, 131, 149, 153,
    220
  internal information, 142
  listening to answers, 16, 27, 78, 89,
    151, 155
  as marketing cycle activity, 76
  methods, 78, 136, 218, 219
  mistakes, 150–152, 155
  need for, 154
  online, 136, 149–150, 155, 173
  public relations distinguished, 161–162
  responders' time, 138
  schedule for, 216, 218, 219–222, 231
  service provision information from, 85

surveys. See surveys
technology for, 179–183
use of information, 136, 152–154
value in, 82
re web site, 176
market orientation, 2, 157
market redefinition, 76, 77
market-based organizations, 13–15, 27.
    See also competitiveness
  becoming, 28, 29
  benefits of being, 30, 38–40, 50
  change process, 40–46
  characteristics of, 38
  support for transition, 30, 40
marketing, 27–28
  big-ticket items, 223–224
  as competitive edge, 12, 27
  difficulty in. See marketing disability
  elements/tasks of, 44–45, 88. See also
    marketing cycle
  expertise, 218
  importance of, 6
  linkage to competition, 2, 50
  as mission promotion, 22
  need for, 13
  as process, 2, 74
  promotion distinguished, 156
  resources for, 11, 232–236
  team approach, 2, 5, 7, 22–26, 27. See
    also marketing effort; marketing
    team
  technology assistance in, 174
  Web resources, 236
marketing committee, 169
marketing cycle, 2, 6, 9, 74, 76. See also
    marketing sequence
  activity order in, 75
  application case studies, 86–88
  competitive application of, 117
  competitors and, 89–94
  continuous nature of, 30, 37–38, 50, 86
  customer as center of, 74
  distribution. See distribution; see also
    service delivery
  evaluation, 85–86
  market as beginning of, 75
  market definition/redefinition. See
    market definition
  market inquiry. See market inquiry

pricing. *See* price setting
  as process, 94
promotion. *See* advertising
service design/modification. *See*
  services
marketing director, 217
marketing disability, 17, 24–25, 75, 88–
  89, 94
  customer service and, 110, 112, 203
  market inquiry use and, 151
  overcoming, 103, 135
  service recipients and, 112
  sources of, 158
marketing effort
  attitude for, 20
  inclusiveness of, 22–23, 26, 27
  staff role in, 24, 153
  targeting, 222–224
marketing materials, 7, 10, 84, 156–171
  boring, 164, 168
  comprehensibility of, 158–159
  costs, 160–161, 165, 186–187, 224
  currency of, 167–168
  desktop publishing resources, 235
  developing, 169
  effect on donations, 72
  evaluating, 168
  flexibility in, 187–189
  focused, 164, 167, 169–170, 186, 224
  for fund-raising, 191
  history in, 158, 159–160, 167
  information source listing, 165–166
  length, 164–165
  look, 169, 189. *See also* appearance
  market connection, 156–157, 162–163,
    164
  marketing disability and, 158–159
  money requests in, 167
  photographs in, 166–167
  problems with, 157, 157–162
  production expertise, 188
  professional, 160–161
  purpose of, 167
  quality of, 160–161, 165, 187
  references in, 165
  resource–problem connection in, 163
  service-oriented, 158, 164
  solving customers' problems through,
    162–164, 165

technology to produce, 6, 160, 161, 173,
  186–189
things to avoid, 157, 166–168, 171, 189
things to include, 157, 164–166, 170–
  171
tradition in, 159–160
types of, 156, 170
updating, 218
varying for different markets, 157, 166,
  168–169
marketing methods and techniques, 2, 19,
  154
marketing plan, 7, 10, 216, 217
  appendices, 228
  coordination with strategic plan, 227
  deadlines in, 229, 230
  draft, 219
  incorporating information into, 154
  outline, 224, 227–228
  responsibility assignment, 225, 226,
    229, 230
  software, 230, 235
  time frame, 226–227
marketing planning process, 215–231
  cycle, 226–227
  definitions, 225–226
  marketing team, 216–219
marketing process, 2, 74
marketing sequence, 157, 161
marketing skills, 1, 2, 18, 231
marketing team, 13, 14
  developing, 216–219, 231
  expertise for, 217
  meeting schedule, 218
  members, 216–217, 231
  outcomes, 218–219, 231
  responsibilities, 217–218, 231
  review of marketing materials, 164
  size, 217
  staff jobs, 24, 217
markets
  attention to all, 105
  categories of, 97–98
  choosing, 96, 106, 107, 113, 123
  competitors' view of, 75
  crucial, 174, 197, 222–223
  disparate, 87
  final interaction with, 148–149
  free, 1, 3–4

254   Index

markets (*continued*)
 future, 223
 growing, 108
 hidden, 81
 identifying. *See* market definition
 income. *See* payer markets
 input opportunities, 210
 internal. *See* internal markets
 marketing plan description of, 227–
  228
 moving with, 30, 33, 33–37, 48–49
 new, 25
 number of, 97–98
 open, 1, 3–4
 payer. *See* payer markets
 referral. *See* referral sources
 responsiveness to, 29, 49
 restricted, 3–4
 retaining, 39, 50
 reviewing, 131
 segmenting, 96, 105–107, 112–113
 sensitivity to, 71, 81, 89
 service. *See* service markets
 service decisions re, 105–107. *See also*
  services
 target. *See* target markets
 targeting, 25, 77, 107–109, 113. *See*
  also market redefinition
 understanding, 13
 wants of. *See* wants
media, representation in, 39
meetings, 62, 177
membership
 marketing materials for, 170
 as payer market, 98, 100, 118
mental health services, 103–104
mission
 avoiding service mismatches with, 32–
  33
 change outcome for, 65, 72
 commitment to, 32
 in fund-raising, 102
 as guide, 30, 31–33, 37, 49
 implementing, 46–48
 maintaining, 30, 33–37, 46
 market opportunities at variance with,
  30, 48
mission statement, 36–37, 49
 in marketing materials, 164

 in marketing plan, 227
 visibility of, 37
mission-based organizations, 29, 37
mistakes, 61, 65
 in market inquiry, 150–152, 155
 in problem solving, 203–205
monopolies, 3, 41–42, 67
 customer service by, 195
 geographic, 3, 77
 loss of, 110
MSOs. *See* management support/service
  organizations
museums, 16, 162–163

National Council of Nonprofit Associations, 235
National Public Radio, 47–48
needs, 76
 assessments, 17, 88
 assumptions about, 17. *See also* marketing disability
 focus on, 10
 having, 15, 27
 knowing, 112, 158
 meeting, 8, 27
 transforming to wants, 17, 27
 wants distinguished, 6, 15–16
new, focus on, 69–70
newsletters, online, 173, 192–193
nonprofit associations, 143
not-for-profit areas, 3–4
not-for-profits
 database of, 126
 expectations re, 70–71, 73, 109
 markets of. *See* markets
 naming, 3
 need for, 237–238
 provider choices, 3–4
 rules for, 99
 successful, 61
 wealth of, 71–72
nutrition, 57

objectives, 225, 228, 229–230
offices, 63
organizational chart/table, 63, 216–217
Osborne, David, 79
outcome measures, 225–226, 229
outcomes, 4, 71

documenting, 55
in marketing plan, 229, 230
from marketing team, 218–219, 231
referral follow-up, 104–105
outsourcing, 4

Parker, Richard A., 144
parking, 205
patience, 67, 72, 212
payer markets, 97, 98, 99–103, 112
competition in, 117, 118–119
e-mail, 178
press, 39
price setting, 81–83, 94
price wars, 92, 94
pricing, 1
competitors', 92, 125, 133
printers, 187, 188, 236
printing costs, 1. See also marketing
materials
prisons, 4
privatization, 4
problem solving, 202–203, 213
asking about wants, 208
customer perspective in, 198–200, 203,
208
documentation for, 208
follow-up, 210
listening to complaint, 207–208
mistakes in, 203–205
promises, 208
speed in, 196, 201, 202
staff empowerment, 201–202
process measures, 225
product cycle, 69
product definition, 22
products
design/modification of, 76
new, 75
profit, entitlement to, 83
promotion, 156. See also advertising; sales
public records, 126
public relations, 156, 161–162

quality, 30, 104
checking, 210
improving, 66
maintaining, 81
perception of, 24

rapid-response environment, 1–2, 12, 68,
176
referral sources, 84
competition for, 119, 121–123
competitor information from, 127
customers as, 121, 196, 211–212, 213
as market, 97, 98, 104–105
marketing materials for, 170
permission for use, 212
surveys of, 141, 222. See also surveys
thanks to, 212
religion, 4. See also churches
rental car industry, 68–69
reputation, 39. See also image
research, 3. See also market inquiry
by competitors, 91
on competitors, 119, 124–128, 133,
236
online, 175–176
resources for, 125–128, 143
statistically significant results, 137
response time, 1, 70, 196, 198–202
Rhea, Louis M., 144
risk taking, 14, 60
for change and flexibility, 61, 72
for customers, 61
by delegation, 202
in informal market inquiry, 149
in problem solving, 201

safety, 205
sales, 17–18, 22, 202
availability, 209
solving customers' problems, 157, 162,
202–203
schools, public, 4
secrecy, 91
self-assessment, 120, 121
service delivery, 84. See also distribution
service, duplication of, 3, 22
service markets, 97, 98, 103–105, 112
competition in, 117, 119–121
service orientation, 45, 157–158, 162
in marketing materials, 164
service population. See also customers;
market definition
advertising to, 84
changing, 36
competition for, 1, 45

service recipients. *See also* customers
  of competitors, 124, 133
  evaluation interviews with, 85
  marketing materials for, 170
  surveys of, 221
  treatment of, 109, 112
services
  adding, 125
  changing, 36, 58, 76, 86
  of competitors, 124, 133
  competitors' use/adaptation of, 91
  in conflict with mission/values, 32–33
  as customer problem solution, 203
  customers' knowledge of, 203, 213
  customers' perspective on, 205–207
  design/modification of, 38, 80–81, 94
  80/20 rule and, 223
  focus on, 10
  ideas for, 130–131
  marketing plan description of, 228
  new, 75
  questioning, 106
  reactive adaptation of, 14, 86
  refusing, 33
  terminating, 132
  traditional, 36, 106
  types of, 104
Simon, Judith, 147
social entrepreneurship, 1, 61
social services, governments' role in, 4
Society for Nonprofits, 235
software, 57
  for development, 192
  for marketing material production, 187
  for marketing planning, 230
  for surveys, 150, 179–181
  upgrading, 62
stability, 71
  financial, 40, 50
staff
  backgrounds of, 88
  changes in, 58
  competition education for, 43–44
  competition for, 1, 115–117, 129
  as customers, 110, 197
  discussion of change with, 43–46, 50
  effect on organization, 24
  e-mail, 177–178

  empowerment, 196, 201–202, 213. *See also* customer service
  informal market inquiry by, 147, 148
  as information source, 128
  information use by, 153
  as internal market, 98–99
  job satisfaction, 141
  listening skills, 89
  as market, 80–81
  marketing involvement, 7. *See also* marketing effort
  marketing materials for, 170
  on marketing team, 217
  motivating, 8, 21, 30, 46
  pay, 116–117
  recruiting difficulties, 41
  resistance to change, 43
  retraining, 43
  skills needed in, 1
  sources of, 116
  surveys of, 141, 221. *See also* surveys
  training, 218
  web-site areas for, 184
standardization, 137, 180
stationery, 188
strategic planning, 34, 97
  marketing planning coordination, 227
  target markets in, 108–109, 113, 222
  time frame, 226
strengths, 45
surveys, 7, 136–144, 154
  administration methods, 143, 179, 239
  consistency in, 141–142
  cost of, 136, 223–224
  of customers, 127
  customer satisfaction, 85, 139–140
  data analysis, 152
  definition, 137
  design, 180, 181
  of donors, 222
  by e-mail, 150, 180–181, 221
  focusing, 138, 181
  frequency, 138–139
  of funders, 221
  help with, 142–143, 181
  identifiers, 139–140, 181
  information best gathered by, 136–137, 145

information desired from, 139–140
instructions for, 138, 142, 239
length of, 138, 144, 181, 239
nondirected answer space, 180
online, 143
population sample, 136–137, 143
question sequence and wording, 139, 143
referral sources, 222
repeat, 141
return rate, 138, 144
sample, 143–144, 239–243
of service recipients, 221
software for, 150, 179–181
staff, 221
tabulation, 179–180, 181
testing, 143, 150
thanks to responders, 142
trend tracking, 140–141
who to survey, 137
SWOT analysis, 132
symphonies, 86

target markets, 106
contacts in, 218–219
80/20 rule, 107–108, 113, 222
focusing on, 96, 107–109, 113, 231
ignoring, 215
marketing materials' connection with, 156–157, 162–163
marketing plan identification of, 228
marketing team assignment to, 219
overlap with competitors, 124
prioritizing, 123, 124
taxation, 185–186
technology, 1, 2, 10, 172–193
access to, 173–174
availability of, 179
changes in, 59
cost of, 178, 179
for information gathering, 175–176
interference with service, 174–175
for market inquiry, 179–183
for marketing assistance, 173–175
for marketing materials production, 6, 160, 161, 173, 186–189
for organizational development, 189–192

overuse, 178
role of, 172
uses of, 173
voice mail, 179, 182–183
telecom, 178–179
telephone service, 41–42, 178
thrift stores, 87
titles, 63
trade associations, 111, 127, 143
trademarks, 91
traditions, 73
trend analysis, 136, 140–141, 180
trends, measuring, 221
truth, 198, 208

United Way, 55, 98, 101, 118
survey help from, 143
unrelated business income, 185–186
urgency, compassionate. See compassionate urgency
user fees, 98, 102–103, 119

value, 92
adding, 57, 176
competitors' offerings, 124–125, 133
of data, 141
of organization, 44
perception of, 14, 83
purchase based on, 81–82, 103
of time, 68–69
values, 38
balancing competing, 48
checkpoints, 32
core, 29, 30, 46
delineating, 8
financial, 48
market wants in conflict with, 31–33, 50
organizational, 34, 49
personal, 31–32
using, 48
vendor-customer relationship, 112
vendors, 148
Veterans Administration, 79
voice mail, 179, 182–183
volunteers
competition for, 1
e-mail, 177

volunteers (*continued*)
  informal market inquiry by, 147
  as information source, 128, 130
  as internal market, 98–99
  marketing team members, 26
  web-site areas for, 184

wants, 31
  accommodating, 56, 153
  asking about. *See* market inquiry
  assumptions about, 17. *See also* mar-
    keting disability
  as change drivers, 54–58
  changes in, 55, 73, 78–79, 80–81
  choice of meeting, 31
  in conflict with mission/values, 30–33,
    48
  discerning, 78, 112, 135, 203. *See also*
    market inquiry
  of donors, 101–102
  of fiscal intermediaries, 102
  focus on, 25
  of funders, 31
  ignoring, 158
  of internal markets, 98
  lumping groups' together, 104
  market expectations, 57
  marketing materials appealing to, 158,
    162
  marketing plan analysis of, 228
  meeting, 8, 13, 27, 39
  of membership, 100
  needs distinguished, 6, 15–16
  of payer markets, 99
  primacy of, 15–16
  of referrers, 104–105, 212
  responding to, 14, 78, 89, 151–152, 155

satisfying, 16
seeking, 15, 27
sensitivity to, 76, 81
re service delivery, 85
of staff, 116–117
targeting, 15
transforming to needs, 18
of users, 103
web sites, 171, 173, 183–186
  for advertising, 83
  affiliations, 185
  of competitors, 126
  content, 176
  costs, 1, 224
  donations via, 189–191
  education via, 185, 192
  evaluating, 176
  as feedback access point, 179, 181–
    182
  information currency, 126, 130
  for information gathering, 136, 149–
    150
  links, 181, 183
  marketing concepts incorporated into,
    6
  for research, 176
  restricted areas, 184
Welfare-to-Work initiative (Texas), 4
*Wilder Nonprofit Field Guide to Conduct-
    ing Sucessful Focus Groups,* 147
work plans, 225, 226

Xerox Corporation, 35–36

youth activities, 16

zoos, 16